Are All Warriors Male?

GENDER AND ARCHAEOLOGY SERIES
Series Editor: Sarah Milledge Nelson, University of Denver

This series focuses on ways to understand gender in the past through archaeology. This is a topic poised for significant advances in both method and theory, which in turn can improve all archaeology. The possibilities of new methodological rigor as well as new insights into past cultures are what make gendered archaeology a vigorous and thriving subfield.

The series welcomes single authored books on themes in this topical area, particularly ones with a comparative focus. Edited collections with a strong theoretical or methodological orientation will also be considered. Audiences are practicing archaeologists and advanced students in the field.

BOOKS IN THE SERIES
Vol. 1, *In Pursuit of Gender: Worldwide Archaeological Approaches*, edited by Sarah Milledge Nelson and Myriam Rosen-Ayalon

Vol. 2, *Gender and the Archaeology of Death*, edited by Bettina Arnold and Nancy L. Wicker

Vol. 3, *Ancient Maya Women*, edited by Traci Ardren

Vol. 4, *Sexual Revolutions: Gender and Labor at the Dawn of Agriculture*, by Jane Peterson

Vol. 5, *Ancient Queens: Archaeological Explorations*, edited by Sarah M. Nelson

Vol. 6, *Gender in Ancient Cyprus: Narratives of Social Change on a Mediterranean Island*, by Diane Bolger

Vol. 7, *Ambiguous Images: Gender and Rock Art*, by Kelley Hays-Gilpin

Vol. 8, *Gender and Chinese Archaeology,* edited by Katheryn M. Linduff and Yan Sun

Vol. 9, *Gender in Archaeology: Analyzing Power and Prestige, Second Edition,* by Sarah Milledge Nelson

Vol. 10, *The Archaeology of Childhood: Children, Gender, and Material Culture*, by Jane Eva Baxter

Vol. 11, *Gender and Hide Production*, edited by Lisa Frink and Kathryn Weedman

Vol. 12, *Handbook of Gender in Archaeology*, edited by Sarah Milledge Nelson

Vol. 13, *Women in Antiquity: Theoretical Approaches to Gender and Archaeology*, edited and introduced by Sarah Milledge Nelson

Vol. 14, *Worlds of Gender: The Archaeology of Women's Lives Around the Globe*, edited and introduced by Sarah Milledge Nelson

Vol. 15, *Identity and Subsistence: Gender Strategies for Archaeology*, edited and introduced by Sarah Milledge Nelson

Vol. 16, *Are All Warriors Male? Gender Roles on the Ancient Eurasian Steppe*, edited by Katheryn M. Linduff and Karen S. Rubinson

Vol. 17, *Gender Through Time in the Ancient Near East*, edited by Diane Bolger

SUBMISSION GUIDELINES
Prospective authors of single or co-authored books and editors of anthologies should submit a letter of introduction, the manuscript or a four to ten page proposal, a book outline, and a curriculum vitae. Please send your book manuscript/proposal packet to:

Gender and Archaeology Series

AltaMira Press

4501 Forbes Blvd Suite 200

Lanham, MD 20706

www.altamirapress.com

Are All Warriors Male?

Gender Roles on the Ancient Eurasian Steppe

Edited by
Katheryn M. Linduff and
Karen S. Rubinson

AltaMira
PRESS

A division of
ROWMAN & LITTLEFIELD PUBLISHERS, INC.
Lanham • New York • Toronto • Plymouth, UK

ALTAMIRA PRESS

A division of Rowman & Littlefield Publishers, Inc.
A wholly owned subsidiary of The Rowman & Littlefield Publishing Group, Inc.
4501 Forbes Boulevard, Suite 200, Lanham, MD 20706
www.altamirapress.com

Estover Road, Plymouth PL6 7PY, United Kingdom

British Library Cataloguing in Publication Information Available

Library of Congress Cataloging-in-Publication Data

Are all warriors male? : gender roles on the ancient Eurasian Steppe / edited by
Katheryn M. Linduff and Karen S. Rubinson.
    p. cm. — (Gender and archaeology)
Includes bibliographical references and index.
ISBN-13: 978-0-7591-1073-1 (cloth : alk. paper)
ISBN-10: 0-7591-1073-5 (cloth : alk. paper)
ISBN-13: 978-0-7591-1074-8 (pbk. : alk. paper)
ISBN-10: 0-7591-1074-3 (pbk. : alk. paper)
    1. Social archaeology—Eurasia. 2. Human remains (Archaeology)—Eurasia. 3. Sex
role—Eurasia—History. 4. Warfare, Prehistoric—Eurasia. 5. Women, Prehistoric—
Eurasia. 6. Eurasia—Antiquities. I. Linduff, Katheryn M. II. Rubinson, Karen Sydney,
1943–

    CC72.4.A743 2008
    930.1095—dc22
                                    2007032391

Printed in the United States of America

⊗™ The paper used in this publication meets the minimum requirements of American
National Standard for Information Sciences—Permanence of Paper for Printed Library
Materials, ANSI/NISO Z39.48-1992.

Contents

v

List of Figures and Tables

FIGURES

TABLES

Foreword

Exploring Unknown Lands and Bringing New Worlds into Gender Studies

Rita P. Wright

My first paper from a gendered perspective was about an unusual group of women, called the *naditu*, who lived in Old Babylonian southern Mesopotamia. There was very little material evidence and I was almost totally dependent on translated documentary sources. What interested me about the *naditu* was that they bought and sold land in substantial quantities in a society always described as dominated by males. I wanted to understand in what ways these women were integrated into the Old Babylonian political economy. Much later, when I was a faculty member in the Anthropology Department at the College of William and Mary, I was asked to write a paper on gender in the Indus Valley. In that context, I focused on divisions of labor among a group of potters whose production area my colleagues and I had discovered at the site of Harappa (Wright 1991). As there are no decipherable texts in the Indus, my challenge was to reconstruct this aspect of the culture's history based solely on its material culture.

These same types of evidence (literary, linguistic, and material) are the primary sources the contributing authors bring to this volume, *Are All Warriors Male? Gender Roles on the Ancient Eurasian Steppe*. Their focus on the ancient steppe takes us to an area less well-known to other Western scholars and the general public than Mesopotamia or the Indus. The authors successfully introduce us to the patterns of subsistence, settlement, social life, and gender issues that are unique to the region and yet bear comparison to other early cultures.

The editors have brought together an international group of specialists in steppe culture to view the region through an engendered lens, filling an important niche not previously incorporated into gender studies. Many aspects of gender studies have changed since a paper published in the *Journal of Archaeological Research* by Meg Conkey and Janet Spector in 1984 broke the ice by opening gender studies to a wide readership, whereas formerly gender papers were circulated among a small group of specialists (Nelson 2006). Since then, methodologies and theoretical approaches have undergone significant advances, opening new areas of research to archaeological investigations. The steppe zone was not a focus of that early research. Study there often requires a background in Russian, Chinese, and other, less well-known languages, and there were few opportunities for Western scholars to conduct research in the region. In that sense, this volume and other recently published books that I refer to later are gifts to those of us who do not command these languages or who are unable to travel to this distant region. Knowledge of its somewhat unique landscape, subsistence practices, and social arrangements contributes a basis for comparative study with better-known regions.

Several reviews of the current state of gender studies can be briefly summarized as an added background to the works presented here. They include Sarah Milledge Nelson's introduction to her *Handbook of Gender in Archaeology* (2006), a monumental edited work that covers just about everything relevant to gender studies, though not the steppe, and Elizabeth Brumfiel's chapter on methods in feminist and gender archaeology in Nelson's volume.

My foreword has two goals: to discuss topics addressed in this volume that are of broad significance to scholars working in other regions and to comment on conditions specific to the steppe and considerations of gender. It includes general issues such as "women warriors," women on horseback, representation, and ornamentation. In addition, the extensive excavations of cemeteries and burials on the steppe are unrivaled in the ancient world and the contributing authors have used this base for discussions of pastoralism and the interconnectedness of its sedentary and mobile populations, topics that are virtually unknown in most other parts of the world at the level of detail possible here.

WOMEN WARRIORS

Nelson (2006) identifies many of the struggles encountered by archaeologists in the days of early publication, some of which persist today. First and foremost is the very idea of "finding" women in the archaeological record. Examining the past has always meant setting aside our own culturally based assumptions and not imposing universal criteria to identify, for example, wealth or ethnicity or, as is the case for the steppe, dealing with confounding accounts of the existence of women warriors.

Brumfiel (2006) highlights some methodologies scholars have employed to avoid pitfalls when ethnohistoric and ethnographic data are used as guidelines to cultures in deep prehistory. Although ethnographic evidence can serve as a first approximation for assessing factors like divisions of labor, they often are poor guides to the social relations in an ancient culture (Wright 1996; Brumfiel 2006).[1]

Several early historic accounts of the steppe zone create similar challenges. While few scholars accept Herodotus' writings (5th century BCE) as whole cloth on many matters, his views about the women who inhabited the steppe have cried out for investigation, as have those of other influential historians (for example, Sima Qian, a 2nd-century BCE Chinese historian). Obviously, these historians and others fell victim to the norms of their own cultures, leading them to understandings that now can be tested against archaeological evidence. Still, the issues they raised are of continuing interest and remain "questions in the public eye" (Nelson 2006). Most immediately, the question, "Are All Warriors Male?" this volume's title, comes to mind. Here, the authors examine this question based on literary sources in the Indo-European world (Jones-Bley), and with archaeological materials from tombs of the 1st century CE in present-day Afghanistan (Rubinson) and artifacts associated with warfare in female burials in the Eurasian Iron Age (Berseneva). For example, 20 percent of female graves in kurgans, richly furnished elite burials, from the 2nd to 4th centuries CE, contained weapons, including arrowheads and, less frequently, "swords, daggers and spearheads" (Berseneva). Fans of the television program *Xena, Warrior Princess*, will be relieved to learn that this idea is not a total fantasy, as shown in the detailed analysis of literary sources brought to this volume (Jones-Bley), though not at all what Herodotus and others had in mind and much more interesting, but see Hanks (this volume) for some interpretive issues requiring additional study.

WOMEN AND HORSES

While general readers may envision the steppe as a featureless grassland, it is not ecologically homogeneous, a factor relevant to women, horses, and pastoral practices. The open plain was a prime location for horse herding, while lands on forested margins were less so and more conducive to specializing in sheep, cattle, or mixed groups of animals. Given the varied ecological conditions and animals exploited, we can expect variation among pastoralists. In general, the term *pastoralism* refers to a "continuum of lifestyles" (Khazanov 1994; Meadow 1996, 401) marked by degrees of mobility. As Barfield outlines (1989), nomadic pastoralists live a "portable" life suited to the frequent movement of animals but within a fixed range. They move about on a seasonable basis, seeking pastureland for their animals. Present-day nomadic pastoralists may trade items they produce (milk products, meat, or textiles, for example) with settled farmers in exchange for agricultural products. Semisedentary pastoralists have a home settlement, which may be in an agricultural community, where they remain the major part of the year; some members or the entire family leave for short periods in order to move animals to areas of preferential grazing. Movement typically occurs during dry periods or when nearby available land is being used for agricultural purposes. Sedentary pastoralists remain in one location throughout the year and may engage in farming and animal husbandry.

The variability of subsistence practices bears directly on the significance of evidence that women rode horseback. As several of the contributors note, artifacts and skeletal remains in some burial contexts link gendered activities to horses and horse riding. While the first thing that comes to mind is warfare and the power behind rider and horse in military incursions, the use of horses and riding included a broader base of activities. For example, Sargat grave goods in a female tomb included an iron bit and cheek piece but was absent of military equipment (Berseneva). The use of horses for herding many different animals on the steppe might account in some cases for the presence of artifacts used for horse riding. Shelach develops this idea in the context of late 2nd and early 1st millennium BCE on the eastern part of the Eurasian steppe when "packages" of artifacts and grave size mark different identities. Grave size, coffin construction, and animal sacrifice signify social and economic prestige; weapons and bone artifacts (arrowheads mostly) "reflect a type of warrior (perhaps masculine) identity." Plaques fastened to clothing "visible on day-to-day interactions" and found in other "packages" are interpreted as expressions of personal or ethnic identity and burials with ceramic vessels and small bronze ornaments "with lower social and economic prestige." In general, horse sacrifice is associated with male burials, while cattle and sheep are present in male and female graves. On the other hand, horse gear was placed in female graves but not in graves of males, singling them out as horse riders but not warriors. In a society devoted to herding horses, cattle, sheep, and goats, the horse-riding gear (given the presence of cattle and sheep in their grave goods but not horse) suggests they may have participated in animal herding. Shelach ties the multiple and overlapping identity packages to a "florescence of identity construction" resulting from a broadly experienced period of instability and increasing sociopolitical change in the late 2nd and early 1st millennia BCE on the eastern edges of the Eurasian steppe.

Finally, horse riding is attested to among the entire population in the Kingdom of Silla (57 BCE–668 CE), based on archaeological evidence and historic documents (Nelson). Men and women, elites and commoners, all rode horseback, the primary mode of transport in the Silla state. While women may have been warriors, warfare and hunting were considered "upper-class male occupations," as represented in tomb depictions and later history. The essential point, as discussed in the above examples, is that horses are ridden for a variety of reasons. Finally, in the case of the Silla, horses and gear associated with riding were strictly prescribed by sumptuary rules according to rank. Within each rank, some types of gear and ornament were not permitted for women, but such restrictions also were applicable to men of inferior statuses.

REPRESENTATION

Steppe cultures that practiced horse herding attached great symbolic significance to the horse. In the only chapter in this volume based upon settlement data, the authors (Olsen and Harding) examine representational objects from north-central Kazakhstan between 3700 and 3100 BCE among the Botai, who lived in pit houses and practiced horse pastoralism.[2] Unlike nomadic pastoralists, who are mobile and travel over large territories, the Botai settled in villages and "practiced radial migration" around their settlements.

The ritual burial of a horse in a Botai house appears to follow a practice known from later tomb burials and their use of horse bones (specifically the phalanges) to produce female figurines complements the religious significance of horses and the figurines themselves. The figurines are inscribed with decorative elements suggestive of cloth and women's garments, and based on the examination of surface textures using high-powered microscopy, the authors have been able to reconstruct weaving and possibly appliqué and embroidery technologies.

The female figurines, some of which are decorated and others not, were found in houses. More specific contexts at various sites include pits outside of houses in which ceremonial offerings were placed. Others were found in semisubterranean floors in small pits and at the center of a house near a hearth. A clay house model placed below a house floor included male and female figurines.

The female figurines clearly had a symbolic importance but cannot be associated solely with females, since they were as likely to be meaningful to both men and women as to females alone. Olsen and Harding interpret them as possible female spirits or deities or alternatively spirits of dead ancestors.

MACRO- AND MICROHISTORIES

The publication of a book on steppe cultures and gender comes at an opportune moment. Asia's ancient history, especially in South Asia, Central Asia, and East Asia, alongside that of other, better-known regions in Asia, such as the ancient Near East, is of interest given the increased opportunities for outsiders to conduct research in those regions. Of no less importance are the currently increasing economic and cultural ties with the region in the growing global economy. These awakened interests in the Anglophone world are providing new understandings and a broadened view of the "possible" in the way humans construct their cultures.

Two books, *The Making of Bronze Age Eurasia* by Philip Kohl (2007) and *The Urals and Western Siberia in the Bronze and Iron Ages* by Ludmila Koryakova and Andrej Epimakhov (2007), together synthesize the prehistories of the regions and time periods covered by this book. Whereas Kohl and Koryakova and Epimakhov adopt what Kohl refers to as a "coarse-grained spatial and temporal macro-perspective on the basic activities carried out by different groups, and then attempt to discern how these various activities relate to one another or are interconnected" (Kohl 2007, 258), the authors in *Are All Warriors Male?* pare these processes down to size, revealing details and providing insights into the different ways they were felt by steppe cultures. These engendered views from local areas afford complementary, but different, perspectives on how pastoralism was experienced within this vast zone.

As noted above, field research in many parts of the steppe zone has focused on the excavation of cemeteries and burials and less on settlements. Although most of the skeletal remains were aged and sexed, few were subject to bioarchaeological examination. As Bryan Hanks points out in chapter 1, the skeletal remains need additional study, given certain issues regarding subadults. Nevertheless, the contributors have put burial evidence to good use by employing multiple lines of evidence involving the elaborate arrangements of tombs, the spatial distribution of skeletal remains, and associated artifacts in order to identify gendered activities, gender equality, and social relations.

Tombs excavated at the site of Daodunzi on the eastern frontier of the Eurasian steppe in a valley at a high elevation better suited to pastoralism than agriculture evince images of life among mobile pastoralists (Linduff). Based on the discovery of sheep, and to a lesser extent bovine, bones in female tombs at Daodunzi, we can safely state that the Daodunzi were not horse herders, as was the case with their neighbors, whose tombs include horse skulls and hoofs. In pastoral societies the presence of sacrificed animals can signal high status, and their presence in women's tombs along with animal plaques may be indicative of their economic roles among pastoralists specializing in sheep. Linduff suggests that the spatial distributions of the catacomb burials in which the women were interred, in distinction to males who were buried in vertical pits, may be indicative of marriage patterns, in which women were from local families and males were intrusive.

Semimobile agropastoralists in the Karasuk region specialized in cattle and sheep (Legrand). No excavations have been undertaken in settlements. Clustered arrangements of tombs, situated on the edges of rivers and lakes, include both local materials and other objects more broadly distributed, an indication of the group's mobility. The spatial distribution of individuals within the clusters, adults at the center, with subadults and infants at increased distances from the center, is interpreted as family groupings by age and gender. Unlike the Daodunzi tombs, there are gender differences in the distributions of cattle offerings, the majority of which are found in male tombs, and sheep (in male and female), possibly indicative of a division of labor. Other grave goods indicative of specialization between males and females include bronze awls placed near the waist of females and bronze knives at the waist of males. The awls likely have multiple implications (Spector 1993), including ritual functions, but may have been used in hide preparation; the richly decorated bronze knives at the waist of males are interpreted as prestige weapons and were possibly used in butchery.

The stock-breeding pastoralists of the western Siberian Iron Age (the Sargat referred to above—Berseneva), although seminomadic, inhabited permanent settlements and fortresses. They specialized in domestic animals, the most dominant being horse, then cow and sheep and goat, and were more rigidly stratified than any of the other groups discussed above. Bioarchaeological examination of female skeletal remains indicates that women spent time on horseback, conceivably for herding purposes or, considering evidence for weaponry, for military purposes. Spatial distributions within the kurgans contain both males and females placed at their center and, based on limited anthropological study and artifact clusters, are interpreted as the remains of elite family burials. Although male burials contain larger numbers of high-status items, especially weapons associated with warriors, female burials also contain these elements and many are identified among the elite segments of society.

As these examples of different pastoral economies document, steppe cultures were not totally undifferentiated, although there are many similarities in artifact styles and a penchant for metal technologies that were widely shared. As Kohl (2007) and several of the contributions to this volume indicate, during periods of transition, cultures appear not to have been totally replaced, and many artifacts, especially those in burial contexts, demonstrate the traces of shared sets of ideas and residues of past lives.

Many burials in steppe cultures contain large quantities of sumptuous goods produced from sophisticated technologies and created with elaborate design elements that can be traced to specific cultural traditions. Artifacts recently recovered from a vault in the palace in Kabul, Afghanistan, where they were hidden during many years of conflict, included sumptuous goods from the excavations at Tillya Tepe in northern Afghanistan. Among them were elaborate gold plaques, ornaments, clasps, and belts (Rubinson). In addition to the golden objects, the six excavated burials contained others produced from nonlocal materials, or based on nonlocal models, or imported from elsewhere. The cultural identities of these individuals have been variously interpreted. The skeletal evidence of one woman with a flattened skull is evidence of a tradition identified with regions to the northeast of the burial site and suggests she may have been born elsewhere, either having brought the objects buried with her when she came to the area or maintained ties with people from her "homeland" through long-distance contacts.

The evidence from Tillya Tepe, the Sargat, and other sites discussed by various authors in this book on gender in the steppe complement Kohl's (2007) and Koryakova and Epimakhov's (2007) emphases on the interconnectedness of Eurasia. They provide hints of the possibilities for travel of ideas, technologies, and peoples across the steppe. The specifics of variability of its subsistence and settlement document this exchange in local contexts.

PROJECTS FOR THE FUTURE

The authors provide us with new pathways for understanding the social construction of pastoral lifestyles. Future studies will build on these works in reevaluating long-held assumptions and adopting new methodologies, such as better sampling strategies, collection of botanical and zoo-archaeological evidence, and excavations of different types of settlement sites to establish social arrangements within houses, villages, and larger communities, where these are available. Artifact analyses involving use ware need to be conducted. Awls and knives and other instruments discussed throughout the book cry out for functional analysis. Here, I am thinking of the types of analysis (for example, Kehoe 1992; Brumbach and Jarvenpa 2006; Weedman and Frink 2006; Gifford-Gonzalez 1992) conducted in connection with the subsistence practices of hunter-gatherer societies.

There is now a significant literature on technological styles (Lechtman 1977, 1994; Hosler 1994) and human agency in the selection and practice of specific technologies (Hoffman and Dobres 1999). The spread of metal technologies, in particular, in various parts of the world, was a dynamic force for societal change, revealing choices made at local levels often resulting in the reorientation of social practices, as Kohl discusses (1989) for the steppe, but with significant variability in different areas of the world, such as Ehrhardt notes with respect to Native American contact with European cultures (2005). Studies of ceramics also lend themselves to similar analyses of the exchanges of technical knowledge and material goods (Wright 1989, 2002), although such evidence is often lacking on the steppe. An engendered approach, such as proposed by Marcia-Anne Dobres (2000), would build on the contributions herein.

Another tantalizing area of research involves stylistic analyses of the objects interred in burials. Although analyses of ornamental styles have long been part of the research of steppe materials, especially so-called animal style and other 1st millennia BCE and CE art (see, for example, Minns 1913, 1944 and Rostovtzeff 1929, or more recently Jettmar 1967 and Bunker et al. 1970), combining such research together with study of the distribution of raw materials and technological styles is of equal interest. For example, Chernykh magisterially did such a study of ancient metallurgy, where cultural context and technological styles are explored on a broad scale throughout the Bronze Age steppe (1992). Calligaro has begun the raw material studies for Tillya Tepe (2006), a site where a study of technological styles in the context of the ornamental styles would potentially be enlightening.

The authors have drawn extensively on the burial evidence from cemeteries, tombs, and pit burials to reconstruct pastoral modes and social relationships. Additional study of human remains, as Hanks notes, should include osteological sexing and aging in cases in which it has not been conducted. In addition, studies of health and nutrition (Lovell 1994, 1997), activity patterns based on signature on bone (Molleson 1994) and genetic relations either through DNA or discrete trait analyses where bone is poorly preserved (Hemphill et al. 1991; Lukacs 1993, 1996), types of studies which have just begun on steppe materials, would contribute important data to the patterns and questions discussed in this volume.

In summary, the contributors to this volume have "broken the ice" (Nelson 2006) and provided benchmark contributions for more extended analyses of an archaeology of the steppe and gender. An array of evidence for pastoral societies and gendered relations on local levels described here will now be the framework from which to engender new evidence, to encourage new field approaches, and to create possibilities for future research. The work justifiably provides a broadened perspective with which to view pastoral societies and brings the steppe into the mainstream of gender studies.

NOTES

1. Long-held views on the relations of early states to kinship groups, based principally on ethnographic analogs, have been discussed extensively in the context of early southern Mesopotamian states by Norman Yoffee (1995). I develop the topic from an engendered perspective in "Gendered Relations in Ur III: Kinship, Property and Labor" in Diane Bolger, ed., *Gender through Time*, forthcoming from AltaMira Press.

2. For a discussion of the Botai and whether the horses there were wild and hunted or domesticated and herded, readers can begin with Kohl (2007, 139) for a review of the evidence and extended bibliography.

Acknowledgments

We would like to acknowledge the encouragement and participation of Sarah Milledge Nelson, especially in the preliminary stages of this project. She supported and challenged our thinking about the undertaking and followed through when we needed her assistance with the publisher. An edited volume is never simple, especially one with authors located so far from each other. We thank each of them for accepting our challenge to write a chapter where no one had done so previously, and for doing so with such care and interest. The large and multiple-language reference list was formed and maintained by Mandy Jui-man Wu, Jiayao Han, Leslie Wallace, and Sheri Lullo. They willingly and conscientiously saved our sanity over and over again. Thanks to the Mary Jane and Richard Edwards Fund at the University of Pittsburgh for supporting the preparation of the index. Our special thanks to Jane Vadnal for undertaking this task so skillfully and thoughtfully. Coediting the book engaged us in valuable as well as unexpected conversations about all sorts of issues about theory, the specifics of the material, and interpretation as well as issues far beyond the contents of the volume. All those discussions strengthened our interest in the subject, while clarifying our resolve that this was a worthy endeavor. We thank each other for the other's patience, wisdom, guidance, and encouragement.

Introduction

The Nature of Nomads, Cultural Variation, and Gender Roles Past and Present

Katheryn M. Linduff and Karen S. Rubinson

Although the study of gender has opened new avenues of research in many parts of the ancient world, one very large area and distinctive lifestyle are often absent from the literature: Eurasia and its ancient nomadic societies. This volume is intended to stimulate thinking about the rich diversity of gender roles among the pastoral peoples found in the Eurasian steppe in antiquity. We sought to take a careful look at this issue by bringing together a set of chapters that not only expands the study of gender in this region, but also provides insight into problems of sorting out the evidence, a task particularly complicated among these cultures where written records are most often absent.

What little we do have in writing about these past cultures is from historians of neighboring literate cultures (Greece and China, for instance) who observed and interacted with them. Both Herodotus and Sima Qian describe these peoples as ruthless "barbarians," who had no permanent homes and whose lifestyles they thought were both incomprehensible and primitive. Men versus women's activities or roles were not of interest and were rarely recorded, and some of the observations, such as those about the presence of "warrior-women," were highly mythologized rather than accurately observed.

The chapters brought together here address issues about the veracity of myths surrounding the nomadic peoples, including the "warrior-women" (Jones-Bley, Hanks, Rubinson), the mobility of pastoral peoples (Legrand, Linduff, Olsen and Harding, Shelach), family life (Berseneva, Legrand, Linduff), and migration theory and the transmission of ideas, objects, and peoples (Jones-Bley, Nelson, Rubinson, Shelach). Many of the chapters rely on the data collected in recent excavations, much of it reported in languages not accessible to most scholars and students of the study of gender and of archaeology. We conceive that this book will change the way we think about pastoral peoples and provide a rich new context in which to understand the shared lifeways as well as distinctive local features of these previously highly romanticized groups.

OBJECTIVES

In their book *In Pursuit of Gender: Worldwide Archaeological Approaches*, Sarah Milledge Nelson and Myriam Rosen-Ayalon note that "women's activities are as important to study as men's and the relationship between them is critical to describe in order to really understand a particular society . . . [and this] has led to far more sophisticated archaeology" (2002, 5). Determining the archaeological correlations that display the concept of gender and its relationship to biological sex has stimulated much discussion and the archaeology of gender, as it has been studied for the past two decades, has brought evidence from many parts of the ancient world under scrutiny. In this volume we hope to bring archaeological remains from Eurasia and its pastoral societies to the discussion on gender, as this region was completely absent from the latest review of gender studies and archaeology in *A Handbook of Gender and Archaeology*, edited by Sarah Milledge Nelson and published in 2006. Consideration of this vast and diverse region simply has not been attempted before in a single volume.

Eurasia forms the largest landmass on the globe, an area that extends from the Balkans to the Yellow Sea and links Europe and Asia. Lying between the fortieth and fiftieth latitude of this enormous land belt is a steppe with a fairly uniform terrain at an average altitude of between five hundred and a thousand meters. The peoples who lived there in premodern times practiced distinctive lifestyles: Most were pastoralists, although many were agropastoralists and semisedentary, while others were more mobile. Some lived near empires, while others crossed the open steppe tending to their herds. Archaeological evidence of the lives of these peoples includes both mortuary and habitation settings excavated in recent decades. Often excavation is carried out on a broad scale, unlike the North American tradition of the past half-century, so that extensive data sometimes come from a single site. That is not to say that research questions were formulated about gender so that information specific to it was sought and collected, therefore conclusions in all chapters here are tentative, and sometimes provocative. Our posing the questions about gender and how to find and assess it in the archaeological record in Eurasia, will, hopefully, stimulate those in the field to develop research projects that include such inquiry and collection strategies.

Exploration of how gender was constructed in several locations within this vast land and at different times has provided an opportunity to place this information into the discussion about gender worldwide and to analyze how to read it archaeologically, while also providing a more nuanced understanding of particular societies and their social structures, especially in relation to the steppe lifestyles. The evidence here is primarily mortuary, so direct association with daily life is risky, but it seems that what we have begun to discover is what women and men did in these societies (especially because women's and men's roles and tasks have been ignored or taken for granted in previous literature), and where possible, how gender roles and families were constructed. Because of some of the apparent commonalities, we have hints about how both may have been distinctive to a mobile lifestyle.

THE HISTORICAL PROBLEM

This volume is based on the expectation that archaeologists and art historians who study ancient Eurasia have important contributions to make to the study of gender. Current archaeological work and research on steppe lifeways has provided enough evidence to show that the peoples described by the Greek ethnographer Herodotus (5th century BCE) in *The Histories*, and the Chinese historian Sima Qian (2nd century BCE) in the *Shiji* (Records of the Historian), were only a subset of those living across the Eurasian steppe, and the details of their ways of life as described by the ancient writers seldom mentioned gender roles. In fact, the ancient as well as contemporary literature on the nomads has emphasized the successes of their male military leadership but do not talk much about women. When they do, such as the discussion of the Amazons (Herodotus 4.110–117; 9.27), the descriptions are idealized and schematic, leading to sometimes wild and often untested speculation about the role women warriors might have played on the steppe. Detecting how gender was actually constructed in these societies as evidenced in the archaeological materials now available is the goal of the volume's contributors.

We have gathered together chapters by people who bring diverse types of expertise: in gender studies (Nelson, Linduff), in Eurasian archaeology (Berseneva, Hanks, Harding, Legrand, Linduff, Olsen, Rubinson, Shelach), in analysis of symbol systems and mortuary remains (Hanks, Linduff, Jones-Bley, Rubinson), in scientific expertise useful for analyzing materials (Hanks, Harding, Olsen), and in reconstruction of lifeways of ancient peoples from archaeological as well as historical materials (Legrand, Linduff, Rubinson, Shelach).[1] We come from many different nations, and together represent training and intellectual depth held by no single person. A well-known archaeologist, Rita P. Wright, who has worked on virtually all issues listed above, and is among the pioneering scholars of gender roles in ancient societies, writes the foreword.

In an effort to understand just what the construction of gender was in each of the locations studied by our participants, and how that played into the daily lives as well as the memorialization at death, we assume that not all nomadic peoples thought, behaved, or lived the same way. Comparative analysis has required explanation, and the authors have been asked to address such issues. Were roles gendered similarly in many, most, or no mobile societies? Why? Did gender roles shift in relation to historical, environmental, or economic circumstances? What role does gender play in selection of leadership? Are roles fixed, or do they adjust according to task? Season? Age? Ethnographic studies have recorded societal patterns for mobile groups that give equal status to men and women, and shifting leadership strategies depending on circumstances and season, for instance (Barfield 1993). Can these patterns be found in the archaeological record for ancient times? Does mobility itself support certain gender roles? What role does gender or kinship play in determining status? Is status achieved or ascribed? Do these patterns differ or complement the sedentary neighbors of the pastoral peoples at the frontiers of the steppe? When and where are women associated with weapons on the ancient steppe? And can we really call them warriors? Such questions have guided the writing of the following chapters.

We have discovered that, as Nelson claims, searching for universals in gender studies turns out to be less productive than concentrating on variables and finding the revealing differences (2006, 19). The authors here, for example, have found social hierarchies among women and men; have found that cultural heritage is marked in burial, especially in elite tombs and where marriage and political change can be documented; have determined that sometimes the most important features to define status at death were age, marital status, and/or lineage, and not gender; have discovered that social status may change with marriage, age, occupation, and/or accumulation of goods or animals. In addition, we found many instances where the definition of gender roles and status proposed in historical literature was not confirmed in archaeological settings. That is, there is often a considerable difference between what the texts say happened and what is documented in burials. And vice versa. For instance, the idealized image of women warriors as professed in texts was sometimes played out in burials, but not often. We also confirmed that we were more successful reading the archaeological setting if we examined the full context, including textual evidence where possible, rather than limiting our investigations to study of a single type of artifact or interpretation. In other words, striving to understand the whole site, tomb and/or household, marriage or lineage leads to richer interpretations of each family member than studying only one feature in isolation.

THE AUTHORS

The authors contributing to this volume are people with different types of training and intellectual backgrounds as well as diverse types of data. All are active and published scholars and include professors and museum personnel, as well as very recent PhDs. The participants present archaeological work in China (Inner Mongolia); Mongolia; the Altai region of Russia; Kazakhstan; Russia, east and south of the Ural Mountains; Afghanistan; Korea; and Ukraine. Time periods considered range from the late Neolithic through the Bronze and Iron ages (c. 6000 BCE–c. 700 CE), and include study of peoples who lived many different types of fully and semimobile lifestyles. We editors anxiously awaited first drafts to come in because we were not sure just how each author would approach the data, what each would find, and what sort of interpretations could be made.

We divided the chapters into three sections that represent the main topics addressed throughout: the warrior ethos, the gendering and marking of identity in pastoral societies and how that changes, and the commemoration of marriage, families, and lineage at death. Each chapter brings an approach particular to the evidence and comes to critical conclusions that may be useful in moving forward to more nuanced interpretation and the construction of field projects that take into account gender issues in a more scientific and systematic way.

Bryan Hanks's (University of Pittsburgh) chapter, "Reconsidering Warfare, Status, and Gender in the Eurasian Steppe Iron Age," deals primarily with interpretive theory. He considers how the tombs of Iron Age Eurasian steppe nomads have become a popular topic among scholars in discussions concerning gender, status, and warrior activities in later Eurasian prehistory. The majority of these social interpretations have been based exclusively on mortuary evidence in the form of human skeletal remains and the inclusion of certain categories of grave goods such as weaponry. He argues that there are two major problems connected with these interpretations. The first is a general lack of acknowledgment of the complexity of mortuary ritual activities and interpretations regarding social status, identity, and gender. It is suggested that recent theoretical trends developed in connection with European Iron Age mortuary studies offer a potentially important conceptual framework for investigating mortuary practices in the Eurasian steppe Iron Age as well. The second problem discussed focuses on the need for stronger bioarchaeological approaches to the analysis of Eurasian steppe human remains, particularly with regard to juvenile sexing, muscle activity stress markers, and trauma patterns connected with violence and warfare. In conclusion, Hanks argues that new conceptual theories and bioarchaeological methods for skeletal analysis must be employed before improved understandings of social organization, status, and gender roles among Early Iron Age steppe societies can be achieved. His chapter reminds us that the conclusions drawn by other authors in this volume are based on the best available data, not perfect data sets.

Karlene Jones-Bley (University of California, Los Angeles), in her chapter "*Arma Feminamque Cano*: Warrior-Women in the Indo-European World," assesses the myth of the "warrior-woman" and its archaeological correlates. It has often been suggested that the Amazon, known from the ancient Greeks, was invented as a kind of sociopolitical bogeyman, who lived a life contrary to all that the Greeks saw as women's roles. Although there is no denying that bearing and raising children was a primary role for most women, recent scholarship has shown that women who spoke Indo-European languages went beyond the boundaries of hearth and home. Jones-Bley's chapter reviews the linguistic and literary evidence, together with archaeological data, that demonstrate that at least some women were indeed warriors in many of these societies and that perhaps, with more careful sexing of remains, more such women can be identified. Further, the role of horse riding and chariot driving among women is examined based on archaeological, artistic, and literary evidence, including the fact that the Greek word for horse, *hippo*, is found in the names of three of the Amazon queens. The evidence indicates unquestionably that some women held military positions in these ancient societies—that enough women engaged in warrior activities that they were not anomalies. Either they stepped in when necessary or lived within societies that did not have the rigid gender roles that were ascribed to them in the 19th century.

Karen S. Rubinson (Barnard College) brings the materials from a well-known cemetery, Tillya Tepe, under the lens in her chapter, "Tillya Tepe: Aspects of Gender and Cultural Identity," to suggest that there are multiple identities for women (and probably men) and that only a full contextual analysis can get closer to seeing how that was displayed, in this case at death. She discusses six burials excavated in northern Afghanistan that are said to be those of the settled descendants of the nomadic Yuezhi, who, according to Chinese texts, came to Central Asia from the Chinese borderlands and are customarily viewed as the ancestors of the Kushan rulers. The graves of five females and one male date to the middle of the 1st century CE. An analysis of the rich materials buried with these individuals suggests both their eastern steppic roots as well as documents the process of creating new cultural identities for themselves. They wear ornaments that point to strong ties to the eastern steppe and one woman even has the flattened skull well-known from the culture of the Huns. Another practice known from nomadic steppe societies, burial of women with weapons, is also apparent in these tombs, but whether one can characterize any of the five women as warriors must await detailed publication of the weapons found with them. Even so, the oldest of the women is buried with "Siberian-style" daggers and a pickax, in contrast to the other women, two of whom were buried with either knives or daggers (tools?) and two with none. This senior woman does not possess in death the weapons of the male (sword, bows and arrows, as well as knives and daggers), but the pickax might be construed as a warrior's weapon as well as a marker of her senior status. The combination of eastern steppe elements with local Central Asian practices implies that a newly formed, mixed or blended, identity was emerging.

The second section of this volume (part II) is titled "Horses and the Gendering of Identity on the Steppe and Beyond," and the chapters address the importance of livestock, especially horses, to the definition of identity, both cultural and sexual. Sandra Olsen (Carnegie Museum of Natural History) and Deborah G. Harding (Carnegie Museum of Natural History) reconstruct clothing of females from materials excavated in northern Kazakhstan in their chapter "Women's Attire and Possible Sacred Role in 4th Millennium Northern Kazakhstan." During the Copper Age of Northern Kazakhstan, the Botai and Tersek cultures manufactured female figurines by incising ornate decorations on the phalanges of horses and more rarely saiga antelope. These objects provide significant details about the clothing of the women of these cultures, as well as shed light on their rituals and the roles of women in the religions of these horse herders of the Eurasian steppe. The context of horse phalanx caches in small pits in the floors of houses may indicate the practice of placing icons there to represent goddesses or female spirits to protect the domicile. Evidence regarding textiles derived from pottery impressions indicates that twined bast fiber cloth, most likely hemp or nettle, would have been available to make clothing. In this chapter, all of the data are compiled to reconstruct both attire and female roles in the Copper Age societies of Northern Kazakhstan. Examples in Russia, Romania, Bulgaria, and Spain suggest that the use of these bones to represent females was widespread in the 4th and 3rd millennia BCE and probably defined gendered attire for all.

Gideon Shelach (The Hebrew University of Jerusalem), in his chapter, "He Who Eats the Horse, She Who Rides It? Symbols of Gender Identity on the Eastern Edges of the Eurasian Steppe," looks at excavated materials from pastoral societies and proposes that identities change as lifeways adjust to local circumstances. He examines the symbols and conception of gender roles among societies located in the eastern part of the Eurasian steppe during the late 2nd and early 1st millennia BCE, a time of vast and meaningful sociopolitical and economic change. He considers the evidence from three cemeteries from different parts of this area, set against a background of related archaeological data. Although the early 1st millennium in this region has long been characterized as fully pastoral, data show that pastoralism was adopted to expand the economic base of these societies, not to replace agriculture. Nevertheless, it was in this period that the groups of the Northern Zone, as it is called, developed an identity distinctly different from their southern Chinese neighbors. The mortuary data demonstrate that not only were apparently new gender identities defined at this time, but also social and economic statuses as well. Using the analytic tool of hierarchical clustering, the data reveal the interrelationships of social/economic, ethniclike, and masculine identities, which, in differing ways in the three cemetery areas, cut across biological sex. Overall, average wealth and prestige are not closely correlated with the sex of the deceased, but it appears that access to the highest sociopolitical strata was a male prerogative. One interesting outcome is that although horse sacrifice at burial is strongly correlated with male identity in these data sets, grave goods associated with horse riding are not associated with that identity. In fact, the earliest representation of horseback riding in the region comes from the grave of a woman.

Sarah Milledge Nelson (University of Denver) moves even further to the east to take careful look at evidence from the Korean peninsula in her chapter, "Horses and Gender in Korea: The Legacy of the Steppe on the Edge of Asia." In the past, Korean history has been seen through the lens of Chinese culture, but this chapter addresses yet another legacy, that of the Eurasian steppe during the Silla period (traditional dates 57 BCE–668 CE). The sumptuary rules of the early Korean state of Silla describe in detail the number of horses and quality of horse trappings that are permitted to all ranks and genders. The implication of these documents is that riding horseback was the primary transportation for everyone in the Silla state, elite and commoner alike, both male and female, in contrast to, for example, China at this time, where we know that particular urban elites (mostly male, some female) and the military rode. The widespread role of horse riding in Silla society can be traced back to the founders of the state, who had strong connections to the steppe. Nelson documents ties to the steppe and forest steppe in the archaeological background of Silla and earlier peoples of the Korean peninsula, including the importance of birch bark artifacts and reindeer leather boots, both of which could only be owned by the top rank of men and women in Silla times. Earlier, mounded burials, a reverence for white horses, and a preference for gold artifacts over other precious materials marked early Korean culture. With these material ties to the steppe apparently came social behaviors, such as the prevalence of horse riding among both men and women, which distinguished the gender and status roles of this state in East Asia from most other Chinese-related states, where women seldom rode horses, except in limited periods, and then only among the elite. It is important to take into account these long-lived steppe traditions when examining Silla culture.

In part III of this volume, "Marriage, Families, and Death on the Steppe," the authors consider gender in relation to commemoration of identity in marriage unions and the construction of families on the steppe. The authors have found multicultural families and also that lineage and age were important in how family members were displayed at death. According to Natalia Berseneva (Institute of History and Archaeology, Ural Division, Russian Academy of Sciences) in her chapter, "Women and Children in the Sargat Culture," gender dimensions can be seen in the Sargat culture as an important part of mortuary analysis. As a social construct, she reconstructed sex-related roles of individuals inside and outside of marriage from mortuary evidence. Among the possible variations, gender may be patterned by sex in relation to the human biological life cycle so that childhood, adulthood, and old age may constitute different and separate genders. These latter patterns are examined here among mortuary remains of the Sargat, a nomadic population which occupied the vast forest-steppe area in Western Siberia from the early 6th century BCE to the 3rd and 4th centuries CE, although a complete picture cannot be formed, since children and females are underrepresented in the burial contexts studied. Sargat burials contain a wide variety of grave goods, many originating far beyond the steppe, including, for example, glass beads from Egypt, the Levant, southwest Asia, and China. In fact, the single diagnostic artifact for Sargat identity is pottery. In approximately one-half of all the burials analyzed, the grave goods are gender neutral, whether male, female, or child. Greater differentiation is seen in the goods found in richer burials at the center of grave clusters; these can belong to men, women, and even children. Horse trappings and armor and most weapons are not found with children; in fact armor and long swords are found only in adult male burials. Some weapons were found in 20 percent of the female burials (bows and arrowheads), and 60 percent of male burials. The absence or inclusion of certain burial goods may suggest a vertical hierarchy among individuals, as well as gender differences. In fact, a few male burials were found containing no weapons and much jewelry, presumably characterizing men with different social roles, at least in death. The rich children's burials confirm that at least some small children had important social roles in Sargat society.

Sophie Legrand (University of Paris) brings material from central Siberia to her chapter, "Sorting Out Men and Women in the Karasuk Culture." She considers family structure of Bronze Age peoples of the Karasuk culture, circa 1400–1000 BCE, in light of gender. The Karasuk culture is known almost exclusively from excavation of cemetery sites and the data set for this study are four hundred tombs from various cemeteries where the burials were anthropologically sexed. Cemetery arrangement, tomb structure, and grave goods, together with age and sex of skeletons, are considered, with the goal of understanding something of family organization in Karasuk society and its relationship to social organization. The arrangements of burials in cemeteries show that kinship is the base of the Karasuk societal organization, since funerary clusters are small family cemeteries. Adults are placed in the central units and other family members arranged according to both age and gender. Age does not appear to influence the grave complexes, but there are differences in gender and social rank markers. On the whole, female burials contain more jewelry and bronze clothing ornaments than male burials, and high-status women are buried with awls placed at their waists, imitations of cowry shells, and body ornaments such as beads. In general, male burials contain little jewelry and few bronze clothing ornaments. Males of high social status are buried with bronze knives placed at the waist, celts, and "bow-shaped" bronze artifacts. Overall, it appears that the Karasuk had a hierarchical social order based on a patriarchal system and, with one exception, the women and children assumed the social rank of the man with whom they were associated in burial.

In her chapter, "The Gender of Luxury and Power among the Xiongnu in Eastern Eurasia," Katheryn M. Linduff (University of Pittsburgh) looks at mortuary data from the Ordos region in present-day China and finds a multicultural marriage pattern that displays particular steppic identities determined by gender. The chapter looks at nine cemeteries of the later 1st millennium BCE from the northern borderlands of China that Chinese texts ascribe as land belonging to the nomadic groups called Xiongnu. The analysis of the graves and their contents, together with the skeletal data, shed light not only on how gender played into the construction of political and economic power, but also on the complex social relationship within the local groupings. Xigoupan, a spot where Chinese records tell us that Xiongnu headquarters were, with its rich male and female burials containing many Chinese goods, probably belonged to regional Xiongnu notables. Examination of other cemeteries of less powerful and/or wealthy individuals reveals regional distinctions among the groups and varied burial practices within cemeteries, and indicates that the Xiongnu was not a homogeneous group, as suggested in the Chinese written records. Furthermore, the archaeological research contradicts the Chinese characterization of the Xiongnu as having no respect for their elders; in fact, the graves of older men and women are consistently richer and larger than those of younger individuals. Women and men of similar age appeared often to have similar social status. Analysis of burial location and contents also makes clear the formation of intercultural families, as well as observation of certain practices, such as bride price, also found among living pastoralists.

AUDIENCE

Finally, the chapters in this volume are written in a style that is, hopefully, readily accessible and about topics that appeal to a diverse audience. Because of the wide geographic distribution of the peoples of Eurasia, they were in contact with neighboring groups from across a vast area. Therefore, scholars whose main focus is on the adjacent regions, including China, the ancient Near East, and Eastern Europe, would benefit from reading this volume. The large group of archaeologists, cultural anthropologists, historians, art historians, and those with concern for gender issues we hope will be very pleased to learn about these new data. In addition to this more academic set of readers, and because there has been such popular interest in "women warriors," including in TV, movies, and even comic books, there could be an audience of a sort not usual to scholarly publications.

NOTE

1. Some of the papers included here (by Linduff, Rubinson, and Olsen) were first presented at the Second University of Chicago Eurasian Archaeology Conference—Social Orders and Landscapes: Interdisciplinary Approaches to Eurasian Archaeology, held in April 2005.

Part I

THE WARRIOR CULTURE: MYTH AND IDENTITY

Chapter One

Reconsidering Warfare, Status, and Gender in the Eurasian Steppe Iron Age

Bryan Hanks

The tombs of Iron Age Eurasian steppe "nomads" have become a popular topic in discussions concerning status, gender, and warrior societies in later Eurasian prehistory. The majority of these social interpretations are based almost exclusively on mortuary evidence in the form of tumulus constructions (kurgans), human skeletal remains, and the inclusion of certain categories of grave goods such as weaponry. This chapter argues that there are two significant problems connected with such interpretations. The first focuses on conceptual issues surrounding mortuary patterning and the interpretation of identity and status. It is suggested that conventional approaches to gender and status among prehistoric steppe societies are too functional in nature and do not adequately account for the agency of the living in structuring mortuary practices and mediating the deposition of specific categories of grave goods. The second problem focuses on the need for more rigorous bioarchaeological analyses of Eurasian steppe human remains, particularly with regard to subadult sexing, muscle activity stress markers, paleopathology, and trauma patterns connected with interpersonal violence and warfare. In conclusion, it is argued that new theoretical approaches and bioarchaeological methods for skeletal analysis must be employed before more valid interpretations of social organization, status, and gender among Early Iron Age steppe societies can be realized.

Much of the recent literature on Early Iron Age mortuary evidence in the Eurasian steppe continues to reinforce rather rigid models of social organization and ethnocultural identity. Variation in tomb construction and grave furnishing are often straightforwardly interpreted as direct indicators of contingent variation in social statuses, roles, and gender for early steppe societies. Since the 1980s, however, such functional perspectives have been increasingly criticized for their lack of awareness for human agency and social practice in the past (Barrett 1994; Miller and Tilley 1984; Pader 1982; Parker Pearson 1982). Subsequently, problems relating to conventional theoretical interpretations have been well illustrated in recent years by scholars investigating prehistoric mortuary practices from a number of case studies around the world. For example, important contributions on social authority and power (Arnold 1991, 1999; Dietler 1990; Parker Pearson 1982; Sweely 1999), cultural identity and ethnicity (S. Jones 1997; Wells 2001; James 1999), grave goods and their relationship to status and gender (Arnold and Wicker 2001a; Arnold 1996; Dommasnes 1982; Härke 1990; Linduff and Sun 2004; Weglian 2001), and the role of human agency (Arnold 2001; Babić 2002; Chapman 2000; Davies 1994) have become prominent themes in the reevaluation of mortuary patterning and its meaning. Such approaches have sought to more effectively identify and explain dynamic processes of identity formation and human intentionality and their connection with the complex relationships created between the living and dead which structure the mortuary event (Parker Pearson 1993).

This chapter draws on these recent trends in social theory in order to evaluate critically how many scholars continue to frame their interpretations of the social structure of early Eurasian steppe societies, as most focus almost exclusively on mortuary evidence and social interpretations drawn from such data. While much of this research has centered on the emergence of warlike "nomadic" societies and the nature of their social organization (Koryakova 1996; Kradin 2002), other works have suggested that women in particular held special status within these societies as ritual specialists and as warriors (Davis-Kimball 1997a,b, 1998, 2000, 2002; Taylor 1997; Guliaev 2003). These interpretations connect importantly with the nature and scale of warfare in the Eurasian steppe Iron Age and with the social category of *warriorhood* and its relationship to cultural constructions of gender and status within these early societies.

PROCESSES OF SOCIAL CHANGE

Archaeological evidence from the Eurasian steppe indicates that during the 1st millennium BCE a period of substantial change occurred that reflects increased mobility and migration, intensified conflict and warfare, and vibrant change in sociocultural identity, particularly relating to a new pattern of warrior lifestyle (Davis-Kimball, Bashilov, and Yablonsky 1995; Rolle 1989). Because of a distinct lack of settlement data for the Iron Age in most regions of the steppe, interpretations of the social, political, and technological conditions of this period have been formed through the study of mortuary remains recovered from the kurgan monuments that dot the Eurasian landscape.

There can be no doubt that the placement of corporate cemeteries, as well as singular tombs and cenotaphs within the landscape, provided a highly symbolic memorialization of the dead (Kroll 2000). In this way, the past was firmly rooted to individuals and communities in the present. While various forms of tumulus burial began as early as the Aeneolithic period in the steppe region, it was particularly with the transition to the Iron Age that greater emphasis was placed on single inhumations and large complex tomb constructions. Such patterns signaled the transition toward new social, political, and material conditions. In fact, unambiguous evidence for the use of horses in mounted warfare dates to around the beginning of the 1st millennium BCE (Renfrew 1998). The widespread diffusion of this mounted warrior pattern, within two to three hundred years, clearly suggests dynamic new social settings where the technological dimension of cavalry warfare and the warrior lifestyle became quickly disseminated and strongly expressed through funerary activities (Bokovenko 1995a,b, 1996; Hanks 2000, 2001, 2003a,b).

In combination, these developments have been framed conventionally in social evolutionary terms as the emergence of chiefdoms and as social processes connected with core-periphery dynamics (Koryakova 1996; Kradin 2002). Such models indicate a trajectory of increasing social complexity and political authority leading toward greater control and exploitation of land, people, and resources. In this way, the emergence of more elaborate mortuary practices is understood as reinforcing new structures of social inequality and more effective forms of political centralization. While these models can be useful for examining a number of broader socioeconomic transitions from a comparative view, such approaches can overshadow many aspects of the social and material vibrancy connected with Early Iron Age societies.

For example, conventional models often view the emergence of warriors as a social category specifically oriented toward the attainment of elite rank, prestige, and authority situated within a "chiefdomlike" setting. Comparatively speaking, such hierarchical models have formed an important part of the interpretation of prehistoric social organization, however, in recent years many scholars have challenged the neoevolutionary connotation of this view by asserting that social power and authority can be variably dispersed within and between early societies (Yoffee 1993). Examples of this include the concept of *heterarchy* (Ehrenreich, Crumley, and Levy 1995) and other dimensions of supralocal power and knowledge constituted through horizontal social institutions such as sodalities and warrior associations, which are common among segmentary or "tribal" societies (Fowles 2002; McIntosh 1999). Overall, there has been a general shift in thinking among scholars concerning the traditional focus on elites within societies. As Steven Shennan recently stated regarding the European Bronze Age, "the emphasis on ranking and stratification has been excessive, driven on the one hand by a desire to see

Bronze Age Europe as a participant in the 'rise of civilization' and on the other by acceptance of the 'myth of control' which pervades social evolutionary approaches and which, in effect, subscribes to the ideology of early elites that everything happens in society as a result of their efforts" (1998, 192).

This reorientation of perspective on social power has been greatly influenced by developments in postprocessual, feminist, and practice theories, all of which have increasingly moved toward a greater focus on individuals within societies and the dynamic relationship between individual agency and larger social structures and institutions of power (Gardner 2004; Sweely 1999). However, this shift in theoretical direction has not been accepted wholeheartedly within the scholarly community and, as a result, significant debate still lingers over the connection between the complexity of social practice and the identification of such actions in the archaeological record. In considering this current state of discourse over archaeological theory, it is worth noting the view of the late David Clarke on the "radical" rise of the New Archaeology in the 1970s. As Clarke stated in 1973, "a new environment develops new materials and new methods with new consequences, which demand new philosophies, new solutions and new perspectives" (1973, 8–9). Such a view seems as pertinent today as it did nearly thirty-five years ago, as current archaeological approaches to human action and intentionality in the past continue to develop in a variety of new directions. Nevertheless, in tandem with the rise of new theoretical pathways into the past, it is crucial that empirical data continue to inform and direct the validity of such interpretive projects. Regarding the study of mortuary data, recent advances in bioarchaeology provide an important avenue of research for examining the biological life histories of individuals, which has the potential to contribute significantly to more traditional social interpretations based primarily on funerary treatment at death (Robb 2002; Saul and Saul 1989). Such multidisciplinary studies offer great potential for a more rigorous investigation of the category of warriorhood in prehistoric societies and the lifestyle activities and cultural identity, including gender, connected with it.

AMAZONS: BETWEEN MYTH AND REALITY

It is difficult to discuss the Eurasian steppe Iron Age without contemplating the myth of Amazon warriors in some way. Since the time of Herodotus, stories of Amazons have figured prominently in Western perceptions of the northern "barbarian" peoples of temperate Eurasia. In recent years, several publications have attempted to address this issue in light of available mortuary evidence in the western and central steppe regions—particularly sites connected with Scythian, Sauromatian, and early Sarmatian cultures, which date approximately from the 8th to the 2nd centuries BCE. Herodotus' travels in the north Pontic region in the mid–5th century BCE, and his discussion of the myth that the Sauromatians were the result of the coupling of Scythian men and Amazon women, have been traditionally used as a starting point for establishing the historical existence of steppe women warriors. While some scholars are comfortable with using Herodotus' accounts as a form of early ethnography (Taylor 1997, 193; 2001, 37), others have taken a much more critical stance concerning their validity (West 1999, 2000).

Much of the discussion surrounding Amazons and the role of women in steppe warfare has challenged conventional androcentric biases that view women as passive actors in social settings of violence and warfare. In recent years, a number of publications have illustrated that women historically have been active participants in combat around the world—particularly in small-scale guerrilla warfare (Goldstein 2001; D. Jones 1997). However, according to Goldstein, based on historical evidence, women fighters have only accounted for 1 percent of all warriors in history (2001, 10). While there are numerous case studies that make up this 1 percent, the seemingly universal gendering of war as a male domain is striking (2001, 10). While historic evidence provides clear contexts for the role of women as fighters and warriors, when considering prehistoric evidence for such activities, the picture becomes much more complicated and is inextricably tied to an evaluation of *direct* versus *indirect* evidence.

For example, interpretations of Amazon women warriors in the Eurasian steppe Iron Age frequently focus on *indirect* evidence from the mortuary domain, such as the inclusion of weaponry and other categories of grave furnishings, instead of *direct* evidence of a warrior lifestyle that may be indicated by specific bioarchaeological indicators. Such direct evidence may include, for example, activity stress markers indicating asymmetry in muscle development and attachment and the osteoarthritis and other pathologies that may be induced by particular repetitive physical activities connected with martial activities. These would include archery, sword fighting, and intensive horseback riding from a young age. Unfortunately, aside from a few scholarly works that have considered such bioskeletal indicators as part of general physical anthropological studies (e.g., Courtaud and Rajev 1998), very few research programs in the Eurasian steppe region have attempted to investigate this issue more systematically.

However, several classic case studies focusing on such skeletal evidence have been conducted on prehistoric and historic period skeletal evidence from North America for spinal pathologies associated with frequent horseback riding (Bradtmiller 1983—as discussed by Larsen 1997; Reinhard et al. 1994) and upper limb bone asymmetry and osteoarthritis connected with archery (Bridges 1990). Studies of osteoarthritis indicators associated with archery have also been carried out in Europe (Rhodes and Knusel 2005; Stirland 1993). Studies of this type on Eurasian steppe skeletal material may provide direct evidence of the range for such activities between sexes and across age groups, and such data would greatly support social interpretations that previously have been based solely on grave goods in defining the status and role of individuals.

Currently, the single biggest problem with many recent interpretations of women warrior burials in the Eurasian steppe is the connection between biological sexing, gendered perceptions of *maleness* and *femaleness*, and the context or *social value* of certain categories of grave goods such as weaponry and personal adornment. These issues will be focused on in more detail below in light of the excavations and published reports of the Iron Age Pokrovka cemeteries, located in the southern Ural Mountains region of the Russian Federation. The Pokrovka mortuary evidence has often been at the heart of discussions over the existence of late prehistoric female warriors in the Eurasian steppe and is therefore one of the most important case studies for interpretations of late prehistoric steppe societies.

WOMEN "WARRIOR-PRIESTESSES" OF POKROVKA

Five Iron Age cemeteries at Pokrovka, comprising approximately fifty kurgans (tumuli) and more than 150 burials, were excavated between 1992 and 1995 as part of a collaborative American-Russian project (Davis-Kimball 1998, 142). Published results from this work have appeared in both English (Davis-Kimball and Yablonsky 1995; Davis-Kimball 2001) and Russian (Yablonsky 1993, 1994, 1995a, 1996) and have been an important source of data for various interpretations of female statuses and warrior activities.

In published works by Jeannine Davis-Kimball (1998, 142; 2001, 245), statuses for both males and females were inferred from a sample of 174 skeletons—comprising 69 females and 105 males. These statuses were determined exclusively on the presence or absence of specific categories of grave goods, as indicated in table 1.1.

Based on these studies, three main statuses were initially determined for women: *hearth women* (75%), *priestesses* (7%), and *warriors* (15%). A fourth category, that of *warrior-priestess* (3%), was deduced by Davis-Kimball based on a combination of weaponry items and *cultic* objects—such as seashells (1998, 43). Statuses for men fell into three broad categories: *warriors* (94%), *males without artifacts* (3%), and *males buried with a child* (3%). Interestingly, children, when buried with adult individuals, were in every case placed with males rather than females. No explanation for this pattern is offered by Davis-Kimball (1998, 146). Furthermore, as the author

Table 1.1. Statuses and associated grave goods based on data from Davis-Kimball (1998, 2001)

Hearth person:	earrings	beads	anklets	bracelets	
Priest/Priestess:	stone/clay altars	shells	bronze mirrors	objects + animal art	ores/pigments
Warrior:	arrowheads	quivers	swords	daggers	amulets

notes, because various combinations of animal bones, iron knives, and pottery vessels were placed in nearly all of the burials, such items were excluded from the study (1998, 142). Based on this analytical approach to the Pokrovka mortuary evidence, Davis-Kimball (1998, 146) suggests that:

> Compelling evidence exists for strong female hierarchical structures that are more diverse than among the males. Included in the female statuses are hearth women—who controlled clan wealth; perhaps a special status for spinners and weavers; priestesses of varying degrees of status—who maintained equilibrium within the family, clan and tribe; female warriors—who assumed a defensive role in nomadic society; and, warrior-priestesses—who may have divined, performed oracles, and bestowed sanctification upon the chieftain's decisions. During the nomadic Early Iron age, feminine power within the social, political and cultural spheres would have been, without doubt, extremely effectual.

While Davis-Kimball makes a persuasive argument for these specific status categories, there are a number of issues regarding her methodology that must be considered more carefully. For example, only specifically chosen grave goods were included in her study and artifact deposits such as animal bone remains, iron knives, and pottery were excluded. While it is entirely possible that Iron Age women held positions of high status—achieved, ascribed, or a combination of both—it is the specific *social* categories that she has developed that are problematic. For example, in a number of publications, Davis-Kimball (2001, 2002) refers to a young *warrior-priestess* burial from the Pokrovka 2 cemetery (kurgan 8, burial 4). She classifies the young female, aged 13–14 years (2002, 58; but cited as 12 years of age by Yablonsky 1995a, 34), as a *warrior* based on the presence of forty bronze arrowheads, an iron dagger, an amulet with a bronze arrowhead inside of it, an animal tusk "amulet," and a quiver included in the grave pit. She also classifies this individual as a *priestess* based on the presence of two oyster shells, a pink translucent stone containing a white dried paste, and a boar's tusk "amulet" (2001, 247). Other female burials have been classified by Davis-Kimball as *priestesses* based on the presence of artifacts such as bronze mirrors, carved stone and clay "sacrificial altars," and colored pigments and ores (1998, 142). To support her interpretation, she suggests that priestesses used colored pigments as "cosmetics applied for rituals; tattooing the skin; dying yarns for textiles; or painting ritual designs on clothing or the body; tattoos, that is, writing on the body, could be signs of 'women's culture'" (1998, 146).

In consideration of Davis-Kimball's status categories, there are three specific areas of interpretation that should be considered more carefully as they relate to Early Iron Age social organization: 1) the assignment of sex to subadult individuals; 2) the direct correlation of grave goods with cultural concepts of status and gender; and 3) models of social organization and their relationship to interpretations of warrior "status" and "lifestyle" in late prehistoric steppe societies. Each of these three areas is considered in more detail below.

BIOLOGICAL SEXING AND AGING

In mortuary archaeology, in many parts of the world including the steppe region, the biological sex of individuals is often assumed from included grave goods rather than actual osteological analysis of human remains. Moreover, when such physical analyses are undertaken, the specific methods used for aging and sexing are not described. This is particularly worrisome when biological sex is so often assigned to subadult individuals, such as the young "warrior-priestess" noted above from Pokrovka. In *adult* specimens, the biological sex can be determined in many cases with around 97–98 percent accuracy if both the cranium and pelvis are available for analysis and are well preserved (Meindl et al. 1985; Molleson and Cox 1993). However, sexual dimorphism among prepubescent children and juveniles is minimal due to lower testosterone levels and therefore the assignment of biological sex is highly problematic at best (Mays 1998, 38). Studies using measurements of children's permanent teeth, typically the lower canine, for biological sexing have been undertaken with some positive results indicated (Perzigian 1976; Molleson 1993), however, it is certainly not a widely practiced method and several authors have argued that a number of factors such as diet and health may affect tooth development and the reliability of this method (Gugliardo 1982; Loth and Henneberg 2001; Schutkowski 1993; Simpson et al. 1990).

In several recent publications focusing on steppe warrior-women, biological sex has been assigned to children buried with weaponry, such as the Pokrovka burial noted above, where the individual was described as a 12- to 14-year-old female. A more recent publication describes a "girl" 7–10 years of age buried with iron armor and two spearheads (Fialko 1991; Guliaev 2003). In fact, in consideration of 112 graves of women with weapons in the region between the Danube and Don rivers, Fialko (1991) notes that about 70 percent of these females ranged between 16 and 30 years of age. Such examples indicate the importance that individuals ranging in age from young adult to subadult have within interpretations of status, gender, and warrior-hood. In a recent publication detailing the results of a bioarchaeological analysis of the human remains from the Iron Age Aymyrlyg cemetery in Tuva, Siberia, Murphy provides a more systematic categorization of subadult and adult aging (Murphy 1998; 2003, 39–40). In her study, a total of 436 adults and 171 subadults were analyzed for the Scythian period (8th to 2nd c. BCE) and 148 adults and 54 subadults for the Hunno-Sarmatian phase (3rd to 1st c. BCE). Of these samples, biological sex was only determined for the adult categories.

While it is certainly feasible among horse-riding pastoralist groups, both historic and prehistoric, for juveniles and adolescents to develop exceptional riding and archery skills, our understanding of their participation in the dynamic setting of actual warfare deserves more attention. The path toward becoming a hunter and/or warrior in most tribal societies begins at a young age, as the skills required to be effective in these activities must be cultivated from youth. This represents a paradox for archaeologists, as it is precisely during the juvenile and adolescent stages that significant age grade transitions and the social construction of identity and gender commonly occur. For example, among males of the Loikop of Kenya (a Maa speaking group like the Maasai), age grade transitions are based on clear divisions and subdivisions and have a close association with weaponry in the form of spear types, styles, and sizes, which are modified accordingly by each age grade cohort as they move through the various stages (Larick 1985; 1986, 274).

While boys do carry spears from the age of 7 in Loikop society, there is a clear hierarchy in the size of spears carried and in the use of weapons for participation in warfare. As Larick explains, "a hierarchy of size and massive-ness climaxes with the spears of senior warriors, who often carry a pair of large spears. Senior warriors have responsibility for the offense and defense of the community; they embody the power of the tribe and they are entitled to carry its most powerful spears" (1986, 275).

Table 1.2. Subadult and adult age categories as noted by Murphy (1998, 2003)

Subadult		Adult	
Infant:	< 2 years	Young adult:	17–25
Child:	2–6 years	Adult:	25–35
Juvenile:	6–12 years	Adult:	35–45
Adolescent:	12–17 years	Mature adult:	45+

Table 1.3. Loikop age grade transitions based on data from Larick (1985, 1986)

Boys:	younger (7–11)	older (11–15)	
Warriors:	junior (15–22)	senior (22–30)	
Elders:	junior (30–45)	intermediate (45–60)	senior (60+)

Even though data gleaned from anthropological studies, like that of the Loikop noted here, cannot be directly mapped onto our interpretations of late prehistoric Eurasian steppe societies, such data do indicate that the construction of warriorhood, and its gendered nature, lifestyle activities, and related material culture, often begin at a very young age. Therefore, even though biological sexing is highly problematic for subadult individuals, detailed studies of weaponry deposits with more specific age categories, as outlined above, may provide important data for identifying patterns of weaponry placement in graves and variable shifts in such practices over time. Nevertheless, in conjunction with such studies the deposit of weaponry and other grave goods must be understood as a complex arena of social practice that reflects the agency of the living within funerary ritual settings. Direct connections between certain categories of grave goods and interpretations of role, status, and gender can be highly problematic. For example, the deposit of weaponry in both the graves of children and adults can be a reflection of ascribed as well as achieved status and may not have any connection with the actual use of weapons in combat by those individuals. Furthermore, other categories of grave goods such as spindle whorls, which are often interpreted as relating to female gendered activities, are also found within male burials (Berseneva this volume). Such patterns strongly suggest that more nuanced theoretical approaches to understanding grave goods as representative of material culture and social practice must be drawn on in order to more effectively understand the wide range of human intentionality represented in Early Iron Age steppe mortuary ritual patterns.

GRAVE GOODS AS MATERIAL CULTURE
AND SOCIAL PRACTICE

Since the 1980s, numerous scholars have discussed the dangers of interpreting grave goods in functional terms because this completely disregards the agency of the living and their actions during the funerary process (Arnold and Wicker 2001b, xv; Härke 1990; Pader 1982; Parker Pearson 1999, 83; Weglian 2001). In fact, Parker Pearson notes that, "as archaeologists, we should be wary of how we separate the material culture *on* the body (clothes) from the material culture *of* the body (posture and body modification) from the material culture *off* the body (weapons, furniture, and other items)," as each of these categories may contribute in different ways to the totality of the individual's social identity (1999, 9). Such patterning may relate both to the way in which identity is constructed during the individual's lifetime as well as how the identity of the deceased is (re)articulated by the living through the mortuary event itself.

Despite recent theoretical trends that highlight the vibrant nature of material culture in funerary settings, scholarly discussions of steppe warriors continue to emphasize the functional notion that grave goods recovered from burial contexts were the property of the deceased and therefore directly represent the activities, tasks, and/or social role of those individuals (e.g., Fialko 1991; Guliaev 2003; Davis-Kimball 1998, 2002). In other words, arrowheads, spearheads, swords, and defensive items such as iron armor, not necessarily found together but also as individual deposits, can be directly linked to warrior individuals—be they male, female, adult, or child. By the same token, the deposit of bronze mirrors, clay or stone altars, colored mineral ores, and objects decorated in "Animal Style" art are connected with "priests" or "priestesses" (Davis-Kimball 1998, 246). In fact, during the Soviet period, O. A. Vishnevskaya was the first to postulate that stone "altars," and bronze mirrors found with them, were the material culture of priestesses or ritual specialists (1973; see also Yablonsky 1995b, 218).

In contrast to these interpretations, recent publications on Early Iron Age grave goods have suggested other possible uses for these classes of objects. For example, Karen Rubinson (2002) notes that the inclusion of bronze mirrors in Early Iron Age burials is a widespread phenomenon within the Eurasian steppe region—stretching from the region of present-day northern China to the Ukraine. Citing a variety of different Iron Age case studies, wherein mirrors are found deposited in both heavily and lightly furnished tombs, with children and adults, and females and males, Rubinson illustrates that metal mirrors and wooden mirror models were deposited in a variety of different mortuary settings (2002, 70–71). As she suggests, it is important to understand the broader social context of mirrors and their placement within graves, as they cannot easily be tied to a single purpose or gender and therefore had multiple meanings in different cultural settings (2002, 70–71).

Two recent publications focusing on the recovery of stone altars, colored mineral pigments, bone artifacts, *gryphaea* shells, and bronze mirrors from Sauro-Sarmatian burials located in the southern Ural Mountains region of Russia and northern Kazakhstan have suggested that these objects were used for bodily ornamentation such as tattooing/painting and cosmetics (Tairov and Bushmakin 2001; 2002, 185–190). The placement of these objects in both male and female graves suggests that their use was not gender specific but was instead connected with individual social and bodily identity constructions. Whether these objects were the personal possessions of the deceased, or were placed with the dead by the living, is not easily determined; however, clear evidence of tattooing has been discovered on preserved human remains recovered from frozen tombs in the Altai-Sayan Mountains region of north-central Eurasia and is associated with both males and females (Polos'mak 1992, 1994; Rudenko 1960, 1979). The application of pigments through tattooing or painting may have been an important part of both individual as well as ethnic identity and status constructions among Early Iron Age peoples. However, the application of paints to corpses may have been practiced during the mortuary ritual as well, as many of the objects (bone pipes and stone altars) recovered from the southern Urals burials yielded strong pigment residues from their last use (Tairov and Bushmakin 2002).

At this point it is necessary to return to a discussion of the deposit of weaponry in burials as this connects importantly with interpretations of gender, status, and warrior activities. As noted above, the inclusion of arrowheads, swords, daggers, and metal armor, either individually or in combination, is often regarded as evidence of warrior paraphernalia. However, the deposit of what we might consider a complete "set" of weaponry, including an iron sword and/or lance with a bow and arrows, is uncommon in most cases. The deposit of arrows is more ubiquitous, although it can be argued that archery was also used for hunting as well as warfare in the Early Iron Age. A recent publication argues that swords, lances, and battle-axes represent "real" warrior gear, while bow and arrow sets, knives, and daggers can be easily attributed to hunting and utilitarian tasks (Moshkova 1994). In fact, regarding the inclusion of swords and lance heads in Sauromatian female burials, it has been suggested that these are possible "mistakes" in the interpretation of the human remains in the original site reports (Bernabei, Bondioli, and Guidi 1994, 167). These views are based on a recent large-scale Russian-Italian collaborative project that began in 1989 and has focused on the creation of a statistical database and analysis of several thousand Sauromatian and Sarmatian grave inventories from the Volga-Don and Samara-Ural regions (Bashilov and Moshkova 1996; Moshkova 1994, 1997, 2002). The key aims of this project focus on the culture-historical chronology of the Sauro-Sarmatian antiquities in four periods, each corresponding to respective archaeological cultures, and the investigation of both the homogeneity and heterogeneity of archaeological patterning that is related to historical ethnocultural formations (Bashilov and Moshkova 1996, 124). In addition to ethnocultural issues, the statistical analysis of grave goods and tomb construction was also used to infer social statuses for males and females. This was done comparatively between the Volga-Don and Samara-Ural regions and then each region was analyzed independently. The general results of the first publication on Sauromatian burials are worth quoting in some detail:

> The male burials [Samara-Ural] are singled out [as] rather compact and are further divided into groups according to a series of features, including the presence of arms [weaponry]. However, the status index could be high both in the burials with and without arms. The results of the studies have shown a considerable social stratification inside the male part of the society. The cluster and seriation analyses of the female burials have not given such reliably defined groups. They

are demonstrating a higher variability and more complicated inner structure of the female burials, which is difficult to explain. However, the status index is better regulated. On the whole, the material from the South Ural region proves a complicated social organization . . . which are seen even in the burials of the children (Bashilov and Moshkova 1996, 127–128).

This collaborative statistical project has generated and systematized extremely significant new data for future comparative research. However, even with the use of statistical approaches, important decisions must be made regarding the classification of grave goods into units of *difference* as well as higher or lower rankings of *value* when considering status or gender. For example, in the project outlined above there is a clear disagreement between the Italian and Russian scholars over whether arrowheads should be considered as representative of "weapons" and therefore indicative of "warriors." While the Russian scholars argue that archery was an important component of steppe warfare, the Italian scholars argue that the frequent placement of arrows in graves, without accompanying lances and/or swords, may indicate archery for hunting rather than warfare-related activities (Bernabei, Bondioli, and Guidi 1994, 174). It is, of course, possible that they represent both activities.

Two of the general results noted above also have important relevance to discussions of status. It is noted that in the male burials from the southern Urals region (112 graves) weaponry does not always correlate with what are considered *high* status burials based on other included grave goods. It is also noted that the analysis of the female burials from this region (ninety-seven graves) has not provided clear definable groups and instead indicates a high variability in terms of mortuary patterning. None of the statistical data from either the Sauromatian or Early Sarmatian burials support the female status categories proposed by Jeannine Davis-Kimball as discussed above for the Pokrovka mortuary data. Rather, what is clear from the statistical data is that funerary treatment varied with regard to the types of grave goods that were included with the deceased, especially weaponry. Certainly, the use of multivariate statistical methods provides a powerful tool for investigating patterns within mortuary data; however, quite often there is already a predisposition toward a specific social model. As Feldore McHugh notes, "[multivariate] methods are no aid to understanding in themselves, since their interpretation is being constrained by what little understanding of social structure already exists through previous qualitative studies" (1999, 63). Therefore, the use of quantitative methods still relies strongly on decisions about the value and meaning of particular categories of grave goods and what their placement with the deceased means in terms of status and identity. Such approaches also make important decisions about what to include and exclude from quantification—such as the exclusion of faunal remains, which was done both in Davis-

Kimball's analysis (1998, 142) and in the Russian-Italian statistical analysis (Moshkova 1996, 165).

With regard to weaponry deposits, it is useful to note that similar concerns regarding the inclusion of weapons in graves, and more specifically what this may indicate in terms of social status, gender, and age grades, have been frequently discussed for the Iron Age and Anglo-Saxon periods of Europe. It is useful to consider these discussions here in the context of the problems surrounding the interpretation of patterns connected with the interpretations of warriors and weaponry deposits in the steppe Iron Age.

In a number of publications, the problems associated with the interpretation of Anglo-Saxon mortuary patterns and the nature of weaponry deposits have been examined in detail (Härke 1990, 1992, 1997; Lucy 1997; Pader 1982; Stoodley 2000). Based on this research there are two areas of relevance to the problems outlined above for Eurasian steppe mortuary material: 1) weaponry deposits and "warrior graves"; and 2) age grade organization and weaponry burial rites. Regarding the first point, in an interesting study undertaken by Härke (1997) on forty-seven Anglo-Saxon (early 5th to late 7th century CE) burial sites containing weaponry deposits within burials, it was indicated that the placement of weapons varied over time, few deposits reflected actual functional military kits, and there was a direct correlation with the intensification of mortuary weaponry deposits during periods of lower levels of fighting (based on the Anglo-Saxon chronicle). Based on this mortuary patterning, and the fact that the burials represent the immigration of a foreign population into England, Härke suggests that the weaponry rites were an important part of expressing and reaffirming martial symbolism and existing "power structures" rather than a functional reflection of actual warrior individuals (1997, 125). For example, 25 percent (N = 3,814) of the burials contained weapons sets that "do not make any practical sense at all: they are made up of a single throwing spear or throwing axe (francisca), an unaccompanied battle knife (seax, usually a small narrow seax), or even a shield on its own" (1997, 119). In total, 48 percent of the male adult burials in Härke's study were buried with weaponry, which does not support the notion that weapons were restricted to elite or noblemen statuses among Anglo-Saxon populations (1997, 119).

In another recent study by Stoodley, based on 1,230 Early Anglo-Saxon (5th to 7th century CE) undisturbed burials from forty-six cemeteries, it was determined that social identity started to form at early ages for both male and female genders (2000). In this interesting study, Stoodley correlated grave goods with six age divisions. Based on his analysis, individuals aged 2–3 years represented an important transition in mortuary rites as from this stage on the quantity, quality, and types of grave goods increase with age (2000, 459). A second important threshold occurred at approximately 18–20 years of age and marked an important change in the status of the individual from youth to adult within the community (2000, 461). With regard to weaponry deposits, a clear pattern emerges. Weaponry, aside from spears and arrows, is in almost all cases deposited with individuals 15 years and older (predominantly males when such data are available). By contrast, single spears were found with all subadult age categories — with the youngest being a 1-year-old (2000, 461). However, 72 percent (N = 13) of the spear burials in the child group were with individuals 10–14 years of age. The majority of weaponry burials (41%) are found with individuals 20–25 years of age and in total 56 percent of deposited weapons are associated with the adult group — aged 20–40 years.

These analyses by Härke and Stoodley provide excellent case studies for the investigation and interpretation of weaponry deposits and their connection with status and the life cycle of individuals. The deposit of weaponry with individuals, including subadults, adults, males, and females can indicate not only achieved social status or role but also importantly ascribed status. Such studies also confirm that mortuary patterning, and the deposit of grave goods including weaponry, can change dramatically over a few generations as new social, cultural, and ethnic conditions form (Härke 1997, 125). When considering patterns of weaponry deposits in steppe Iron Age mortuary practices, a number of important questions can be asked about the actual nature of warfare, its frequency, and how changes in these areas may have impacted the social construction of warriorhood and its connection to concepts of status and gender.

TOWARD A SOCIAL ARCHAEOLOGY OF WARFARE

As outlined above, there are a number of conceptual problems surrounding the interpretation of warrior burials in the Eurasian steppe region. However, even with a greater awareness of these issues, how can we move forward more productively with interpretations of such archaeological patterns? This author suggests that there are two key factors that must be considered in future archaeological studies: 1) more nuanced anthropological interpretations of warrior agency and lifestyle; and 2) more systematic bioarchaeological analyses of human remains. Regarding the first point, in recent years anthropological approaches to understanding warfare and violence have become much more focused on the active role that warriors occupy within societies. For example, Ferguson and Whitehead (1992) suggest that it is necessary to acknowledge the complexity associated with contact zones occurring between state/nonstate entities and between individual nonstate groups. These historically situated dynamics result in the creation and re-creation of social structures in a dynamic process they term *tribalization* (1992, 12). Such a view rightly acknowledges the scale of individual activity that exists when new structures of internecine tension and warfare emerge between societies. At a broader level, this perspective provides an anthropological awareness for large-scale sociopolitical processes and the creation of new ethnocultural formations. On a smaller scale, this perspective acknowledges the specific material and social conditions that come together in the form of warriorhood as a category of social meaning. The problem, of course, is how we as archaeologists conceptualize this meaning and interpret it through archaeological evidence.

Archaeological interpretations of prehistoric warriors have ranged from an emphasis on rigid models of chiefly power to the glorified aesthetics and expressive behavioral characteristics of this lifestyle (Kristiansen 1998; Shennan 1986; Treherne 1995). Both interpretations suggest that warriors exist as real social categories, traditionally perceived in terms of individuals with higher rank and status within communities. However, Deborah Shepherd, commenting on available early historic evidence for the Iron Age Celtic and Germanic groups, argues that warriors have also existed at the edge of the ordered community and when not engaged in warfare often participate individually or in small cohorts in raiding and stealing (1999, 219). What is important here is Shepherd's emphasis on warriors acting outside the normative category of societal elites, as this emphasizes the fluidity of warrior agency and its connection to the specific age set of young males. In fact, it is possible to argue that there is a wide range of activities that could be equated with the warrior lifestyle that is infrequently considered by scholars, for example, the role of warriors as mercenaries within and outside their communities (Arnold 1988, 2005), the formation of warrior sodalities, engendered perceptions of warriorhood relating to masculinity and femininity (Hanks, forthcoming), and the impact of age grades that structure transitions into and out of the "warriorhood" category within an individual's life cycle (Gilchrist 1999, 2000).

It is important to note that in many cases these sociocultural categories and actions represent horizontal rather than vertical social gradations. And such activities, which are well documented ethnographically, may sharply contrast with conventional interpretations of mortuary data that focus on ascribed and achieved statuses based on a vertical and hierarchical model. This clearly has been the traditional approach for understanding the Early Iron Age of the Eurasian steppe region. While there is still much to overcome conceptually with how the mortuary record of this region is understood, it is suggested that new directions must be developed.

This author suggests that one area that must be more thoroughly investigated is the impact that warrior activities may have had on Early Iron Age steppe societies. It is informative, for example, to consider a number of the publications focusing on the Early Iron Age of Europe, wherein Bettina Arnold has examined processes associated with the mobility of men and women away from their home territories (1995, 1996, 2005). The factors stimulating such activities can include "male out-migration" as specialist warrior mercenaries, marriage alliances, and political or economic oriented movements (2005). The outward migration of warriors, be they male or female, and the impact that this may have on their societies is an issue that crosscuts several important aspects of late prehistoric/protohistoric societies. For example, in the case of the early La-Tène in Europe, Arnold suggests that the rise in elite status markers (gold neck rings, bronze drinking vessels, daggers, wagons, etc.) in female burials, with a corresponding shift in fewer elite male burials, may represent the impact that male out-migration had as Celtic mercenary activity increased around 400 BCE (1995, 159). As she argues, the basis of social power and status within these communities shifted to women as males (sons, brothers, and husbands) became increasingly drawn away from their home territories (1995, 159).

Processes such as these that can initiate fragmentation within communities, and more specifically the ways in which warrior agency may work, have not been discussed for the Eurasian steppe Iron Age. With the strong evidence for martial equipment, and its symbolic significance within such societies, it would seem that much greater attention should be placed on theorizing the nature of warrior mobility and the effect that out-migration and interregional marriage patterns may have had on these early societies. However, such approaches bring us even closer to investigating the impact that *individuals* have on early societies rather than focusing primarily on larger social structures and their concomitant patterns in the archaeological record. Such a project connects in a number of important ways with recent trends in archaeological theory.

PEOPLING THE PAST?

In his recent book, *The Archaeology of Personhood*, Chris Fowler remarks that the broader agenda of postprocessual archaeology has become synonymous with attempts to "people the past" (2004, 5). As a result, much greater emphasis is being placed on conceptualizing personhood and identity. This trend toward placing a greater focus on *individuals* in the past would seem to be congruent with rapid developments in bioarchaeology and forensic studies, both of which have provided new methods for the physical and chemical study of human remains and the reconstruction of lifetime activity patterns and specific biological events. Therefore, with new analytical tools at our disposal we seem now, in many ways, transfixed on trying to illuminate the life history and personhood of individuals in the past. However, this emphasis on finding, or perhaps more accurately *constructing* individuals in the past, suffers from important conceptual problems. For example, as Julian Thomas notes, we must be cautious about our archaeological imagination, which is inherently coupled with our understanding of the material nature of human practice (1996). Thomas's use of *imagination* in this case represents the important distinction of understanding material objects as evidence of past human practice outside of their original contextual settings. As he states, "what we produce is an interpretation, which is not of the past, but which stands for the past" (1996, 64). This view is important when considering the context of mortuary remains and their use by archaeologists for modeling broader perceptions of social organization, on one hand, and the reconstruction of individuals on the other. Death and burial represent very unique moments in time where the identity of the deceased can be, and often is, actively (re)negotiated by the living through communicative action and display. Concerning this, Bettina Arnold has recently questioned the degree to which such human intentionality can be identified and understood. As she states:

> The question is not "Are the patterns we as archaeologists see real?" but rather "Do the patterns we see matter?," that is, would they have been recognized as significant or "real" to the study population? If the answer to the final question is "No," what does this imply for the application of concepts like agency to archaeological interpretation? (2001, 221)

Arnold's cautionary comments are significant when considering how we as archaeologists of the present hope to understand and reconstruct the human intentionality of the past. For example, mortuary studies at once engage with what might be termed the *biological condition*, the *social condition*, and the *material condition* of the past, all of which coalesce in complex ways in the dynamic creation of human lifeways.[1] In fact, it may be more accurate to suggest that mortuary archaeology as a practice regularly vacillates among these conditions—and in so doing, sustains them as arbitrary categories of meaning. However, as a discipline, archaeology is unavoidably divided into different arenas of study. In the examination of mortuary evidence, the context of the remains always will be deconstructed at the site level and assigned to different fields of analysis—broadly representing the biological, social, and material dimensions.

Andy Jones discusses this problem more generally with regard to postexcavation analysis in archaeology (2002). He suggests that, "due to the fragmented nature of archaeological practice, post-excavation analysis is in fact at the periphery of the interpretative process" (2002, 48). This seems to be an extremely important conceptual and methodological point of view, particularly since many scholars actively subscribe to the view that human dynamics in the past exist only as historically situated realities. Such realities are understood as being negotiated through material culture and therefore cannot be reconstructed outside of that context of meaning. In this sense, social conditions are only brought into *being* through engagement with a material world and therefore are constantly being created and re-created. Moreover, one may suggest that the biological condition is a product of social relationships and structures that are highly situational throughout the lifetime of the individual—from birth until death. As such, the death event only reveals one specific moment in the process of life and the creation of personhood—and so does not readily provide a fixed social meaning that can be readily unpacked. Nevertheless, even with this cautionary view, biological data provide an extremely important line of information about past human behavior and activity, which may co-vary significantly with social interpretations based solely on funerary treatment at death (Robb 2002; Sofaer 2006). Therefore, if we are indeed moving toward a broader agenda of *peopling the past*, and in so doing drawing more heavily on bioarchaeological data to conceptualize personhood, we must continue to acknowledge and confront these significant epistemological problems and strive to draw evenly from all available evidence to inform our interpretations.

CONCLUSION

This chapter argues for a greater awareness of how mortuary archaeology connects with recent trends in social theory and with new analytical methods currently available. It has been suggested that it is necessary to move forward from traditional approaches to understanding gender and social identity, and their relationship to the category of warriorhood within early steppe societies, to focus more critically on the actual meaning of these concepts and the social processes that shape them. The material dimension of gender is important for archaeologists, as this represents one of the predominant areas of recoverable information. However, understanding the dynamic relationship between material culture and the social categories mediated through such objects is a realm of interpretation that still requires much greater attention. The use of more detailed bioarchaeological analyses seems promising; however, even though important developments have been achieved in this area of study in recent years, the application of such research within archaeological interpretation has not become as widespread as one would hope. Nevertheless, social interpretations of gender and warrior lifestyle in the steppe region must be examined through the use of biological indicators of activity, such as skeletal stress markers and paleopathology. With the wide range of analyses now available, biological information may help to more critically evaluate both the agency of the living and their manipulation of material culture during burial and to provide a clearer perspective on specific individuals, their life-ways, and how these connect with the broader patterns of their social groups. In conclusion, and echoing the sentiments of the late David Clarke (1973) from nearly thirty-five years ago, I believe that with the development of new pathways into investigating the past we must continually seek to redefine both the questions that drive our research and the theories we use to construct our perceptions of people's lives in the past. And we must always remain considerate of our archaeological imaginations.

NOTE

1. A version of this chapter was first presented at the seventy-first Society for American Archaeology meeting in San Juan, Puerto Rico. In the discussion following the session, Bettina Arnold rightly pointed out that there is also an important *political* dimension that influences mortuary archaeology.

Chapter Two

Arma Feminamque Cano: Warrior-Women in the Indo-European World

Karlene Jones-Bley

Few words conjure more immediate or specific images than the word *Amazon*. A modern audience sees her as Wonder Woman—champion of justice. The ancient Greeks, from whom we get the term, saw her as a large, well-built woman dressed in warrior garb wielding a sword or dagger and perhaps lacking a breast. To the Greeks, the thought of Amazons brought fear of chaos. Amazons were a symbol of female assertion, and this was no way for a woman to behave. Women belonged at home bearing and caring for children. They were the mothers of soldiers or the mothers of mothers of soldiers—this was the natural order. Women taking on the role of warrior were beyond the pale, and there are even those who suggest that the Greeks invented the Amazons as a kind of sociopolitical bogeyman. It is, however, difficult to believe Amazons were made out of whole cloth. They must have had a prototype, and indeed they did.

The perceived position of women in ancient Indo-European societies, and here I mean societies that spoke an Indo-European language, such as Greek, Latin, Celtic, Iranian, or Slavic,[1] has been, for the most part, based on what we know of Greek and Roman women and influenced by 19th-century attitudes (see Katz 1995). As a result, women have been pictured as having little impact on society except to bear and raise children. While there is no denying this was a primary role for most women, recent scholarship has shown that women, even Greek and Roman women, went beyond the boundaries of hearth and home (see, for example, Blundell 1995 and Savunen 1995).

Nevertheless, despite the many inroads made by recent scholars, the idea of women taking up arms has generally remained in the fields of mythology, folklore, or satire. There is, however, a large body of evidence pointing to females bearing arms. Moreover, the evidence comes from many parts of the Indo-European-speaking world and clearly clashes with the traditional view of women as a passive, even oppressed, segment of society. Despite this evidence, much of which has been known since at least the early part of the 20th century, the idea of women as warriors has been denied, overlooked, dismissed as a figment of the imagination, or reinterpreted as an instrument to keep society (read women) in line. An abbreviated catalog of women involved in warfare illustrates my thesis that ancient women, or at least female figures, were more actively involved in warfare than previously thought. The catalog can be broken down into several categories, although some figures overlap these categories:

CATALOG OF FEMALE FIGURES INVOLVED IN WARFARE

Goddesses of War

Irish—Medb, Badb,[2] Macha,[3] Nemain,[4] and the Morrígan
British—Andraste,[5] Brigantia[6]
Greek—Athena, Enyo[7]
Roman—Minerva,[8] Juno,[9] Bellona[10]
Slavic—Zarya,[11] Zorya[12]
Indic—Devi[13]

Warlike Figures

Irish—Fedelm,[14] Scáthach, Aife
Germanic—Gondul, Skogul[15]
Roman—Nerio[16]
Greek—Aphrodite[17]

Legendary Figures

Irish—Luachar[18]
Germanic—Brynhild
Roman—Camilla
Amazon Queens—Andromache, Thalestria, Penthesileia, Hippolyte

Figures with War Connections but Not Actually Warriors

Celtic—Epona
Germanic—Freyja[19]
Greek—Eris[20]
Iranian—Anahita[21]

Historical Figures

Celtic—Boudica, Cartimandua
Germanic—Velenda,[22] Hetha and Visna,[23] Rusila/Rusla[24]
Iranian—Atossa,[25] Tomgris[26]
Saxon—Æthelflæd[27]

These are the names of only some Indo-European female figures—mythical and historical—who are directly or indirectly related to war.

There are also groups of women whose predominant aspect is war related, such as the nine witches of Gloucester, Valkyries, and, of course, the Amazons. Classical authors including Strabo, Tacitus, Dio Cassius, and Caesar regale us with the military prowess and physical strength of Celtic women. The iconography also provides us with many representations of women in battle or sporting weapons (see for example Boardman 1993, figs. 19A, 56B, 96, 97, 154). Just what are we dealing with?

To paraphrase Strabo, Indo-Europeans were madly fond of war (see Strabo IV.4.6), so if the society was fond of war, does it seem reasonable that women would have been completely excluded? That women, at least in part, shared this taste for war can be seen in the Spartan women, who neither lamented their men who died in battle nor brooked cowardice in their sons. Celtic and Germanic women were also known not only to stand on the sidelines but also to cheer their men and taunt the enemy (Caesar, *The Gallic War* 1.51; Tacitus, *Germanica* 7-8; *Annals* XIV.30, 34).

In order to objectively examine both the question of what is going on and the evidence, we must set aside the comfort and supposed order of the 19th-century views that have shaped our vision of the Indo-European-speaking female (Bachofen 1861; Harrison 1903). It is not enough to say that these views no longer apply—they were wrong in the first place. Nor is it sufficient to replace this view with an early-21st-century feminist view that would have divisions of female warriors or to manipulate evidence creating women where, in fact, there are men. What I propose here is an objective look at the evidence, one that makes a serious attempt to set aside preconceived ideas and prejudices—not to exchange one dogma for another.

EVIDENCE FOR WOMEN AND WARFARE

The types of evidence are divergent. Interestingly, the best evidence for warrior-women is found most abundantly in two extremes of the Indo-European world—the Celts in the far west and those referred to as Amazons in the east. This distribution, which if linguistic, would point to archaic survivals on the periphery, is not a matriarchal substrate as is commonly supposed. It is on these two groups that I will concentrate.

Let us first take up the east. A great deal of scholarly (and popular) ink has been spilled on the subject of Amazons, particularly on the question of whether or not there really were Amazons, and if they were real, how we can more directly identify them.

CLASSICAL EVIDENCE

Herodotus (IV.114) tells us that these women warriors did not engage in or even know how to do women's work; they lived without men (being with them only to beget children), and they dressed like men as well.[28] They rode horses, shot bows, threw spears, and hunted. He further tells us that no girl married before she had killed an enemy. If this was not fulfilled, the woman died a spinster. Apollodorus gives us the story that "they pinched off the right breasts, that they might not be trammeled by them in throwing the javelin, but they kept the left breasts, that they might suckle" (*The Library*, II. v.9). Strabo (XI.5.1), however, tells us that the Amazons spent their time plowing, planting, tending cattle, and particularly training horses. Moreover, they mated at random with the Gargarians, a neighboring people in the northern foothills of the Caucasus.

All of these things were presented to the Greeks (here read Athenians) as abnormal and aberrations. At least one scholar (Tyrell 1984) writes that the myth itself was designed to keep Athenian society (or perhaps just Athenian women) under control, and that the myth was used to show what happened in society when women did not keep their places as wives and mothers. In other words, women behaving like men resulted in a world of chaos, despite the fact that the deity who watched over Athens was the spear- and shield-bearing Athena herself. This obvious contradiction has been rationalized: "her warlike attributes were geared more to protectiveness than to aggression" (Bell 1991, 85). This, I would say, begs the issue as few aggressors see their actions as aggressive. Furthermore, Athena's actions and interference in the *Iliad* cannot be termed defensive (*Iliad* 5.12–132, 5.78–863, 20.41–53). The view that society balances on the edge of devastation when women take the lead is also mirrored in the Celtic literature (as we will see) despite what is generally thought to be a more liberal view of women by the Celts, leading O'Connor to state that the original purpose of the author of the *Táin Bó Cuailnge* was to "warn his readers against women, particularly women in position of authority" (1967, 34).

Until quite recently many scholars believed the Amazons were just a Greek myth having little if anything to do with reality and that Herodotus, who did sometimes have trouble with geography, made up the Amazons about whom he wrote at length. But other classical authors contributed to the Amazon myth as well. Aeschylus referred to them as flesh eaters who rode on "steed-like camels" (*hippobamosin*), but he also said they were nomadic (*Suppliant Maidens* 283–287), and in *Prometheus*, he tells us that Amazons hated all men (*Prometheus* 726). Myths inevitably contain some truth, and in this case it is becoming more and more clear that there was at least some truth in the Amazon myth. Nevertheless, the contradictions within the myth served to strengthen the unreal status of the Amazons. Amazons were virgins who hated men—but met with men to beget children. Apollodorus (*The Library*, II. v.9) said they pinched off their right breasts; Hellanicus said the breasts were cauterized; Philostratus said they fed their children horse milk in order to keep their breasts from enlarging (Fantham et al. 1994, 131). The implication of the Amazons' life to the Greeks may have been that Amazons lived in a world of nature and thus, to the nature-taming Greeks, unnatural chaos. This unnaturalness seems to be emphasized by the fact that their sexual activity was random and conducted outdoors. There is, however, nothing to indicate that the Amazons lived in a state of chaos. Indeed, the Amazons had a queen (the names of several are known, e.g., Thalestria, Penthesileia, Antope, Hippolyta, and Andromache), enough organization to go to war, founded cities (Ephesus, Smyrna, Cyma, Themiscyra, and Myrina are attributed to them [Strabo XI.5.4]), and according to Lysias (*Funeral Oration* II.4–6) ruled over many nations and enslaved those around them.

Amazons appear on the Greek scene prior to Herodotus. They are first mentioned by Homer in the *Iliad* and, in iconographic form, they appear on dozens of black-figure vessels with Herakles, Achilles, or Theseus. The earliest known depiction of an Amazon appears on a terra-cotta shield found at Tiryns, dating to about 700 BCE,[29] fighting a warrior whose identity is unclear (see Bothmer 1957, pl. I.1a; Hampe and Simon 1981, fig. 95). They are, however, despite the assertion by Taylor that "Amazons are depicted in Greek sculpture and painting with the right side of the chest draped to cover this missing breast" (1994, 395), never depicted as having only one breast and the right breast is fully formed under the draping (see, for example, Bothmer 1957, pls. LXXXVII.4, 9, LXXXIX.1–3, 5–6, XC.1, 3; Hampe and Simon 1981, fig. 95; Boardman 1993, figs. 94A–B, 97, 127A–B). In 1996, Taylor gave a plausible explanation for the removal of the left (as opposed to his earlier discussion of the right) breast. He suggested that the left nipple would have been in danger when using a "composite reflex bow fired from horseback [where] the draw is short and across the body" (Taylor 1996, 200). Another view is taken by Marazov, who interprets the draping of the right breast as "some specific semiotic value of this attribute . . . [which] . . . denotes the Amazon as a sexless creature" (1996, 94). Marazov further claims that to ancient people the breast signified a social not erotic function which connects with the etymology of Amazon as the "non-breast feeding one" (Marazov 1996, 94). This, however, is contradicted by numerous Greek epigrams, such as:

> Oh, would I were the wind, that walking on the shore thou mightest bare thy bosom and take me to thee as I blow. Anonymous (Paton 1916, 169, no. 83)
> Oh, would I were a pink rose, that thy hand might pluck me to give to thy snowy breasts. Anonymous (Paton 1916, 169, no. 84)
> Eluding her mother's apprehensive eyes, the charming girl gave me a pair of rosy apples. I think she had secretly ensorcelled those red apples with the torch of love, for I, alack! am wrapped in flame, and instead of two breasts, ye gods, my purposeless hands grasp two apples. Paulus Silentiarius (Paton 1916, 281, no. 290)

Clearly the Greeks also found erotic pleasure in women's breasts. Furthermore, the lack of one breast does not preclude breast-feeding, and as we have seen, according to Apollodorus the left was used specifically for this function.

Although the Greeks may have been reticent to represent this deformity, a more likely reason for the two-breasted Amazon is linguistic. While the Greek's own folk etymology for Amazon is "un-breasted," this cultural mastectomy would have left the Amazons "one-breasted," *monomazones*. A more likely etymology would be "without-husband," from Proto-Indo-European *ņ-mņgʷion-es . The first element of this compound is a negative marker cognate with the English prefix *un*. For the second element of the compound compare Old Church Slavic *mǫžǐ* to Russian *muzh*, "husband" (Huld 2002). But the word for a woman to become married combines the prefix "to follow" with the word for husband, *zamuzh*—literally to follow a husband—something Amazons clearly did not do. This linguistic suggestion of "without husband" follows Aeschylus's assumption that Amazons were "mateless and flesh-devouring" (1938, *Suppliant Women* 287–289).

In support of this argument that the Amazons did not remove their breasts, it might also be noted that although Athena wielded a spear and Artemis a bow, there is never a suggestion that they were deprived of a part of their female anatomy in order to improve their skill with these weapons.

EVIDENCE FROM THE EAST

That contemporary women not only engaged in battle but were also buried with what is often called warrior equipment (knives, spears, bows and arrows) can be seen from burials of Scythian, Sauromatian, Sarmatian, Sargat, Saka, and other peoples across the steppe.[30] Moreover, many of these skeletons show injuries typical of combat (see Rolle 1989). The key to recovering women warriors is the anthropological sexing of skeletons. These burials, mostly discovered since the 1950s, give us undisputed evidence of women buried as warriors and also give new meaning to the stories of Amazons told by Herodotus and others.

In the steppe region of southern Ukraine, a number of kurgans dating to about the 4th century BCE have revealed women, identified anthropologically, who are of interest. These women were buried with earrings, necklaces of bone and glass, bracelets, bronze arm rings, pottery, clay spindle whorls, and mirrors. Note that spindle whorls, which have traditionally been considered typically female items and deal with the woman's work of spinning, seem to contradict Herodotus's statement that they did not know women's work.[31] While mirrors might be thought of as a female item, they are also found in Scythian (Bokovenko 1995a, 278) and other male burials on the Eurasian steppe. Nevertheless, all the bronze mirrors in a Saka context from Kazakhstan are from female graves (Yablonsky 1995b, 205). We thus see that mirrors cannot be used as a sex indicator (also see Rubinson 2002) any more than weapons can. In addition, typical warrior items including bows and arrows, iron knives, armor, and lances[32] have been found in women's graves (Rice 1957; Rolle 1989; Polos'mak 1994a; Melyukova 1995; Barbarunova 1995; Davis-Kimball 1997a), but without anthropological examination, these would certainly have been labeled male burials. Any idea that these items were placed in the grave as ritual items or offerings from a grieving husband can be dismissed by the fact that these women also showed evidence of head and body wounds typical of battle (Rolle 1989, 88; Davis-Kimball 1997a, 48).

One of the best and most interesting examples of a female warrior grave comes from Cholodny Yar and dates to the 4th century BCE. In the central burial of kurgan 20 under a timber ceiling lay two skeletons (both anthropologically sexed). The main skeleton was clearly a female. She wore large silver earrings, bronze arm rings, and a necklace of beads made of bone and glass. She also had a bronze mirror, pottery, a clay spindle whorl, and food offerings together with the usual iron knives. (Knives are not necessarily considered weapons as they were also used for eating.) What are more likely weapons were the two iron lance points, a quiver with forty-seven bronze arrowheads, and five "pebble missiles." The second skeleton, a male, lay at her feet and had only "two small bronze bells, two ornamented pipes and an iron arm ring" (Rolle 1989, 88). He might well be thought of as another of her grave goods.

Another female grave with a sword was found at Volnaya in kurgan 22 in Ukraine (Melyukova 1995, 46), and at Akkermen I, in kurgan 16, a female skeleton was found with armor. The latter lay supine, wore bronze and silver arm rings, and a necklace of glass beads. She also had a bronze mirror, a decorated lead spindle whorl, and food offerings in wooden vessels. Her weapons included a quiver containing twenty arrows, two lances, and a heavy fighting belt covered in strips of iron. She also had "severe head injuries from blows and stabs, and a bent bronze arrowhead still embedded in the knee" (Rolle 1989, 88). The fighting belt reminds us that it was the belt of the Amazon queen Hippolyte that was the ninth labor of Herakles.

Burials of women equipped as warriors are not confined to Ukraine but have been found eastward across the steppe as far as the Altai Mountains (Mamontov 1990, 1991; Polos'mak 1994a; Melyukova 1995; Davis-Kimball 1997a; Berseneva this volume; Rubinson this volume). Women with military equipment have also been found in the Caucasus (Rice 1957, 48–49). Within these female burials, a wide range of weapons has been found including daggers, lances, spears, swords, and pebbles (possibly for slings) but the bow and arrow seem to have been the favorite weapon of women. Sometimes the only remaining evidence is that of a quiver hook (Mamontov 1991). The choice of the bow and arrow may have been to compensate for the lesser strength of women, and/or because they could be used from horseback.

The idea of riding horseback should not be overlooked nor underestimated. This is mentioned numerous times by the ancient authors and should in no way surprise us. It was not unusual for women to ride horses during the Iron Age, and we have iconographic evidence of it for non-warrior-women as well, such as on the Hallstatt ceramic vessel from Sopron in Hungary, which is roughly contemporary with the Amazons. This vessel also shows a woman driving a wagon, and we have iconography of Mycenaean women driving wagons as well (Megaw and Megaw 1989, figs. 16, 17; Hampe and Simon 1981, fig. 20). From a grave in northeast England at the cemetery of Wetwang (Dent 1985), we have the remains of a woman and her two-wheeled vehicle. On the Russian steppe, the tradition of burying a horse or horses with the master or mistress was not an uncommon occurrence and continued into the medieval period (Mamontov 1990, figs. 49–51). Even women who claim no warrior aspect have been found with horse harnesses in their graves (Petrenko 1995, 12; Yablonsky 1995b, 203; Treister 1997, 50). Certainly these are all indications of what women did in life, but placed in the grave, horses and wheeled vehicles should be interpreted as transport to the Otherworld (Jones-Bley 1997, 2006).

We are, of course, also reminded of the connection between horses and Amazons by the names of three of their queens Lysippe, Hippo, and the more famous Hippolyta. The connection between men and horse names is well-known, such as Philip, Hippocrates, and Eric, but that there was a connection between women, as well as men, and horses is also clear. Bell, in his *Women of Classical Mythology* (1991, 241–247), lists at least thirty-four women with the element *hippo*, "horse," in their names.

The location of the Amazons, based on Herodotus, is generally placed in the area north of the Black Sea. Although Homer (*Iliad*, 3.184–189, 6.173–187) implies that the Amazons came from Anatolia, there is little if any evidence for this. Strabo (XI.5.1) comments that they lived not only in Albania[33] (located in the Caucasus) but also in the foothills north of the Caucasus. This is probably the most accurate as it is in the lower Volga region where the largest number of graves of armed women have been found—accounting for about 20 percent in the Sauromatian area. In Scythian graves of southeastern Europe, E. P. Bunyatyan calculated that during the 4th–3rd centuries BCE, 27–29 percent of female burials contained some sort of armament (Melyukova 1995, 43). Although the ancient authors place the Amazonian homeland in various places, they generally agree that it was on the borders of the "civilized" world.

Despite the literary evidence for this North Pontic location for the Amazons, there are female warrior burials farther east. In 1990, excavations in the Altai Mountains of Siberia at Ak-Alakh uncovered a frozen grave of some interest. In one part of the grave the badly preserved remains of horses were found. In another part of the grave two wooden coffins, each made of a single larch log and dating to the 4th to 3rd centuries BCE, were found side by side. The larger coffin contained a middle-aged man and the smaller one a 17-year-old female dressed in trousers. The finds in her coffin were very similar to those found in the male's and included a headdress of felt, topped with a bird's head covered with gold leaf; a torque decorated with wooden figurines of wolves, also covered with gold leaf; beads; cowry shells; and a bronze mirror. "By her right thigh lay an iron dagger in a wooden scabbard, and by her left a wooden quiver . . . [and] [n]earby, as in the first coffin, there were seven bone arrowheads and some pieces of a compound bow" (Polos'mak 1994a, 350–351). Some might say this is an example of suttee, but even if it was, the woman had all the attributes usually interpreted as a warrior.

Another question to be addressed: Were the Amazons the "wild tribe" outside the scope of other tribes—did they live without men? Archaeologically this does not seem to be the case because the burials we have are in the context of Scythian, Sauromatian, Sarmatian, Sargat, and Saka cemeteries, which also contained men. Nevertheless, that these women commanded special respect and honor can be seen by their primary placement in kurgans (Melyukova 1995, 36; Berseneva this volume; see also Linduff this volume). These mounds were often reused for secondary burials, but it was the person in central position for whom the mound was built and who would thus have been of greatest importance. This feature was typical of Indo-European burial (Jones-Bley 1990, 1997).

EVIDENCE FROM THE WEST

At the opposite end of Europe, we find reports of fighting women among the Celts. Celtic literature and mythology are replete with examples of the powerful woman and the female warrior. And again, we have modern authors who dismiss them: Ehrenberg (1989, 152) suggests that it was the Roman need to see the Celts as barbarians that caused Roman writers to portray Celtic women in battle, because, of course, it was barbaric for women to go to battle. While I have difficulty believing this was the root of this literary tradition, there may be some truth in the thought. This theory might be supported by a marble relief that can be found in the British Museum. The marble relief commemorates the release from service of two female gladiators, appropriately named Amazon and Achilla (BM Cat. Sculpture 1117; see Pringle 2001). The relief is Greek, showing two gladiators, and is inscribed with their names. The relief dates to the 1st or 2nd century CE and comes from Halicarnassis. Also at the British Museum is a Roman bronze parade mask (BM Cat. Bronzes 877) of a woman dating to the 2nd century CE.

Unfortunately for us, the Celts were more literary than iconographic. The literature, however, includes not only the classical authors but also legends and Celtic laws.[34] Nevertheless, we need go no further than the first few lines of the great Irish epic *Táin Bó Cuailnge* to find the quintessential example of the female Celtic warrior—Medb, who straddles this world and that of myth, was the warrior queen who commanded an army, and was the leader of Connacht. During a conversation in bed between Medb and her most current (much younger and complacent cuckold) husband, Ailill, he tells her how much better off she is now that she is married to him. She protests, claiming that she was well enough off without him. She then goes on to list all the things she had; he counters with his possessions. In the end, their possessions are equal except that Ailill has a large bull the equal of which she does not have. In order to solve this problem, Medb sets out with her army to capture the Brown Bull of Cooley that was in Ulster. Clearly, Medb was both a warrior and a woman of great power.

The Celts, particularly the Irish, had an affinity for warrior goddesses who engaged in battle, albeit often in a metamorphosed form. The war goddess, the Morrígan, is nearly a match for the great Irish hero, Cú Chulainn, and as in the case of Medb, she is as comfortable on the battlefield as she is in the bedchamber. However, while Medb may have been a towering figure in the mythical, political, and military spheres, the Irish annals give her no historical counterpart (Kelly 1988, 71). Moreover, her lover Fergus decries the leadership of women when he tells her: "That is what usually happens . . . to a herd of horses led by a mare. Their substance is taken and carried off and guarded as they follow a woman who has misled them" (Kelly 1992, 79). Thus, like the Morrígan, Medb can be interpreted negatively.

In Irish and Welsh stories, the great heroes were taught not only wisdom but also feats of arms by women. Cú Chulainn was trained in all the warrior arts by two warlike queens—Scáthach, who was also a *fáith*, namely, "a prophetess," expert in supernatural wisdom, and Aife. In the Welsh story of Peredur, the hero was trained by the nine witches of Gloucester. They wore helmets and armor, instructed Peredur in chivalry and feats of arms, and supplied him with horse and armor. These women also trained other young men and lived with them in a *llys* or court. These establishments seem to have been something in the nature of a military school.[35]

The role played by these Celtic trainers is somewhat similar to that played by Athena in regard to Greek heroes like Perseus, Theseus, and Odysseus. While Athena did not actually train such Greek heroes, she frequently came to their aid, by guiding both their actions and weapons. Furthermore, she often provides equipment to further their endeavors such as the sword and shield with which Perseus dispatches Medusa; similarly, the Irish Scáthach provides Cú Chulainn with and instructs him in the use of the *gae bolga*, Cú Chulainn's special spear. Thus, both the goddess and these trainers play similar roles in the careers of the Irish and Greek heroes.

The Celtic legends give examples of women taking up arms when provoked: 1) King Conchobar's mother, Assa, "docile, gentle," was taught by twelve tutors. These tutors were one night slain, but Assa did not know the name of the slayer. In revenge, she takes up the sword and destroys and plunders. As a result, her name is changed to Niasa "ungentle" ("Birth of Conchobar" in Cross and Slover 1936, 131–133). The pugnacity of Celtic women can also be seen in the "Feast of Bricriu"; when a quarrel is instigated among the wives of three Ulster champions, none will back down and a physical battle ensues (Cross and Slover 1936, 254–280).

The classical authors substantiate this warrior aspect of Celtic women, noting on numerous occasions their ferocity. Ammianus Marcellinus describes how difficult it would be to defeat a Celt, particularly if he called in the aid of his wife, as she is stronger than he is and could rain blows and kicks upon the assailants equal in force to the shots of a catapult (XV.12.1); Strabo tells us the entire race was madly fond of war (IV.4.2); and, according to Diodorus Siculus, "the women of the Gauls are not only like the men in their great stature but they are a match for them in courage as well" (V.32).

When the Romans abused Boudica, queen of the British Iceni, and ravished her young daughters, Boudica gathered an army that consisted of not only the Iceni but also the Trinovantes (Tacitus, *Annals*, XIV.31) and led a rebellion the likes of which the Romans had never experienced. During one battle of the rebellion, Tacitus tells us that Suetonius Paulinius admonished his troops to take heart and to "ignore the din made by these barbarians and their empty threats, [as] there are more women than men in their ranks." Conversely, Boudica, while gathering troops, shouted that it was customary for Britons to fight under a woman, and that the British did not recognize a distinction of sex among their leaders (Tacitus, *Annals* XIV.35–36; *Agricula* 16).

While Boudica came to the throne at the death of her husband, Cartimandua of the Brigantes had been placed in power by the Romans during the early days of the Roman occupation of Britain. Cartimandua was queen in her own right, and her consort did not hold the title of king.

Celtic females, like their Amazon sisters, also had numerous horse connections. The war goddess Macha had three aspects—war/horse/mother goddess, and like Medb dominated her husbands. It is Macha who, after being forced to run against the royal horses of the king of Ulster while she was late in her pregnancy, laid a curse on the Ulstermen that they would be as weak as a woman in childbed at their time of greatest need. And so it happened that when Medb attacked Ulster to capture the Brown Bull of Cooley, it was left to Cú Chulainn, who was not an Ulsterman, to defend the province against the might of Medb and her Connacht troops. The swiftness of foot of Macha can be compared with the Volscian "Amazon" figure, Camilla, from *The Aeneid*, who outraced the wind with her swift feet. She was trained as a warrior, carried a Lycian quiver and shepherd's pike tipped with metal, led her horsemen, was not accustomed to the skills of Minerva (i.e., women's work), and was, of course, a virgin (Virgil, *The Aeneid* 7.1055–1072). One might also make a case for a connection with Myrina, an Amazon for whom the city was named, who, according to Strabo, had the epithet "much-bounding," due to the speed at which she drove her chariot (Strabo XII.8.6). Camilla's tomb is mentioned as a landmark (*Iliad* 2.814), confirming her fame much like other heroes (see Jones-Bley 1990; Jones-Bley and Della Volpe 1991).

The Gaulish horse goddess, Epona, was quite popular in the Romano-Celtic world, particularly with the army (Linduff 1979). Her cult centered around the region of Alesia in eastern France (an area which has many rich female burials). She is usually depicted riding a horse sidesaddle and may be accompanied by a bird, dog, or foal. Coe (1997, 61) interprets the female horse rider and charioteer on the Sopron vessel to "be early representations of a psychopompic Celtic horse-goddess." But as she earlier reminds us, "mythical traditions generally reflect . . . societal norm[s]" (1997, 58).

Epona had insular counterparts. As we have seen, Macha has horse associations—running in the race against the king's horses. Medb also has horse connections—one of her lovers is Fergus Mac Roich, "Fergus great horse," and one of her husbands is Eochaid, "horse-like." Medb's name is derived from the Proto-Indo-European word for "honey," *medhū. Puhvel says her name means "intoxicating from drinking mead (made from honey)" and can be related onomastically to the horse-sacrifice ritual, the *aśvamedha*, and further relates to "her involvement with horses" (1987, 261). On one dedication Epona is referred to in the plural *Eponabus* (*Corpus Inscriptionum Latinarum* III, 7904, quoted in Ross 1967, 323) indicating that she, along with Medb and Macha, too, may have been a triple, which would strengthen the comparison with Medb and Macha.

The Welsh goddess Rhiannon, whose name probably means "ruling goddess" (Proto-Celtic *rīgantonā; the suffix -onā means "goddess," as in the names Bellona and Epona), also has horse connections. She is first seen in the *Mabinogi* when Pwyll, Prince of Dyfed, encounters her as a mysterious lady riding a white horse. Rhiannon bears Pwyll's son, but the son is spirited away by her maids who say that she killed the child. She is punished by being made to sit by the horse block and carry visitors to the palace on her back.

Coins from northwest France dating to the 1st century BCE seem to depict female warriors. One coin shows a nude woman warrior riding a horse and carrying a bow, and another coin shows a horsewoman whom Duval describes as dressed and riding as an Amazon, also carrying a bow (Duval 1977, 173, figs. 389, 390).

Despite the writings of classical authors and the mythological evidence, the question remains: Where are the Celtic women warriors? We know women fought side by side with men at the hillfort of Maiden Castle in southern England against the Romans. This is evidenced in the war cemetery outside the eastern gate where ten of the thirty-four skeletons were females (Harding 1985, 124–125). Nevertheless, it is generally concluded throughout Europe that when swords, armor, shields, and helmets are found in the grave, they are considered almost exclusively male items. We have seen that contemporary Eurasian women not only engaged in battle but were buried with their warrior equipment, and it is, therefore, possible to identify the female warriors, but it must be done in a scientific manner and with an open mind. Without anthropological sexing, which can be difficult depending on the condition of the remains, archaeologists have depended on grave goods to determine sex. This is not the first call for anthropological sexing (Arnold 1991, 1995). Recent investigations have shown that grave goods are not as reliable as previously thought, as evidenced by the discussion of mirrors and spindle whorls above (see Berseneva this volume).

Nevertheless, in the West we are still left primarily with literary and some historical evidence. However, this is so compelling I would suggest that more rigorous anthropological sexing needs to be done on those burials which are designated male by way of grave goods only. It should, however, be expected that the number of female warrior graves would be fewer than male. It may also be that despite their warrior aspects, women were not, by choice or custom, buried with weapons. The ability to find women (or if one prefers, gender) in the grave requires that a sound methodology be used. Arnold (1991, 1995) has taken steps in this direction in terms of elite women with power. She has proposed the "Rosie the Riveter" phenomenon. This same hypothesis can be applied to women warriors. Perhaps what we have are not professional female soldiers but women who did not shirk battle when it was necessary. But then, if this is so, why do we have stories of women as teachers of the warrior arts? Is this just part of early societies' war ethic? Nevertheless, in light of the literary evidence and analogy from the Eurasian steppe, it is fallacious to assume that all burials with weapons are male.

CONCLUSION

It should be clear that the concept of the woman warrior is not as rare as one might initially believe. Examples can be drawn from many societies, for example, the Egyptian queen Hatshepsut, and historical examples include Empress Mathilda of England, Zenobia of Palmyra, Georgian queen Tamara, and Joan of Arc. More modern examples could include Margaret Thatcher of Britain, Golda Meir of Israel, and Indira Gandhi of India—all heads of state who took their countries into war. Nelson (1997, 139–140) reports that an entire troop of the famous pottery army in Qin Shihuangdi was female and that the king of Dahomey had an all female army, who were not allowed to engage in sex. Despite the widespread presence of female warriors, the attitude toward fighting women has rarely been one of acceptance. Indeed, even as late as 2007, according to an article in *Newsweek*, women who have trained, behaved, and died as soldiers are not fully accepted by the U.S. government (Quindlen 2007).

The conclusion that some women held military positions in these ancient societies is unquestionable. Not only do we have literary and iconographic evidence, but we also have burials of women who were clearly warriors. I do not by any means think that European society was filled with women who rejected the more traditional female roles for one of warrior. What I do believe, based on well-documented evidence, is that enough women engaged in warrior activities that they were not anomalies. These women either stepped in when society needed them or their society simply did not have the rigid gender roles which we have subscribed to since the 19th century. It is this view that has blinded us to the evidence and prevented us from seeing the obvious.

NOTES

I want to thank V. I. Mamontov for giving me such generous access to his unpublished excavation reports. I also want to extend my appreciation to Martin Huld for our many conversations on this chapter and his suggestion for the title.

1. Because these and other languages are derived from a common protolanguage, it can be assumed that they also share a common protoculture, some aspects of which have been reconstructed in Mallory and Adams (1997).

2. Irish war goddess. Only those less well-known names (or aspects) not mentioned later in the text are footnoted.

3. Irish war goddess.

4. Irish war goddess. For the Irish and British goddesses see Green (1996).

5. British goddess of victory.

6. British tribal goddess associated with Victory and Minerva. On at least one relief, she is shown carrying a sword (Green 1996, 36).

7. Companion of Ares, and one of the three Graeae whose name means "warlike."

8. While not primarily a warrior goddess (this aspect seems to be late), she takes on Athena's warrior-goddess aspect and is later worshiped with Mars (Guirand 1959, 209).

9. Juno's warrior aspect is not emphasized, although it is made clear in the first lines of *The Aeneid*—describing Carthage, which waged war fiercely, as her favorite land and where she kept her shield and chariot (Virgil I,19–26). She has deep Italic origins and is found in the Sabines, Oscans, Umbrians, Latins, as well as the non–Indo-European Etruscans. When armed with spear and shield, she is Juno Sospita but is also invoked at the time of childbirth (Guirand 1959, 203–204).

10. The Roman equivalent of Enyo, war goddess, and companion to Mars.

11. Slavic virgin dawn goddess dressed as a warrior.

12. Slavic dawn goddess who when found with Pyerun, the god of war, assumed the aspect of a well-armed virgin warrior, patroness of warriors whom she protected (Guirand 1959, 294).

13. War was only one aspect of this multifunctional goddess.

14. Armed Irish prophetess, who drove a chariot drawn by two black horses (Kelly 1992, 90–91).

15. Gondul and Skogul are both Valkyries.

16. Roman goddess borrowed from the Sabines. She was the consort of Mars, and her name may mean "masculinity" from the Latin root *ner-* meaning "man."

17. Although Aphrodite was the goddess of love, Ares, the god of war, was (among others) her lover, and in Sparta she, along with other divinities, was portrayed as a warrior (Pomeroy 2002, 19).

18. Druidess, who reared the Irish hero Finn MacCumaill.

19. Norse goddess of love and beauty, who receives half of those killed in battle.

20. Greek goddess of discord, who, while not having a warrior aspect, delighted in creating conflict that caused war.

21. Iranian multifunctional goddess, who bestowed warrior prowess (Dexter 1990, 155).

22. Germanic prophetess, who foretold the German success over the Romans (Tacitus IV, 61).

23. Leaders of the army from Schleswig during the battle of Bråvalla (probably 8th century but could have been as early as the 6th century). They are described as women "whose female bodies Nature had endowed with manly courage" (Saxo Grammaticus 1979–1980, 238 and n. 11). We should remember that Saxo is not always clear about who is an actual person and who is legendary.

24. She is mentioned three times by Saxo and may refer to Inghen Ruaidh (red daughter), who was a leader of the Vikings who attracted Munster in *The War of the Gaedhil with the Gaill* (Saxo Grammaticus 1979–1980, 71, n. 48, 246).

25. Daughter of Cyrus, who, along with Hystaspes, son of Darius, commanded the Amyrgian Scythians and Bactrians (Herodotus VII.64).

26. Queen of the Massagetae, a Saka people, who killed Cyrus the Great (Herodotus I.214).

27. Daughter of Alfred the Great and wife of King Æthelred. She ruled Mercia after Æthelred's death (c. 910) and led the Mercian army against the Danes (Stenton 1968, 324).

28. Although we have numerous depictions of Amazons in male dress, namely, trousers (see, for example, Bothmer 1957, pls. LXI.5, LXII.5, LXIv.1–4b, LXV.4; Rolle 1989, 90–91, figs. 64–65), the Greek painters did not confine the Amazon wardrobe to trousers. They are frequently in the more conventional chiton, although of a less conventional length (see Bothmer 1957, pls. X, XIII, XXVI.2, XL.2), a knee-length chiton (Bothmer 1957, pl. LXXXI.8), and even a long (ankle-length) chiton (Bothmer 1957, pl. LXXXI.4). Furthermore, the short chiton was sometimes worn over what appear to be long stockings or leggings (see Bothmer 1957, pls. LXXIII.3, 4, LXXIV.3, 4, LXXV.a). For a more in-depth discussion of the Amazon wardrobe, particularly regarding the exposed breast, see Cohen (1997, 74–77).

29. The Scythians were the earliest of the Iron Age steppe people of concern to us here, and they date roughly from the 9th to the 3rd centuries BCE. The Sargat date to the second half of the 1st millennium BCE to c. 3rd century CE. The Sauromatians date c. 7th–6th centuries BCE–c. 4th–2nd centuries CE, the Sarmatians from c. 4th–2nd centuries BCE–5th century CE, and the Saka c. 6th century BCE to c. 400 CE.

30. This phenomenon extends even into China during the Wu Ding period (1250–1200 BCE) with the burial of Lady Hao, concubine of the king and, according to oracle bone inscriptions, a famous military leader. She was buried with numerous weapons including many *ge* halberds. A second concubine of the same king, Lady Jing, was also buried with military equipment (Linduff 2002, 266–267).

31. However, spindle whorls are also found in male graves that also contain weapons (see Berseneva this volume and Parker Pearson 1999, 108).

32. Bows and arrows, knives, and lances can all be used as hunting tools. In fact, only swords can be classed only as weapons, but armor must be classed as a defensive item.

33. The mention of Albania brings us to an interesting note that Coon and others observe of Albanian (the one in the Balkans) customs. They report that even in the 20th century, women who reject matrimony must take an oath to remain a virgin and that from then on they dress and are referred to as males (Durham 1909, 36; Lane 1922, 172–175; Coon 1953, 24–25).

34. See Kelly (1988, particularly 68–79) for a discussion of the legal status of women in early Irish law. It should, however, be remembered that these laws originate, at least in written form, in the 7th–8th centuries CE after Christianity had a firm hold in Ireland. In his introduction, Kelly discusses some of the inconsistencies that appear to conflict with earlier times.

35. Huld (1997) suggests that the training of boys by female warriors may be part of a larger Indo-European male puberty ritual.

Chapter Three

Tillya Tepe: Aspects of Gender and Cultural Identity

Karen S. Rubinson

In 1978–1979, an Afghan-Russian archaeological team under the direction of Victor Sarianidi excavated a small cemetery dug into the remains of a citadel that had existed from the 10th through the 5th centuries BCE, located in northern Afghanistan near the town of Shibargan, not too far from the Amu Darya River (figure 3.1).[1] The archaeologists excavated six burials, all extremely rich, that contained individuals covered with golden ornaments. The graves contained goods from the length of Eurasia, including glass from the Roman west and mirrors from the Han Chinese east. These burials date to the middle of the 1st century CE, a period between the political authority of the Greek kingdoms that were the legacy of Alexander the Great's foray into Central Asia and the establishment of the Kushan Empire sometime in the late 1st or early 2nd century CE. In the last few centuries BCE and 1st century CE, nomadic groups from the steppe moved into Central Asia from the north and east and those called Yuezhi[2] were recorded in Chinese texts as located just north of the Amu Darya in the period about 130–125 BCE.[3] The individuals buried at Tillya Tepe have generally been considered to be settled descendants of the nomadic Yuezhi and most scholars have described them as "proto-Kushans," that is, ancestors of the kings who ruled in what is today northwestern India and adjacent areas of Pakistan and Afghanistan from the 1st to the 3rd centuries CE.[4]

From the time of excavation, the woman in the second burial in the small elite cemetery at Tillya Tepe was notable for the battle-ax and Siberian daggers found in her grave (Sarianidi 1985, 23; 1989, 56, 66). These weapons have led to descriptions of this woman as a "woman-warrior" (Yatsenko 2001, 83) or a "warrior-priestess" (Davis-Kimball 1997–1998, 21–24; 2000, 277).[5] Characterizing some nomadic women as "warriors" has a long history (see Jones-Bley this volume; Jettmar 1967, 60; Yatsenko 1987), and one can

Figure 3.1. Map of Afghanistan indicating location of Tillya Tepe. Prepared by Karen S. Rubinson.

find cases of steppe women buried with military equipment even earlier than the 1st millennium BCE (Linduff 2003a, 70, and fig. 4.7). The interest in women as warriors extends well beyond those scholars who work with these primary data (see, for example, Parker Pearson 2000, 100–101). So, in fact, the social role of the woman buried in grave 2 at Tillya Tepe is an interesting question in the context of this volume. I will also ask other questions of the data. Is the "warrior" identity, if it is in fact appropriate, the only identity for this individual? Can we see multiple identities here, as is the case in other mortuary settings (Parker Pearson 2000; S. Jones 1997; Shennan 1989)?

THE NATURE AND PROBLEMS OF BURIAL DATA

Hanks (2000, 25) notes in a discussion of nomadic burials of the Iron Age (c. 6th c. BCE–4th c. CE) on the Eurasian steppe that "as one approaches the burial evidence, it is necessary to consider that the material remains of the burial may indeed represent not only the rank and status of the interred individual, but also a multitude of possible characterizations of the roles which this individual may have assumed." His discussion of the complexity of the factors when looking at nomadic burials was stimulated in part by a publication of Davis-Kimball in which she "argued for an increased awareness for the role of status relating to women with the Early Iron Age nomadic groups" (Hanks 2000, 20). Ultimately, Hanks notes "[i]t is therefore, of utmost importance that one attempts to engage in contextual studies which incorporate all of the materials . . . associated with burial patterns as well as seeking to develop an awareness for the relationship between burials within similar kurgans, mortuary sites and across the landscape" (Hanks 2000, 25). Hanks's comments are perhaps especially relevant here, since they were stimulated by Davis-Kimball's assignment of statuses that had been based on her excavations at Pokrovka beyond that site where these statuses were determined into the theoretical realm (Hanks 2000, 20). It is these very statuses, expanded by further work and extended to the individuals excavated from Tillya Tepe (Davis-Kimball 1997–1998, 21–24; 2000, 226–228) that prompted this investigation.[6]

Since the identification of "women-warriors" in death is usually bound to the appearance of weapons in the burial (Davis-Kimball 1997a, 334; and see Jones-Bley this volume), I quote at length a discussion by McHugh about case studies of burials containing weapons[7]:

> The question of misrepresentation in the mortuary domain applies not just to the separation of individuals into different rank levels, but also is relevant when it comes to considering the social identities that may be presented (or interpreted by the archaeologist) as appropriate in burial. For example, amongst the Bontoc Igorot burial with a spear and battleaxe represents status as an unmarried male, rather than the warrior status that an archaeologist may infer (Saxe 1970). Härke (1991) raises a similar point when he interprets the weapon burials of the early Anglo-Saxon period as symbolizing ethnic differences, rather than role differences; this explains the presence of weapons with the very young and very old, and with individuals suffering various diseases, such as osteo-arthritis, that would have made the use of weapons in a warrior role impossible. Thomas (1991) also notes the occurrence of a Beaker burial with a bow and archer's wristguard, despite the individual having suffered from ankylosis of the spine; the artefacts therefore possibly identified idealized roles, relating to resources important to the community. Obviously the danger here lies in attempting to make a direct connection between particular objects placed in the grave and a function that they might have performed during life as used by the deceased (1999, 14).

This last caveat is directly relevant to the weapons—and other grave goods—in the Tillya Tepe burials.

The historical identification of the individuals based on the Chinese and other texts still remains debated (Enoki et al. 1994; Pugachenkova et al. 1994,

350, 353–355; Bernard and Abdullaev 1997). The inscribed objects in the tombs, including coins (Zeymal 1999) and a few objects of precious metal (Sarianidi 1985, 28, 36, 241 no. 3.41, 251 no. 4.31) do not explain who the interred are. Thus, interpretations of use and meaning of the objects found buried at Tillya Tepe based on direct analogies with other, different, groups, such as the "statuses" proposed by Davis-Kimball, must be carried out with special caution, since the cultural, social, and ethnic identifications may be wholly different.

BURIAL DATA, GENDER ROLES, AND THE ISSUE OF CULTURAL IDENTITY

In the specific instance of the Tillya Tepe material, as already noted, it is the presence of weapons in at least one female burial[8] (see discussion below) that has driven identification of gender roles there. In fact, weapons in burials anywhere seem to cause particular difficulties with identification of both sex and gender, as effectively summed up by Parker Pearson (2000, 97). And historically, on the steppe, grave goods have often been used to define the sex/gender of the grave occupant, without anthropological sexing.[9] Together with the possible ambiguities of interpretation of gender roles inherent in data analysis, the Tillya Tepe data are further burdened by the application of the Amazon myth to its interpretation (Parker Pearson 2000, 100–102). However, as Arnold and Wicker suggest, women warriors might best be identified by skeletal trauma patterns (2001b, xiii); the possibilities are demonstrated in Hollimon 2001. But in the Tillya Tepe case, the burial inventories are our only evidence.

Burials, by their very nature, are static moments that capture and display messages from the living societies that create them. At Tillya Tepe, the grave goods may in fact present differences in gender roles, but in addition, in this time and place of cultural and political transition, they may also display other sorts of identity. For the purposes of this discussion I posit that the specific contents of the tombs are chosen deliberately to indicate elements of, among other categories, cultural identity.[10]

Although the construction of identity in much anthropological literature is seen as the construction of ethnicity (McHugh 1999, 47–48), at Tillya Tepe, suggested to be a manifestation of the historical story of the Yuezhi in Bactria becoming the Kushans, that is, in a time of historical transition, we might rather query if what is being constructed is a *cultural* identity, which I conceive of as a broader concept.[11] If these elite individuals represented a transitional phase between their nomadic past in regions to the north and east and the initiation of a powerful settled state at the edge of Central Asia, these disparate lifeways and political transformation may possibly be expressed in these graves. Can we see the construction of a new cultural identity in process? I think we can.

Although written in the context of modern political change, looking toward historical and archaeological pasts, the words of Jones and Graves-Brown are applicable to the period and place of the Tillya Tepe burials, in my view. They state: "Questions of identity often come to the fore at times of social and political change: the destruction of existing socio-cultural patterns and shifting power relations lead to the re-evaluation and re-presentation of identities as new communities arise." And further, they note "[s]ince the past is often central to the construction of identity, periods of radical social and political change are often a time of 'inventing traditions.' . . . Ethno-histories provide the authenticity and legitimation which cultural groups desire and require in their claims for self-determination and/or secession" (1996, 1). In contrast to the reconstruction of past histories, however, the cultural identities at Tillya Tepe can be viewed as being constructed from both real ethnocultural pasts and present ethnocultural circumstances, to be seen as the process of "becoming."[12]

Initially, as part of this investigation, I reviewed the motifs and styles of the elaborate plaques, temple ornaments, clasps, belts, and other gold pieces adorning the deceased, to explore how they might refer to gender and identity. But the difficulties of reading and interpreting these published images led me down other paths with the data. John Boardman has made many recent astute observations about the material but expressed caution because of the same difficulties (2003a, especially 133; 2003b, 350). It is clear that even the glorious photographs of Sarianidi's 1985 publication leave many questions of detail ambivalent or unanswered, and it is best to wait for sustained firsthand observation before such an undertaking.[13] Rather than looking at the "art," then, we will look at the "archaeological" contexts of these burials.

THE DATA SET

The data set of which these questions are asked is small. Sarianidi excavated six graves: one male and five female.[14] The burials at Tillya Tepe (Golden Mound) are dated by objects in the graves, especially coins, to the middle of the 1st century CE (Zeymal 1999, 243).

Because of the small number of burials, my approach here is to record as completely as the publications allow the presence/absence of various elements that might be signifiers of gender roles or cultural identification. Only a small subset of the material is included in the discussion here, based in large measure on what others have seen as components of gender roles (table 3.1).

Table 3.1. Distribution of selected grave goods and practices at Tillya Tepe.

Burial	Sex	Age	Orientation	Mirrors	Weapons	Gold Circlets	Horse	Metal Belt	Shoe Buckles	Chin Strap	Flattened Skull
1	F	25–35 or 20–30	head north								
2	F	30–40 or 20–30	head north	Chinese on chest	two Siberian-style daggers and pickax	two anklets				x	no
3	F	18–25	head north	Chinese on chest and handled outside coffin	gold-mounted iron dagger handle	one torque, two bracelets, two small circlets			yes	x	
4	M	30 or 20–30	head north		sheath with three daggers, sheath with dagger, sword, two bows, two quivers, arrows	two armlets	horse	yes	yes	xx	
5	F	15–20 or about 20	head west	handled by right hip		two anklets				x	
6	F	25–30 or 20	head west	Chinese on chest and handled at feet	iron knives	two anklets				x	yes

We must keep in mind that the data set is not complete and even the two major publications by the excavator have inconsistencies; the differences in the ages assigned to the deceased are entered into the "Age" column of table 3.1, the age given in Sarianidi 1985 listed first, followed by the age given in Sarianidi 1989.[15]

Before addressing gender roles, let us look at the possible cultural markers of some Tillya Tepe burial goods and practices. One factor to keep in mind is that it may be hard to separate deliberate practice from the background noise of cultural exchange in Central Asia. For example, I am assuming that the glass flasks in burial 6 (Sarianidi 1985, 259, no. 6.38), which must have originated in the Mediterranean world (Boardman 2003b, 372), do not have specific association with gender or identity, but rather represent the exotic and the rare, reflecting the elite status of this individual as such glass does in burials all the way across Asia to China.[16] Similarly, the Hellenistic substrate that was brushed across Asia with the passage of Alexander may contribute to the presence of many seals and cameos in the graves, among other materials.[17]

MARKERS OF CULTURAL IDENTITY

In contrast to the elaborate gold ornaments, often encrusted with turquoise, lapis lazuli, garnet, carnelian, and pearls, that adorned the clothing and equipment at Tillya Tepe is plain gold jewelry of simple annular shape with flared ends. It was worn on the bodies of all individuals except the woman in grave 1, and I suggest that because of its simplicity, in sharp contrast to the ornamented and figural gold, as well as the fact that it is worn directly on the body rather than attached to clothing, these pieces are markers of identity. The women in graves 2, 5, and 6 each wear a pair of anklets, the woman in grave 3 a torque, two bracelets, and two small loops of undetermined function, the male in grave 4 a pair of armlets. Such jewelry is well known beginning in somewhat earlier times farther north and east on the steppe, as for example a torque from the cemetery of Besoba in western Kazakhstan, dating to the 6th–5th centuries BCE (Popescu et al. 1998, 146), and the torque dating to about the turn of the BCE/CE millennia from Sidorovka cemetery, kurgan 1, grave 2, of the Sargat culture (Koryakova 2007, fig. 7, nos. 1, 3). These simple ornaments appear to refer to the ancestral origins of the people buried at Tillya Tepe.[18]

Another object that implies reference to the north and east, in this case the Altai, is the shape of one dagger sheath of the male in grave 4 (Sarianidi 1985, 247–248, no. 4.8). Designed to be tied to the leg, this form of sheath is found at many sites, among them many burials at Ulandrik and Tashanta, dating to the 2nd–1st centuries BCE, where it is made from wood. In fact there the form is so significant that some individuals were buried with wooden models of the dagger in its sheath, rather than omit it altogether (Kubarev 1987, among the many examples are pl. 4, no. 8; pl. 16, no. 13; pl. 48, no. 9; fig. 21; and see Bernard and Abdullaev 1997, 72). Highly elaborated gold and bejeweled variations on this form are found not only at Tillya Tepe, but also in the Sargat culture, Isakovka 1, cemetery, kurgan 3, grave 6 (Koryakova 2007, fig. 12), and to the north and west, in middle Sarmatian contexts, such as the Dachi cemetery on the Lower Don (Gubuev 2005, pl. 2) and Porogi in western Ukraine (Simonenko 1991, fig. 1). In these latter contexts it is a much richer object for a more elite male than those in the Altai, like the one from Tillya Tepe. Although it might be seen as strictly a status symbol, at least in the context at Tillya Tepe together with the many other eastern elements that occur, the form may likely be associated with some ancestral identification of the male.[19]

Xiongnu burials in the Ordos of the 4th through 2nd centuries BCE have also yielded objects that find resonance in certain artifacts found at Tillya Tepe. The woman in burial 3 had golden boot/shoe soles (Sarianidi 1985, no. 3.40); silver ones with curvilinear cut-out designs were excavated at Shihuigou (Linduff 1997, 54 and fig. A68). The practice of placing highly elaborated soles on the bottoms of nomadic boots of the elite is preserved as early as Pazyryk (Rudenko 1970, pl. 64A), but these are the only two examples I know from this time in precious metal. The crown worn by the woman in burial 6 (Sarianidi 1985, no. 6.1), together with her temple pendants (Sarianidi 1985, 6.4), has the same glittering dangles and overall structure of a headdress from a Xiongnu noblewoman buried in tomb 4 at Xigoupan (Sun 1991, fig. 5, no. 2).[20]

One striking pattern in three women's graves at Tillya Tepe (nos. 2, 3, 6) (Sarianidi 1985, nos. 2.43, 3.70, 6.31) is the placement of the same type of Chinese bronze mirror on the chest of each woman. That these mirrors likely have symbolic meaning in these graves, given their placement, is reinforced by the fact that two of these women also have Central Asian mirrors elsewhere in their graves (Sarianidi 1985, nos. 3.71, 6.30). The woman buried in grave 5, who does not have a Chinese mirror on her chest, also has a Central Asian mirror by her hip (no. 5.12), a location which is common and may be more practical than symbolic.[21] The Chinese mirrors are the type known as cosmic mirrors and were widespread in China in the earlier part of the Eastern Han (25–220 CE). They were made beginning in 8 CE.[22] In China such mirrors are not placed on the chest of the deceased. However, such a mirror placement can be found in women's graves in the Karasuk period in Southern Siberia, in the 14th through the 10th centuries BCE (Okladnikov and Sunchugashev 1969, 80). The practice continues in the Tagar period, which follows Karasuk, in burials that date to the 8th through the 6th centuries BCE (Bokovenko 2006, fig. 4). Therefore, the placement of this eastern mirror type also has a cultural significance that links the individuals at Tillya Tepe to burial practices with a long tradition in the regions to their north and east.

In contrast with these proposed eastern connections, there is one practice at Tillya Tepe that clearly seems to point to local practice, the placement of a coin in the hand of the deceased, known in the ancient Greek world as the payment for passage to the underworld. Unlike objects from the Hellenistic world in the graves, which were likely widely available to elite individuals, the deliberate practice of placing the coin in the hand, certain in burial 6, where there is also a coin placed in the mouth (Sarianidi 1985, 52–53),[23] and possibly in burial 3 (Sarianidi 1985, 28), may have been an explicit act of adoption of a local custom. Alternatively, these women, both with Chinese mirrors on their chests and plain gold annular ornaments, may have come from a background where the coin in the hand and/or mouth was their native custom and the mirror and jewelry may have marked acculturation. I would note that at least in the case of the woman in burial 6, it is more likely that the placement of the coin in the mouth and hand indicates someone who is defining or who is having defined a new place for herself in the social order, for she has the flattened skull of Hunnic practice[24] (Sarianidi 1989, 130, fig. 46), again pointing to an eastern origin for the woman or her ancestors. At this stage in my analysis, burial 6 seems to most clearly document the process of transition, of construction of a new identity, at Tillya Tepe, of becoming more Central Asian/Hellenized. Note that this is in direct contrast to Boardman's suggestion, where he speculates that the woman in burial 6 was possibly "an Indo-Greek princess in the royal household of the King of Emshi Tepe," based on his assessment of the preponderance of Greek subjects in her jewelry, the presence of the glass flasks, and the coins in her hand and mouth (2003b, 372).

The use of gold chin straps, another funerary practice found in all burials except number 1 at Tillya Tepe (Sarianidi 1985, 22, 28, 35, 45, 47) and presumably used to keep the jaw closed in death, may also be a practice of eastern inspiration. Although apparently a Greek practice in the 2nd millennium BCE, by the 1st millennium BCE fabric chin straps were widespread in Xinjiang, while straps of metal and fabric continued to be used in the Greek world (Müller 2003, 45–46, 51).[25] Whether the practice at Tillya Tepe reflects a Western tradition or was a practice remembered from the East is an open question.

Before passing on to the issue of gender roles, I have one last question to raise about the eastern-inspired elements found at Tillya Tepe. The dagger sheath with four round attachments and the Chinese mirrors, as well as simple annular gold armlets, are also found in elite burials of the Sarmatians on the European steppe in the middle Sarmatian period (c. 2nd century BCE–2nd century CE), together with polychrome gold work and mirrors of the Central Asian type also found at Tillya Tepe. It is hypothesized that at least some elements of these Sarmatian groups came from areas east of the European steppe (Moshkova 1995, 137) and the similarities of some of the material culture of Tillya Tepe and the Sarmatians and areas to the east have been often noted (e.g., Kato 1991; Moshkova 1995, 147; Treister 1997/1998, 56; Simonenko 2001; Boardman 2003b, 368–369; Koryakova 2007, 111–112).[26] At a minimum, it seems possible to say that some elite markers of both the Sarmatians and the individuals buried at Tillya Tepe appear to have eastern origins, and these elite markers appear in the Tillya Tepe burials and in rich middle Sarmatian tombs at about the same time. Their appearance in both contexts may reflect the marking of cultural identities by the elites who had moved out of their homeland into new areas and who buried themselves with these reminders of affiliation and/or affinity.[27] Alternatively, they could have been adopted by local elites to mark their social positions, but given the broad outlines of the Greek and Chinese historical documentation of the origins of these groups,[28] this appears a less likely explanation.

GENDER ROLES

Davis-Kimball assigned "statuses" (which can be interpreted as societal roles) to all of the female burials at Tillya Tepe (2000, 226–227 and table 1), suggesting that burials 1, 5, and 6 contained "priestesses" and burials 2 and 3 "warrior-priestesses." Davis-Kimball's demarkation of "statuses" was developed based on data from excavations of cemeteries lying on the steppe well north of the Caspian Sea that date from the 6th through the 2nd centuries BCE. Whether these categories extend diachronically and spatially across the entire steppe in the 1st millennium BCE is an open question. As my study of the distribution of mirrors in burials in a variety of 1st millennium BCE nomadic contexts has shown, each region, if not cemetery group, can display distinctive patterns of age and gender association that need to be evaluated in their own, local, terms (Rubinson 2002).[29] In fact, mirrors are, according to Davis-Kimball, a significant marker of "priestess" status. That may be the case in the context where she formulated these categories, and indeed mirrors could have had a ritual function at Tillya Tepe, but Davis-Kimball's assumptions are a stretch of the evidence and far too generalizing to be effective explanations of different local settings, in my view.

The explicatory category of "woman-warrior" assigned to burial 2 by many (e.g., Yatsenko 2001) and both burials 2 and 3 by Davis-Kimball (2000), is, as mentioned above, extrapolated from the presence of weapons found in the burials. Burial 2 is said to contain a pickax and two Siberian-style daggers, placed in a basket at her feet; the objects themselves have not been published (Sarianidi 1985, 23; 1989, 56). Burial 3 contained an iron dagger handle with gold and stone mounts (Sarianidi 1985, no. 3.49), although Sarianidi states that there were "absolutely no weapons of any kind" in the grave (1985, 27). Burial 6 contains what appear to be two knife handles, although the written description associated with the photograph describes only one of them (Sarianidi 1985, no. 6.35). The burial description does not elaborate, calling them "miniature knives" (Sarianidi 1985, 47) or, in the later publication, "iron fragments" (Sarianidi 1989, 116). Although we may construe the pickax was a weapon, we might also consider the knives and perhaps even the daggers as tools. The male burial contains an extensive weapon set, including a sword in a sheath, several daggers in sheaths, two bows, two quivers, and arrows (Sarianidi 1985, 35–36). The women's equipment is certainly much less extensive.

Certainly the weapons found with burial 2 distinguish her from the other women at Tillya Tepe, and it seems safe to say that at least in death, her gender role differed from the other women here. Further, the weapons accompanying the male are different from hers.[30] So she is marked as different in some respect from all other Tillya Tepe individuals. Further, she is likely the oldest woman in the group (table 3.1). It is possible that the weapons mark her as a warrior, since the military role is certainly a possibility within the sociohistorical steppe context, but perhaps these weapons designate her position as a senior female, and perhaps, as with the mirrors, they represent identity, or some mixture of explanations.

The ambiguities in the published data about the daggers and knives in the other two burials make it impossible to determine whether these are weapons at all. Complete publication of all the grave materials may make it possible to expand this discussion.

At this point, the only further comment on gender roles that I might note is that the three women who are buried with any kind of weapon or knife are also the three women who had Chinese mirrors placed on their chests. How these two categories of practice might relate to each other is a question that the data are insufficient to answer at this time. From the published drawings of the burials, it seems that the woman in burial 2 had a round skull (Sarianidi 1989, fig. 16.3), in contrast to the flattened skull of the woman in burial 6.[31] In burial 3, the skull shape remains undetermined from the available data. This very question illustrates the complex intersection of cultural identity and gender roles at Tillya Tepe and the rich potential of this site for exploring both.

NOTES

1. Sarianidi 1989, 3, 39, 46–48.

2. We are using here the Chinese pinyin transliteration of the spelling for both "Yuezhi" and "Xiongnu," since many of the chapters in this volume concern more easterly areas. Most scholars who study Central Asia from a West Asian perspective use "Yueh-chih" and "Hsiung-nu." That this choice must be made is a commentary on the complex influences and central historical and geographical position of Central Asia.

3. Enoki et al. 1994, 180.

4. Boardman 2003b, 348 has a useful summary. See also Bernard and Abdullaev 1997; Enoki et al. 1994.

5. The "priestess" assignment by Davis-Kimball is based on other categories of artifacts, such as mirrors.

6. For a brief summary of Soviet-era work on the statuses of females in the Eurasian nomadic sphere, see Jacobson 1987, especially p. 17. Some of the statuses mentioned there are included in Davis-Kimball 1997b, 332.

7. And see also Jacobson 1987, 6–7, and Hanks, this volume.

8. The skeletons were anthropologically sexed, although the skeletons were poorly preserved (Sarianidi 1985, 18).

9. This is not a problem strictly in the study of Eurasian Iron Age nomads. See, for example, Weglian 2001, 137.

10. And see Wells 1998, 243 and Lucy 2005, 86, 109.

11. By "cultural identity" I do not mean here the construction of past identities in service of modern politics (see, for example, Kohl and Fawcett 1995 or Meskell 1998).

12. See Wells 1998, 283–285 for another example of that process.

13. See Schiltz 2006.

14. There was at least one more burial in the group, left unexcavated at the end of the season, as winter and war came to Afghanistan (Sarianidi 1985, 14; Yatsenko 2001, fn. 8; Davis-Kimball 2000, 226 posits an eighth). A full report of these excavations has not been published. The two most comprehensive compilations are Sarianidi 1985 and 1989. Additional details are found in Yatsenko 2001. The burials were very complex and were excavated under difficult circumstances. Yatsenko, with access to the field notes (2001, 74), modified costume reconstructions that had been published earlier. Errors have found their way into the literature about the original locations of objects from the burials. Pugachenkova and Rempel call a pair of plaques in burial 3 belt buckles, although they were actually found near the neck (1991, 16). Davis-Kimball follows them and bases an argument about status of the individual in which the belt is a significant indicator (2000, 227). Yet Sarianidi had published that they were found in the region of the neck (1985, 28, 29; 1989, 69). This is confirmed by Yatsenko 2001, 78. Another misidentification is that the shoe buckles of burial 4 (Sarianidi 1985, 41) are called belt buckles by Pugachenkova and Rempel (1991, 13). These examples are not exhaustive; rather, they are cautionary.

15. The female in burial 3 has an assigned age only in Sarianidi 1985.

16. In contrast, Boardman attributes great identity significance to these objects (2003b, 372). For a similar flask excavated in China, see Watts et al. 2004, 113.

17. For an in-depth discussion of Greek Central Asia, see Bernard (1994), where he specifically takes note of the Tillya Tepe cemetery (1994, 128).

18. For an example from another time and place, see Rubinson and Marcus (2005).

19. Schiltz (2006, 279) comes to the same conclusion.

20. This crown recalls Korean examples from later periods as well, see Nelson this volume and Cambon 2006, 294, 297. Cambon also illustrates gilded bronze shoe soles from a Silla context (2006, 296).

21. Sarianidi comes to the same conclusion. He says, in translation, "it is possible that it is not by chance in the burial where two mirrors are encountered, always the mirror with the handle is found at the foot/leg, but the Chinese mirror, without the handle, is on the chest and it marks a more important significance to the deceased" (1989, 131).

22. Sullivan 1984, 74–75. Boardman 2003b, fn. 52 uses them to support the dating of the burials. Certainly these mirrors are of the same period as the burials and are not heirlooms.

23. Sarianidi states that the coin in the mouth is the fee for Charon. Boardman suggests both coins be viewed as the fee (2003b, 372). Stevens (1991) notes that although texts specify coins in the mouth, in the Greco-Roman world the coin or coins could be placed variously on the body, including in the hand, as well as elsewhere in the grave, and, in fact, may have had a broader meaning than simply Charon's fee.

24. Cf. Jettmar 1967, 178. The skull had remains of small ornaments made of mica covered with black lacquer. Sarianidi reasonably observed that these, because of the lacquer, reflected an "eastern influence" in Bactria (1989, 131). These ornaments were found on the forehead and cheekbones of the deceased (1985, 47). See also Berseneva, this volume.

25. Müller's article contains a complete catalog of the Xinjiang finds in English.

26. Calligaro notes some technical analogies as well (2006, 293).

27. Just such a case has been argued about the consort Fu Hao, who was probably married into the royal clan during Shang period China (Linduff 1997).

28. Whether or not one agrees with specific details of the naming of these groups or their ethnic identities, the outlines of the textual sources agree on the relatively more northerly and easterly origins of both the Sarmatians and those buried at Tillya Tepe.

29. And see Lucy 2005, 109.

30. Although we do not know for certain what Sarianidi means by "Siberian style," if the woman's daggers had been as elaborate as the "Siberian style" sheath found with the male, it is probable they would have been published.

31. My thanks to Fredrik Hiebert for assistance with this question.

Part II

HORSES AND
THE GENDERING OF IDENTITY
ON THE STEPPE AND BEYOND

Chapter Four

Women's Attire and Possible Sacred Role in 4th Millennium Northern Kazakhstan

Sandra Olsen and Deborah G. Harding

The Copper Age (Aeneolithic) Botai culture of northern Kazakhstan is most famous for its early focus on horse domestication and the vast collections of horse remains from its large settlements (Akhinzhanov et al. 1990; Anthony 2003; Anthony and Brown 1998a,b; Levine 1999a,b; Levine and Kislenko 1997; Olsen 1996, 2000a,b, 2001, 2003, 2006, and 2007; Zaibert 1993). However, our research since 1993 has taken a broader approach to reconstruct the lifestyles of these early horse pastoralists (Olsen et al. 2006). By observing patterns in the archaeological record, especially regarding context of and relationships between certain objects, it has been possible to recognize a number of rituals and thereby shed light on the Botai belief system (Olsen 2000a,b; Olsen et al. 2006).

This chapter will discuss the combination of data from different materials that makes it possible to reconstruct feminine attire and present a hypothesis for the possible ceremonial role of female figurines in the Botai culture. Through the analysis of different lines of indirect evidence, many aspects of Botai clothing have been identified, even without preservation of the actual perishables. Pottery impressions provide significant information regarding fiber technology, bone figurines made on equid and saiga phalanges inform about dress construction and design, and context of groups of phalanges within houses elucidates their use in rituals.

The Botai people lived within the Ishim River's basin, in north-central Kazakhstan, between 3700 and 3100 BCE (Olsen et al. 2006). Previously, only four settlements were recognized as belonging to the Botai culture, despite extensive survey of the region through the years. These are Botai, by far the largest, with over 160 pit houses; Krasnyi Yar, with 54 houses; Vasilkovka, with 44 houses; and Roshchinskoe, of unknown size (Olsen et al. 2006). A fifth site, Troitskoe 5, recently underwent surface collection,

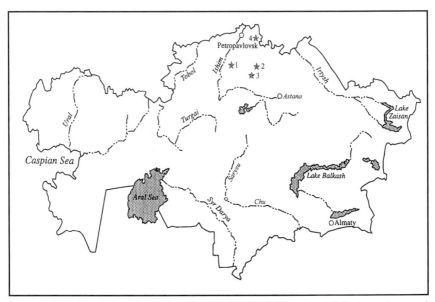

Figure 4.1.   Map of Kazakhstan showing Botai culture sites: 1. Botai, 2. Krasnyi Yar and Vasilkovka, 3. Troitskoe 5, 4. Roshchinskoe

and magnetic gradient imaging indicates that it had between fourteen and eighteen houses.

The Botai possessed a very focused economy based on horse pastoralism. Over 90 percent of the identifiable faunal material from Botai sites was derived from horses. Although harpoon wounds in two horse bones from the site of Botai indicate that wild tarpans were still being hunted occasionally, the overwhelming evidence supports the idea that horses were domesticated and that these people possessed substantial herds (Olsen 2006).

The Botai culture is part of a much larger tradition, which Olsen has coined the Geometrically Impressed Pottery Province (GIPP) (Olsen et al. 2006), that covers a vast area from the southern Urals to at least eastern Kazakhstan. It begins in the Neolithic Age and continues on through the Aeneolithic, or Copper Age, until it is replaced in the Bronze Age. During the Neolithic and Copper ages, the pottery typically has geometric designs impressed in its surfaces by means of various materials. Many of these are perishable and are preserved in no form other than by their impressions. Subsequent Bronze Age pottery typically has decoration restricted to fine comb impressions, which are also arranged in geometric patterns. Unlike the pottery, the stone tool assemblages change markedly between the Neolithic and the Copper ages, from those dominated by delicate blades to ones consisting mainly of small thumbnail scrapers, large bifaces, spear and arrow points, and *pieces esquilles*.

By the Copper Age, evidence for ceremonial behavior begins to emerge in this region. Many of these rituals have traits shared with other cultures of the Eurasian steppes from the Bronze and Iron ages and on into historical times. The ritual of burying horse heads and necks facing east, noted at the Botai site of Krasnyi Yar, is also found in the Mongolian Bronze Age (Allard and Erdenebaatar 2005). The identification of this practice in the 4th millennium BCE in the Botai culture may provide evidence for the antiquity of the association between the horse and the Sun or Sky God, a trait that is common among subsequent Indo-European cultures over a vast geographic region (Parpola 2005; Olsen 2000a). The placement of pairs of dogs on the west side of Botai houses may also signal the beginning of the ceremonial role of dogs as guardians or protectors. Later, Indo-European cultures regarded pairs of dogs as the guardians to the gates of the afterlife, which also lay to the west (Olsen 2000b). The Botai practices of making a bowl from a human skull and covering a skull with a clay mask are also rituals that have large temporal and geographic distributions (Olsen 2000a).

Contributing to this Eurasian steppe religious milieu are female figurines made on ungulate (primarily horse) phalanges. Easily identifiable ones have been found in Romania (Gimbutas 1989) and western Russia (Kuzmina 2003). More abstract decorated horse phalanges have been recovered in Spain (Almagro Basch 1966; Ayala Juan 1985). In Great Britain (MacGregor 1972–1974), The Netherlands (Roes 1963), and Turkey (Obladen-Kauder 1996), proximal phalanges of cattle have been found with abstract designs carved on one surface. One ox phalanx from the Orkneys had a person wearing a knee-length tunic carved on it (Lawrence 2004). In northern Kazakhstan, Copper Age Tersek settlements (Kalieva and Logvin 1997) as well as the Bronze Age site of Balandino, have produced decorated phalanges similar to those from the Botai culture.

GENDER ROLES IN THE BOTAI SOCIETY

There is no concrete evidence to identify the gender of those who produced particular handmade items or conducted certain types of work in the Botai culture, to date, and it is always risky to revert to stereotypes regarding division of labor by sex. In the Botai society, the daily activities, tasks, and crafts that can be readily identified from the archaeological record are provided in tables 4.1 through 4.3.

The social roles or professions listed in table 4.4 are more derived than the activities given in tables 4.1 through 4.3, which are closely linked to the archaeological evidence. Those roles with question marks in table 4.4 may or may not have existed in Botai society, because so far the evidence indicates

Table 4.1. Procurement of raw materials and assets

Animal	Plant	Mineral	Other
wild game	wild plant food	clay (ceramic, adobe)	water
fish/shellfish	wood	sand, quartz temper	
domestic horses	bast fibers	stone	
domestic dogs			

Table 4.2. Routine tasks (based on raw-material type)

Animal	Plant	Mineral	Other
hunting	house construction	water haulage	
fishing	collecting		
horse herding	food processing		
butchery	fiber processing		
mare milking			
food preparation			

Table 4.3. Crafts (based on raw-material type)

Animal	Plant	Mineral
hide/leather working	cord making	pottery making
fur working	cloth weaving	stone knapping
horn working	basket weaving	
bone/shell working	sewing	
	woodworking	

that they lived in egalitarian, communal villages with relatively little accumulation of personal property. There is much stronger evidence for military, commerce, and craft production in the subsequent Bronze and Iron ages. The amount of weaponry from those later periods also signifies inequality and a struggle for access to wealth and power. Among nomadic pastoralists, this is strongly tied to the amassing of large herds of livestock by certain individuals or families and control over grazing rights in optimal locations. The Botai, on the other hand, appear to have had few competitors, were settled in permanent villages, and probably practiced radial migration of the herds around their settlements, instead of long-distance seasonal migration of herds and families. Among the Botai, livestock may have been controlled by the whole community, rather than through personal ownership. There is also little need for craft specialists, since metallurgy was still relatively rare and did not require sophisticated knowledge or skill for production. There is no definitive evidence for the trade of goods from the outside, although small numbers of copper artifacts and some stone raw material may have been brought in from elsewhere.

Table 4.4. **Possible Botai social roles and professions**

Kinship	*Community/Political*	*Economic*	*Spiritual*
family head	village head/tribal chief	land and/or livestock owner?	shaman/priest(ess)
caregiver	adviser	trader?	
child care provider	warrior?	craft specialist?	

At this stage in our knowledge, the assignment of individual tasks, roles, occupations, and so forth to a particular gender among the Botai would be based solely on ethnographic trends rather than actual archaeological evidence, and there are always notable exceptions to our preconceived stereotypes. Any of these activities and roles could have been performed by either gender in the Botai society. Perhaps, as more Copper Age graves begin to appear, the accompanying grave goods will elucidate the roles of men and women within the Botai culture.

Even the professions of warrior and religious leader are not exclusively male domains in the Eurasian steppes. Amazons, or female warriors, have been documented (Davis-Kimball and Behan 2002), although they were probably never present in large numbers. Although there is a general perception that the role of shaman is andocentric, female shamans exist in cultures around the world and are often equally or even more powerful than their male counterparts (Tedlock 2005). Most Korean mondang, or shamans, are female. Female shamans are known as znakharka in Ukraine and voelva in Norse mythology. Siberian and Mongolian cultures, including the Buryat, Yakut, Altaians, Turgout, Kirgis, Tartars, and Tungus, have related linguistic terms for female shaman, derived from a common root of uncertain origin. In Mongolian it is *utagan,* which is etymologically related to *Etugen-eke,* or "hearth goddess." This concept of the hearth goddess is one we will address later in this chapter regarding the bone figurines from Botai sites. These interesting objects provide important clues about Botai females, both in terms of their outward appearance and their possible sacred roles.

THE NATURE OF PHALANX FIGURES

A total of fifty decorated phalanges of horse (n = 44), kulan (n = 1), saiga antelope (n = 4), and roe deer (n = 1), have been recovered from the eponymous site of Botai. All of those made from roe deer and saiga bones and all but two of those on equid bones from Botai were manufactured on proximal phalanges. Only two intermediate phalanges of horse were made into figurines.

The Botai phalanges were altered first by smoothing and preparing the bone surfaces, and then by incising fine geometric patterns on those surfaces. Some of the lines seem to represent the construction of a woman's dress or tunic, and others appear to indicate ornamentation that was applied to the clothing either by weaving a pattern into the cloth or by embroidering, appliquéing, or painting a design on the cloth. Although the practice of incising phalanges was widespread, nowhere is it as developed and common as it was among the Botai.

GEOGRAPHIC AND TEMPORAL DISTRIBUTION OF DECORATED PHALANGES

One of the oldest examples of decorated horse phalanges was reported from Cuina Turcului, a rock shelter above the north bank of the Donau River, in the Iron Gate region of Romania (Gimbutas 1989). It is remarkably similar in design to those from the Botai culture, but is very far removed both temporally and spatially. The earliest date for occupation, Level I, at Cuina Turcului is around 10,600 BCE, and a second layer, Level II, dates to 8,120 BCE. Gimbutas (1989) and Bolomey (1973) assign it to the younger, Epipaleolithic layer. The site was first excavated in the mid 1960s by Romanian archaeologist Dr. Vasile Boroneant (Bolomey 1973). Only three horse bones total were found in Level II, so the fact that one is made into such a fine artifact is somewhat remarkable (figure 4.2).

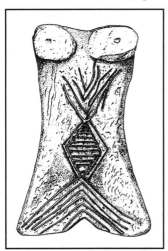

The illustration of the decorated horse phalanx from Cuina Turcului published by Gimbutas shows two small, incised circles on the distal condyles, representing nipples on a woman's breasts. These circles do not appear in other illustrations and are not visible in photographs, but the lighting in the image may fail to enhance such subtle surface details on the condyles. Most likely, Gimbutas, or the artist who drew the illustration in her volume, was able to study the piece under adequate lighting to see the faintly carved symbols. These indicators of breasts are important, although not necessary, to the hypothesis that the decorated phalanges are indeed female figurines.

Figure 4.2. Decorated horse phalanx from Cuina Turcului, Romania, c. 8100 BCE. (after Gimbutas 1989)

Closer to home and more likely to have shared a common ancestor with the Botai is the example from the Late Neolithic/Early Aeneolithic site of Varfolomievka (figure 4.3), in the North Caspian steppes of Russia (Kuzmina 2003, 210). This specimen places the breasts farther down on the shaft of the bone, implying that the distal condyles in this case were considered the figurine's shoulders.

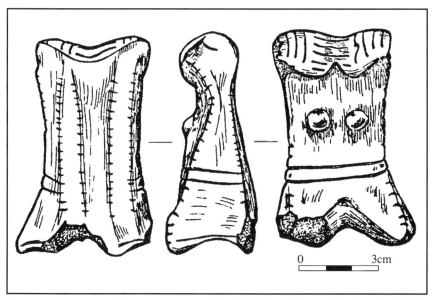

Figure 4.3.   Decorated horse phalanx from Varfolomievka, Russia. (after Kuzmina 2003)

The decorated phalanges that are most similar to those from Botai appear in sites assigned to the Copper Age Tersek, a contemporaneous culture that is related to the Botai, located in the Turgay Depression of northwestern Kazakhstan (Kalieva and Logvin 1997). The Tersek ones are generally simpler and fewer in number (figure 4.4). Some are made on intermediate phalanges, as is the case for two of the Botai figurines.

Sixteen decorated phalanges were recovered from a house and its immediate surroundings at the Botai site of Krasnyi Yar, but these have not been thoroughly analyzed or published to date.

Decorated horse phalanges have also been identified at Neolithic and Bell Beaker sites in Spain (Almagro Basch 1966; Ayala Juan 1985; Cardoso 1995). The Spanish ones are more simply and abstractly decorated, primarily by series of dimples drilled into the front (volar) surface. In these examples it is not possible to discern whether they represent females.

An interesting proximal phalanx of an ox, assigned a cultural affiliation of Late Iron Age/ Pictish (200–800 CE), was collected along

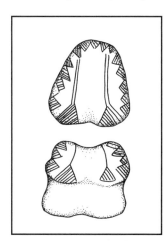

Figure 4.4. Tersek figurine from western Kazakhstan (top and front views), c. 3300 BCE. (after Kalieva and Logvin 1997)

with other archaeological materials from the Bu Sands, Burray, the Orkneys (Lawrence 2004). It is delicately incised on one side with an image of a person wearing a knee-length tunic. The sex of the individual is equivocal, although the author interpreted it as male and concludes that a circle below the elbow is a shield. It is possible, however, that it is meant to indicate decoration on the tunic, or a container that the person is carrying. Lines on the head are thought to depict a helmet, however, they could just as easily represent hair, especially since the posterior part of the lines could be interpreted as a "ponytail." Lines over much of the surface of the tunic may also represent decoration on the clothing. There are a series of circles on the back (dorsal) surface of the phalanx, behind the human figure.

Three other examples of incised cattle phalanges have been found in Great Britain. Two ox phalanges were found at the Broch of Burrian, in North Ronaldsay, the Orkneys (MacGregor 1972–1974, 1985); one has a small design incised on the back (dorsal) and the other has one on the front (volar) surface. Another from Saxon Southampton has Frisian runes inscribed on it (Addyman and Hill 1969; MacGregor 1985). These appear to be Pictish and date to the 7th–8th centuries CE. Terp mounds in the Netherlands have also produced ox phalanges with concentric circles, like the one from Bu (Munro 1889; Roes 1963).

At the Bronze Age site of Demircihüyük, in Anatolia, Turkey, one pig and two cattle proximal phalanges had deep annular incisions around their middle (Obladen-Kauder 1996). One of the cattle phalanges also had two pairs of chevrons on the proximal end of the shaft.

It is unclear whether any of these examples, apart from the Russian and Tersek ones, were somehow remotely related to those from the Botai culture via diffusion of ideas or direct migration of cultures. The practice of using ungulate, especially horse, phalanges as figurines could have been conceived quite independently by craftspersons in distinct cultures who similarly envisioned the easy transformation of these elements into a female torso. Based on temporal and geographic proximity, it is certainly less problematic to argue that the Russian one is an example of a cultural tradition shared with the Botai. However, other religious ceremonies, including those involving horse skulls facing east, dogs buried on the west, and the treatment of human skulls, were equally widespread, particularly among European steppe and Indo-European cultures.

CULTURAL MODIFICATIONS TO THE PHALANX

It is often clear that prehistoric people examined a particular bone and saw the potential for modifying it slightly to enhance natural features and achieve the appearance of an animal, person, or some other subject (Olsen, 2007). The proximal, and even to some extent the intermediate phalanx of an ungulate,

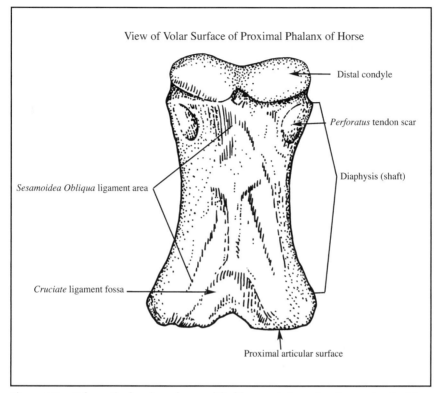

View of Volar Surface of Proximal Phalanx of Horse

Distal condyle

Perforatus tendon scar

Diaphysis (shaft)

Sesamoidea Obliqua ligament area

Cruciate ligament fossa

Proximal articular surface

Figure 4.5.   Schematic drawing of unmodified horse phalanx showing anatomical features. Illustration by Sandra Olsen.

such as a horse, deer, cattle, or antelope, have a natural morphology that is quite suggestive of the female torso. The distal condyles may represent either the breasts, as was probably the case for the example from Cuina Turcului, or the shoulders, as in the example from Varfolomievka. Despite their makers' different interpretations of the bone's morphology, both are important in building a case that these elements were selected to represent females, since both of these examples may have breasts depicted. The diaphysis or shaft of the phalanx is naturally waisted near the midpoint, like the body of a woman, and the flair of the shaft toward the proximal end is reminiscent of that of a skirt or the bottom of a tunic. The proximal articular surface provides a relatively flat base on which the figurine can stand upright.

Figure 4.5 is a schematic drawing illustrating a horse phalanx in its natural state in order to show the rugosities that must be removed when the craftsperson converts it into a figurine. Its parts are labeled with the proper anatomical terms (Camp and Smith 1942), in contrast to figure 4.6, in which the figurine is labeled using terms relevant to its orientation as an artifact.

Throughout this chapter, the figurine terms will be used to describe the various faces and areas, but it is important for the reader to make the distinction between anatomical terms and those used to describe the artifacts. Table 4.5 shows the equivalent anatomical and artifactual terms for the various parts of the decorated phalanges.

The phalanges from Botai were first prepared by smoothing and flattening the volar surface, removing the rugosities for the attachment of the various ligaments and the *perforatus* tendon (Camp and Smith 1942). This was done by scraping longitudinally with a burin or similar stout-edged stone tool in most cases, but occasionally the surface was abraded with sandstone or similar granular stone. The medial and lateral surfaces and the dorsal surface were also prepared by scraping or abrading if decoration was to be added. The surfaces of twenty-eight, or slightly more than half of the total from Botai, were further prepared by polishing. Bone can be very quickly polished, simply by rubbing the bone surface with wet leather covered in fine sand. Most of the polish was focused on the front surface, where the most elaborate designs were applied. The incised lines are today visible because of the dark sediment in them, but some show faint signs of red ochre that would have been used to accentuate the designs on the otherwise stark white background of the fresh bone.

The incisions vary in width and depth, with the simpler figurines often having the wider, deeper incisions. The most basic ones have only side notching, whereas the more complex ones have decoration on the front, back, sides, and, rarely, even on the top and bottom. Figure 4.6 illustrates the percentages of phalanges from Botai that have decoration on the various surfaces. These will be discussed in more depth shortly.

Design elements include dashes, zigzags, crosshatched zones, ladders, chevrons, hatched triangles, hatched diamonds, and chains of diamonds. Dashes, or notches, are the most common and are found on all of the various parts of the phalanx. Among the Botai specimens, only dashes were used to decorate along the rim of the proximal articular surface (base) and on the edge of the distal condyle (top). They were also applied in rows down the intersections between the front and sides, and, more rarely, between the sides and back.

Table 4.5. Equivalent anatomical and artifactual terms of reference for decorated phalanges

Anatomical Term	Artifact Term
proximal articular surface =	base
distal articular surface =	top
medial and lateral surfaces =	sides
volar surface =	front
dorsal surface =	back

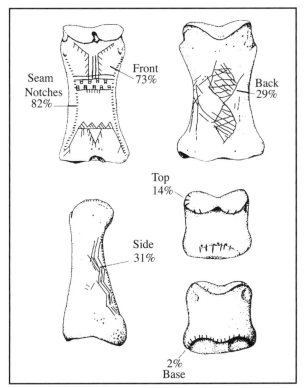

Figure 4.6. Examples of Botai decorated phalanges showing frequencies of decorative elements on different parts of the figurines. Illustration by Sandra Olsen.

FEMALE CLOTHING IN THE BOTAI CULTURE

Although there are no indications of gender-based differentiation of labor or skills at this point, evidence for the wardrobe of Botai women can be derived from the female figurines made on ungulate phalanges. The incised lines on the figurines are interpreted as dress designs, with some lines representing the garment structure itself and others indicating decorations applied to the clothing by some as yet undetermined method. Additional evidence about clothing can be derived from cloth and other fiber impressions in pottery.

INTERPRETATION OF DESIGNS ON PHALANGES

If one accepts that the decorated phalanges are female figurines, then the ornamentation can yield considerable information about Botai women's clothing. Figures 4.7 and 4.8 are examples from the site of Botai. Figure 4.7 shows a recon-

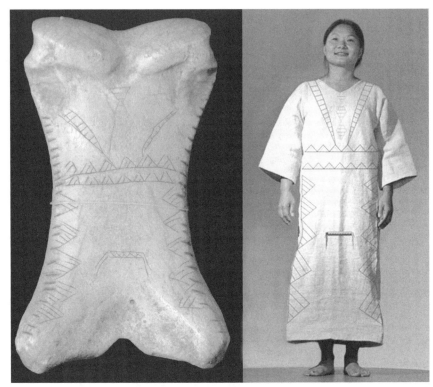

Figure 4.7. Botai figurine and a reconstructed dress of hand-spun hemp. Photo on left by Sandra Olsen; photo on right by Ron Lutz.

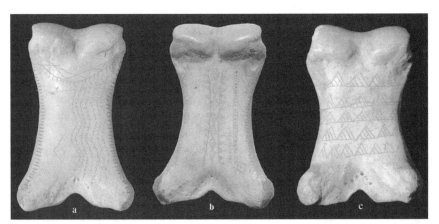

Figure 4.8. Examples of Botai decorated horse phalanges, c. 3300 BCE. Photo by Sandra Olsen.

struction of a dress, made with hand-spun hemp cloth with decoration applied to the front panel similar to that found on the Botai phalanx shown with it.

Dashes, or short incised horizontal notches, running down both sides of the phalanx were the most common design element. Typically, they are four to six millimeters long, under one millimeter wide, and spaced three to five millimeters apart. It might be tempting to interpret these as some form of accounting devices, such as a calendar or livestock counter, but that seems very unlikely. The numbers of dashes are not consistent, either from one specimen to the next or even between the left and right sides of the same specimen. Instead, their frequencies coincide with the coarseness or delicacy of the maker's touch. Those that are broad and deeply incised are fewer in number and more widely spaced. Those that are fine and shallow are closer together and more numerous. Also, the finer ones correlate with high amounts of polish and more elaborate designs on the front face.

The nearly ubiquitous rows of notches down the sides are interpreted here as the whipstitched side seams that unite the side panels with the front of the dress. If the side seams join two pieces of cloth with selvages, then, because they will not unravel, the edges do not need to be turned under. Whipstitching would be the most likely and easiest way to join selvage pieces and could be very visible on the outside of the dress.

Necklines apparently varied on the Botai examples, but some appear to be a typical V-shape (figure 4.6, front view). Ten of the figurines from Botai indicate V-necks. This is understandable if the distal condyles represent shoulders, rather than breasts, as in the Russian example, rather than the Romanian one from Cuina Turcului.

Four phalanges had two marks on the front face that may have depicted the left and right edges of the opening of a jacket or coat. Two have curved vertical lines that nearly meet in the middle, and two have lines that angle in toward the waist and flair back out.

Belts are sometimes depicted (figure 4.6, front view), but they are never shown going all the way around the dress, so they may have been small panels sewn directly on the dress. Nine examples were found at Botai, and all are associated with V-necks.

Some dashes on the fronts of the figurines may represent fringe, given their positions (figures 4.6, front view, and 4.8, below neckline). There are also many geometric designs that could have been embroidered, appliquéd, woven, or possibly even painted on. The hatched

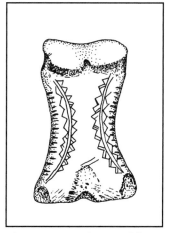

Figure 4.9. A decorated horse phalanx with possible coat opening depicted. Illustration by Sandra Olsen.

triangle is the most common design element for female figurines, as well as Botai pottery and other artifacts, but other geometric elements also occur.

Two phalanges (figure 4.7) appear to show a horizontal braid in the pubic region attached to the front of the dress. Another has a triangle that is reminiscent of a pubic apron. Aprons are found on the front and back of figurines in many regions of Eurasia, most often on otherwise nude bodies (Gimbutas 1989). These examples from Botai may simply be vestigial design elements added to the dress in the pubic region that harken back to the days when more revealing string aprons were worn alone. Alternatively, the pubic apron may have still been in vogue during the summer months, but less practical during the long winters of the South Siberian Plain.

It is interesting to examine the relative frequencies of design placement on the phalanges (figure 4.6). The most common, and therefore probably most necessary, incisions were the side notches, which we interpret as seams. These are the clearest marks that appear to indicate dress construction, other than the necklines found in a few examples. The decoration on what we identify as the "front" of the dress, based on where breasts are depicted in examples from other regions, was more common, at 73 percent, than that found on the "back" or the sides. Notches on the top and bottom were the least common. These may represent stitching around the neck and skirt hem.

DRESS DESIGN FEATURES

To summarize, below are the basic features that we can reconstruct on the women's dresses with some confidence.

- The neck is sometimes V-shaped.
- The side seams were probably done by whipstitching selvages of the front and side panels together, as well as, presumably, the side and back panels, although this is typically not shown.
- Geometric designs are common on the dress front, but only occasionally on the sides or back.
- A belted waist was optional, but the belt does not wrap completely around the dress. Instead it is restricted only to the front.
- Fringe may have been added at the neck, waist, or skirt.
- Pubic aprons or braids were occasionally placed over the pubic region.

HOW POTTERY IMPRESSIONS INFORM ABOUT CLOTHING

Botai ceramics, like those from other cultures within the Neolithic and Copper ages Geometric Impressed Pottery Province (GIPP) (Olsen et al. 2006) of the

Central Eurasian steppes, are decorated using a variety of instruments and materials pressed into the soft clay surface before firing. The retention of fine details from these materials reveals much about fiber technology, woodworking, and bone technology. Notched rib, cord, punctate, incised line, and comb impressions are commonly found in all of the Botai sites. In a study of over ten thousand pottery shards from Botai, Martinuk (1985) found that 15 percent had cloth impressions and even more had cord impressions. Olsen performed a study of a select sample of shards from the main site of Botai in 1996. Silicone rubber molds were made of surface impressions on eighty shards and scanning electron micrographs were taken to record the details of the different techniques. Although this represents only a small portion of the total Botai ceramic assemblage, this sample has been quite fruitful in terms of understanding fiber technology.

The ceramic collections made during excavations at the sites of Krasnyi Yar and Vasilkovka in 2000 and 2002 are also small by some standards, but nonetheless display a wide range of decorative techniques. It is significant that in the samples from both these sites, 20 percent of the shards had cord impressions (table 4.6 and figure 4.10). The main focus of this chapter is on fiber impressions, so the various other techniques that employed bone or wooden implements will not be discussed here.

CORD IMPRESSIONS

One in five of the potsherds from both Krasnyi Yar and Vasilkovka excavations exhibited impressions made by wrapping a cord around a paddle or stick. This technique was also common at the main site of Botai. Horse scapula paddles suitably shaped to have cords wrapped around them are plentiful in the as-

Table 4.6. Decorating techniques on potsherds from
Vasilkovka and Krasnyi Yar

Decorative	Vasilkovka		Krasnyi Yar	
Technique	N	%	N	%
Notched rib*	97	41	7	8
Cord	49	20	18	20
Plain	37	15	36	41
Punctate*	21	9	5	6
Incised line	12	5	6	7
Comb	4	2	15	17
Rocker stamp	0	0	1	1
Indet.	25	10	0	0
Total potsherds	239	100	88	100

* Six potsherds from Vasilkovka had both notched rib and punctate designs.

Figure 4.10.   Cord impressions on ceramic shard from Botai. Photo by Sandra Olsen.

semblage from Botai, but wooden paddles or sticks could also have been used. Details about cordage technology are important because they shed light on thread manufacture, and cord impressions are both more common and more readily interpretable than the small number of shallow cloth impressions. No actual fibers have been recovered from Botai sites yet; so all interpretations of fiber technology are necessarily based on impressions in ceramics.

Weavers define twist direction by the slant of the fibers in relation to the axis of the cord. S-twisted cordage slants down to the right (figure 4.11), whereas Z-twisted cordage slants down to the left (Hurley 1979). Twist is not apparently influenced by the type of fiber used, the method of spinning, or handedness (Minar 2000). Spinning can be done easily in either direction with a spindle or on the thigh. The dominance of an S-twist may therefore have been a stylistic preference rather than a technical one. According to Maslowski (1996), direction of cordage twist can be used as a cultural marker at times. Botai cordage uniformly had an S-twist. In addition, the cord diameter ranged from one to two millimeters and the cords were moderately tightly spun. All of the cord impressions that have been observed are two-ply.

Cord-impressed ceramics are widely distributed across the Eurasian steppes, especially in the Neolithic and Copper ages (Aeneolithic). However, they also occur independently in many parts of the world at different times (Petersen and Hamilton 1984). Because a number of characteristics, like the type of fiber used to make the cordage, diameter of cords, number of plies,

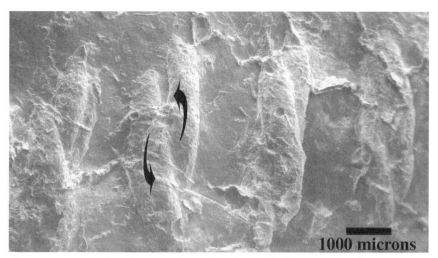

Figure 4.11.   Scanning electron micrograph of a mold of a ceramic shard from Botai, showing cord impressions with two-ply S-twists. Photo by Sandra Olsen.

and direction of twist can vary, it would be useful if scholars would record these data and compare them crossculturally and through time.

CLOTH IMPRESSIONS

Significantly, 15 percent of the more than ten thousand shards from the main site of Botai exhibit traces of cloth impressions, according to Oleg Martinuk (1985). Our small study sample has yielded exciting results, but much work remains to be done on identifying the types of weaves used at Botai. Cloth impressions have been reported from numerous sites across the Eurasian steppes, including the Bronze Age site of Arkaim (Zdanovich 1995), for example, but systematic studies have not been done over a large geographic area. Some of the earliest hemp-type cloth impressions come from Yangshao Neolithic sites in northern China, such as Banpo, in Shanxi Province, where large quantities of hemp pollen have also been identified. These date to the late 5th and early 4th millennia (Barber 1991, 17). Similar cloth impressions have also been found at 5th-millennium sites in Tibet, so it would not be surprising if the Botai had hemp cloth by 3300 BCE.

Based on the appearance of the Botai cloth impressions (figure 4.12), they probably represent simple twined cloth made from a bast fiber. It appears that two-ply S-twist threads were used, just as was the case for the cordage. To attempt to replicate the cloth, we used spun hemp, although the ancient cloth could also have been done with nettle or some other bast fiber. Our experi-

Figure 4.12. Cloth impressions underlying ladder pattern of comb impressions on a ceramic shard from Botai (image rotated for easier interpretation of impressions). Photo by Sandra Olsen.

ments indicate that the Botai wet their fibers during spinning. Ours were not moistened while spinning and the experimental cloth appears fuzzy in comparison with the smooth fibers of the Botai impressions.

In twining, two or more weft threads pass around and are twisted between the warp threads. The impressions from twining are typically rows of lozenge-shaped indentations made by the weft, if it is weft-faced. Twining is one of the oldest known forms of weaving cloth. Examples of simple twined cloth or flexible baskets have been preserved in fired clay from the Upper Paleolithic site of Pavlov I, dating to between 24,000 and 27,000 years ago (Adovasio et al. 1996).

TYPES OF BAST PLANTS IN EURASIA

Based on the experimentation done in this study on a range of materials, it is likely that the Botai used bast fibers from plants to make their cordage. The Botai did not have domestic sheep or goats and the impressions look nothing like experimental ones made with wool yarn in any case. They did, however, compare closely to experimental cordage made with American Indian hemp bast (*Apocynum cannabinum*). There are four major kinds of plants typically known for yielding bast fibers for fine cordage and cloth in Eurasia: hemp, nettle, flax, and ramie. Ramie, also known as China grass, grows in East Asia, notably southern China, but does not range as far west as Kazakhstan.

Flax

According to Zohary and Hopf (2000, map 12), the wild progenitor of domestic flax, *Linum usitatissimum bienne*, has been found along coasts of the Mediterranean Sea, Atlantic Ocean, Black Sea, and the south end of the Caspian Sea, and in the Zagros Mountains of Iran and Iraq. Linseeds have been found in the Epipaleolithic (pre-agriculture) levels at the Syrian site of Tell Abu Hureyra (Hillman 1975; Hillman et al. 1989). Linen fibers dating back to 7000 BCE have been found in Israel, and these probably represent the harvesting of wild flax. Based on changes in seed size, flax cultivation had begun in the Near East by 6000 BCE (Zohary and Hopf 2000, 132). Genetic studies indicate that it was probably initially domesticated for its oil, rather than its fibers, and that it probably had a single origin of domestication (Allaby et al. 2005). From southwest Asia, it then gradually spread outward.

According to our current knowledge, the prehistoric distribution of wild flax appears to have been too far south for it to have been harvested locally in northern Kazakhstan by Botai weavers. The date for the earliest flax domestication precedes the Botai culture by about 2,500 years, making it theoretically possible that it could have reached northern Kazakhstan by the time of occupation. However, there is no evidence for plant domestication of any kind at Botai and the domestic animals that originated in the Near East (cattle, sheep, goats, and pigs) are also absent.

There are two possible indications of diffusion of ideas from the Near East and its periphery to northern Kazakhstan. The first, a copper dagger from Krasnyi Yar, closely resembles those found in Iran at about the same time or somewhat earlier, and ones found in the Transcaucasus slightly later (Chernykh 1992). The second possible piece of evidence for diffusion of ideas is a skull from the site of Botai that was covered with a clay mask (Rikushina and Zaibert 1984). This was similar to ones found in the Tahunian culture of Israel, but the Near Eastern examples date to between 7300 and 6000 BCE (Ben-Tor 1992, 30). The tradition of placing clay over a skinned skull was probably much more widespread than is currently known, however, as it has been well documented in the Catacomb culture of Russia and Ukraine (3000–2200 BCE) (Mallory and Adams 1997, 92), somewhat later than Botai, and the much later Iron Age Tagar and Tashtyk cultures in the Minusinsk Basin of Siberia (Chard 1974, 162; Jettmar 1967; Jacobson 1987). Given the lack of evidence for any Near Eastern domestic grain or animals at Botai sites, however, it is probably unlikely that domestic flax had diffused to Kazakhstan and was being grown there for the purpose of making cloth. Other indigenous plants suitable for producing bast fibers would have been much more readily available and without all the efforts required for cultivation.

Hemp

The original natural range of *Cannabis sativa* is uncertain, but Central Asia is thought to be the epicenter by experts like botanist Mark Merlin, who has spent much of his career investigating the hemp plant (1972; personal communication 2005). Today, Kazakhstan is one of the major producers of marijuana and the wild *Cannabis* grows over much of the steppe and forest steppe there. It has been found in sites belonging to the Tripolye culture of Ukraine between 5300 and 3500 BCE as seed imprints in clay floors. Hemp has turned up in seed form in the Bandkeramik culture of Germany between 5500 and 4500 BCE. Hemp parts have been found in the Siberian Iron Age frozen tombs of Pazyryk (Rudenko 1970, 199). And, as noted above (Barber 1991, 17), hemp spread to China by the late 5th or early 4th millennium BCE. Bast fibers used in making cloth and cordage at Botai could easily have been derived from *Cannabis*.

Nettle

The stinging nettle, *Urtica dioica*, as well as other species of nettle, was widely used to make strong cordage and fine cloth that is difficult to distinguish from linen or hemp cloth. Nettle cloth has been identified in Neolithic contexts in Denmark and Britain. In fact, nettle cloth found in numerous Scandinavian sites was mislabeled as linen until recent reexamination set the record straight (Barber 1991). Nettle cloth has been identified in northern European burials from the Bronze Age and continued to be manufactured in Northern, Central, and Eastern Europe through the 19th century. When cultivated cotton was in short supply during the two world wars, the German army substituted nettle cloth (*Nesseltuch*) from an estimated two thousand tons of wild plants to make their uniforms. It took around forty-five kilograms to make a single shirt, which means that a Botai weaver would have had to collect quite a large amount to make a long dress. Nettle bast fibers are extremely strong, even when spun into quite thin threads, and they are silkier in texture than hemp or linen.

Today, *Urtica dioica* can still be found in the forest steppe of northern Kazakhstan where the Botai culture lived (Komarov 1985). So far, only a small sample of pollen has been analyzed from Krasnyi Yar and Vasilkovka, and the macrobotanical and phytolith studies are only just beginning, so neither hemp nor nettle has been identified from any of the Botai sites yet.

Feather Grass

Of course, there may be other alternatives for coarse cordage, including some types of grasses. Our experiments in making coarse cordage from unprocessed grasses of an unknown species were successful. One possibility might be feather grass, of which there are a number of species in Kazakhstan. Pollen from the family Poaceae to which feather grass belongs has been identified in our palynological samples from Krasnyi Yar. *Stipa,* the genus for feather grass, is also the genus to which esparto belongs. Esparto (*Stipa tenacissima*) is used to make paper, ropes, baskets, and mats, but is restricted to the Iberian Peninsula and North Africa. The *Stipa* that grows in Kazakhstan has not yet been tested to see if it would produce suitable bast fibers for cordage. It is unlikely that *Stipa* would have been suitable for making fine threads for making cloth, however.

PREPARATION OF BAST FIBERS

The plants that produce bast fibers are usually collected in the fall after they have reached their maximum height. They are gathered in bundles, and sometimes split with the thumbnail into strips. They are then retted either in water or by laying them out in the open to be exposed repeatedly to the dew (known as "dew retting"). This loosens the bast fibers from the rest of the stalk. After the retting process is complete, the stems are broken, so that the long outside fibers can be pulled away from the soft, spongy inner pith. To finish cleaning the fibers, they may be laid out on a mat and scraped with a rib, shell, or other smooth-edged tool. The fibers are then allowed to dry. When the craftsperson is ready to make a cord or thread, he or she will soak the fibers to make them pliable. Taking two separate bunches of a few fibers in one hand (usually the left), the person then uses the palm of the opposite (usually right) hand to slowly roll the two bunches of fibers over the thigh so that they are twisted independently. Then, the hand is quickly pulled up to allow the two bunches to twist together, making a two-ply cord or thread. Alternatively, a spindle could be used to spin the thread.

EVIDENCE FOR BOTAI WEAVING
TECHNOLOGY AND CLOTHING

To summarize the information available for Botai fiber technology, we can identify the following features regarding cloth and clothing at Botai sites.

- Two-ply S-twist cord and thread were made from bast fibers. Hemp and nettle are the most likely sources for the vegetal fibers.

- Cloth probably had a simple twined weave.
- The Botai had sewn clothing with elaborate ornamentation, but it is not clear how the decorative elements were applied—either by weaving them into the cloth, or through appliqué, embroidery, or painting.

THE ROLE OF FEMALE FIGURES IN THE BOTAI CULTURE

More intriguing than the phalanges used in the manufacture of these figurines or even the decorations applied to them is the symbolism that may have been associated with them. Interpreting the role or roles of female figurines in any prehistoric culture is problematic because it relies primarily on the image itself and its context at the time of final deposition. There is no indication of where or how the object was employed during much of its use life, however, so a significant amount of information is usually missing from the archaeological record.

For the most part, the female figurines from Botai and Krasnyi Yar that were found in situ were reported from houses (table 4.7), but little further contextual data beyond the domestic association of the objects has been published. Nine out of sixty-eight excavated houses at Botai yielded decorated phalanges. Ten decorated phalanges were found together in one house (house 140) at the site of Botai, whereas the other eight houses only had one or two decorated phalanges, each. Eight of the ten decorated phalanges from house 140 were discovered resting on the floor, while another was in a floor pit, and the last one was recovered just in the house fill dirt. Thirteen decorated phalanges were recovered from a single house (house 1) at Krasnyi Yar, and at least six of those were on the floor.

Some decorated phalanges were found in pits outside houses, and our recent research indicates that extramural pits often contained ceremonial offerings (Olsen 2000a,b). A cluster of three phalanges from one pit at Botai had flakes driven off them from the ends, as if to intentionally destroy or "kill" them. Other phalanges were found between houses, with no particularly obvious association or intentional placement. Little can be said about the original provenance of those found in the disturbed zone at Botai. It is an area of extensive erosion where the riverbank is collapsing and destroying countless houses in the process.

Careful excavations conducted recently may shed some light on the placement of female figurines in the domicile. Botai houses sometimes have small pits in their semisubterranean floors. At the Krasnyi Yar settlement, two houses excavated in 2000 (Olsen et al. 2006) had such pits, containing caches of horse phalanges. One contained twenty-eight proximal phalanges and the other contained six (Olsen 2000a). Although none was incised, one had been

Table 4.7. Distribution of decorated phalanges at Botai and Krasnyi Yar

Provenience	Botai	Krasnyi Yar
House	22	13
Pit outside house	5	3
Between houses	10	
Disturbed zone	13	
Total	50	16

smoothed probably in preparation to do so. Unfortunately, there is no record available for caches of unmodified phalanges at the site of Botai, which has had the largest number of houses excavated.

It is possible that these phalanges were simply being stored for future use, either to extract the tiny amount of marrow and bone grease contained in them or to make decorated figurines at some later date. Alternatively, these bones could have represented female figurines even if they were plain. Perhaps cloth was wrapped around them to represent clothing or it was not always necessary to illustrate the clothing. Peoples of the Eurasian steppe today sometimes equate certain unmodified bones with animals or people, as in the Mongolian and Kazakh game played by boys with sheep astragali (Birtalan 2003; Humphrey and Onon 1996). In this case, one face of an astragalus may represent a sheep, one a goat, one a horse, and one a camel, but the bones usually completely lack any surface modification.

The larger horse phalanx cache pit at Krasnyi Yar was located near the center of the house, just to the west of the hearth. The regular ritual pattern of placing two dog skulls or whole skeletons in paired pits just outside the west sides of houses (Olsen 2000a,b) suggests that the entrance was typically on that side. The dogs may have served as guardian spirits protecting the family inside. At least for this one particular house, the cache might then be located between the doorway and the hearth, an area that would benefit greatly from spiritual protection. The orientation of the cache in the second house is more difficult to determine since only a trench was dug through the middle of the house.

The practice of placing female idols in the home is a widespread one that probably has a very ancient history. Such idols could be placed in the home as part of a building ceremony, to honor ancestors or certain deities, or to offer protection from particular gods or spirits.

A well-preserved clay house model found buried below a house floor at the site of Platia Magoula Zarkou, a Middle Neolithic site in northern Thessaly, Greece, dating to the Tsangli phase (5700–5900 BCE) (Whittle 1996, 87–88), contained eight clay human figurines, some male and some female. These have been interpreted as representatives of ancestors, and the placement of the house model may have been part of a foundation ceremony at the time of construction. These are mentioned partly because they were found in a floor, but also because some of the figurines have a shape that resembles a horse phalanx and they are headless and armless, just like the Botai figurines.

One might also consider the "teraphim" in the Old Testament. These were sometimes clay idols that were kept in the home. Such was apparently the case with the one that was stolen by Rachel, in the story about Jacob, to prevent it from telling her father where she had gone. Whereas seraphim guarded the throne of the god in the sky, teraphim were divinities of the earth that were kept in houses.

The concept of a "hearth goddess" may be useful to consider while investigating depositional patterns for phalanges in the archaeological record at Botai sites. The hearth goddess protected the hearth and the home, and even sometimes the community as a whole. Examples include the Greek goddess Hestia; the early Roman goddess Cacia, who later became known as Vesta; the pan-Celtic Brighid; the Lithuanian Gabija; the Gaulish Nantosuelta; and the Mongolian *Etugen-eke*. The hearth goddess was attended by women, especially the female heads of the household or clan. Festivals were held in her honor at certain times of the year, such as during the renewal of the fire. Offerings such as salt or food might be thrown on the hearth to acknowledge her, and on family occasions, prayers were directed to her. According to Celtic tradition, Brighid was invited into the home by the head female by way of bringing in a doll or corn dolly (straw figurine) dressed in maiden white.

CONCLUSION

It is probably too early to determine the kinds of tasks, occupations, and roles associated with either women or men in the Botai culture, although tremendous strides have been made in reconstructing the lifestyles of these early steppe horse pastoralists. However, the female figurines made on ungulate phalanges offer our first insight into the possible religious significance of women in that society. If the deposit of these figurines in houses, and more specifically in caches in house floors, is an indication of ceremonial offerings, then it is likely that female spirits or deities were assigned important domestic roles. Whether these represent foundation offerings placed at the time the house was built or ones introduced repeatedly during the occupation is still not understood since the cache pits excavated at Krasnyi Yar in 2000 were made near the center of the floor rather than under a wall or other structure. In any case, these figurines may have served to protect the domicile in a way similar to the paired dog sacrifices so typically placed on the west, just outside Botai houses. Hearth goddesses perform more missions than protection, however. They are also associated with increasing fertility. Another possibil-

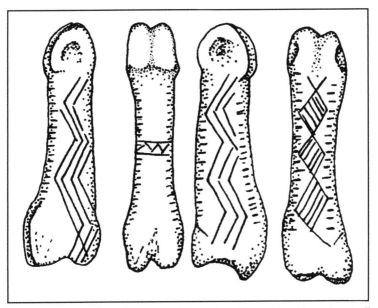

Figure 4.13.   Saiga antelope decorated phalanx from Krasnyi Yar (four views). Illustration by Sandra Olsen.

ity is that the female figurines represent the spirits of ancestors of the family living in the dwelling. There is still much to be learned about these elusive objects and only further exploration with precise attention to context can help resolve our understanding of them.

Preference was given to proximal horse phalanges; however, the same elements of saiga (figure 4.13), roe deer, and kulans could also be used, as well as, more rarely, the intermediate phalanges of horse. These choices undoubtedly reflect the recognition of the similarity between the natural morphology of these bones to a human figure and the ease with which they could be adapted to make figurines.

NOTE

This research was made possible through the generous support of the National Science Foundation, grant BSC-0414441. The core of this chapter was presented at the Second Eurasian Steppe Archaeology Conference, at the University of Chicago, in 2005. This project was inspired by the work of Olsen's Russian colleague, Olga Chenchenkova, who studied the Botai phalanges from an artistic point of view. Our discussions provided much insight and stimulated Olsen's curiosity about these objects. We also want to extend our appreciation to Alice Choyke for providing us with Hungarian hand-spun hemp for our reconstruction of a Botai dress. We wish to thank the editors of this volume, Katheryn M. Linduff and Karen S. Rubinson, for all of their efforts to bring this interesting group of authors together to discuss the very pertinent topic of gender in prehistory.

Chapter Five

He Who Eats the Horse, She Who Rides It?

Symbols of Gender Identity on the Eastern Edges of the Eurasian Steppe

Gideon Shelach

This chapter addresses the symbols and conception of gender roles among societies located at the eastern part of the Eurasian steppe during the late 2nd and early 1st millennium BCE. This period saw vast and meaningful sociopolitical and economic changes among societies located throughout the Eurasian steppe lands, from the Danube River in the West to the Liao River in the East (Hanks 2002, 183; Honeychurch and Amartuvshin 2005, 259; Khazanov 1994, 92–93; Renfrew 2002, 4–7; Shelach 2005). Pastoralism became a dominant, though not the only, economic mode, and many societies which inhabited this huge area adopted a more mobile lifeway. Horseback riding, which became common, if not actually initiated, during this period (Drews 2004, 65–98), is associated with herding as well as with the military capabilities developed by these societies.

In what follows I attempt to unpack gender symbolism and understand better the position of women in these steppe societies. Especially, I hope to demonstrate the complex nature of gender roles and to shatter some of the stereotypic assumptions about male and female roles in early pastoral societies. Because of the prominent role of the horse—real and symbolic—in pastoral societies, much of the discussion focuses on gender associations with horses and with the attributes of horseback riding. One of my conclusions is that rather than being a clear masculine symbol manipulated by males as the dominant group in these societies, horses were used symbolically by individuals of both sexes, though differently for each gender, perhaps.

Like many other studies of "gender archaeology" (cf. Linduff and Sun 2004) my work is based mainly on the analysis of mortuary data. Because graves are one of the few archaeological contexts where structures, artifacts, and individuals are clearly associated with each other, this is a convenient place to address gender issues. However, as many researchers have pointed out, reliance on mortuary data, especially without any supporting evidence, can be misleading. The data uncovered from such contexts are, after all, the result of ritualistic behavior—the construction of the grave and the funeral and burial rites—and therefore are not necessarily a mirror image of the society that produces them. For example, as Hodder pointed out twenty-five years ago, "a change to a less complex or less differentiated burial rite does not necessarily entail a change to a less complex society" (1982, 199). Studies of both past and living societies confirm that in some societies, mortuary ritual emphasizes and even exaggerates the social, political, or economic status of the deceased, while in others differences among members of the population are de-emphasized after death (cf. Cannon 1989; Parker Pearson 1982).

In much the same way we can assume that mortuary data pertaining to gender relations are biased by ritualistic demands. However, while taking such warnings to heart, I also concur with the opinion that mortuary rituals, and their materialistic expressions, are never completely divorced from social, political, and economic realities (cf. Brown 1995; McHugh 1999; Shelach 2001). Thus, although we should be cautious about the patterns of gender relations elucidated by our analysis of mortuary data, we should not reject them out of hand as merely "ritualistic." Rather, we should adopt a common-sense approach to evaluate the meaning of such patterns through comparison to nonmortuary aspects of the material culture. Moreover, we should bear in mind that symbolic and ritualistic aspects, such as those apparent in mortuary practices, are not "just" epiphenomena, but are at the core of gender relations. After all, we are not asking what people are (biologically) or even not necessarily what they do (economically), but how they view themselves and are viewed by others. Gender is mostly about ideology and identity, and such issues are always symbolically loaded.

SOCIETIES OF THE NORTHERN ZONE DURING THE LATE 2ND AND EARLY 1ST MILLENNIA BCE

The geographical focus of this chapter is an area called the "Northern Zone,"[1] located at the easternmost fringes of the Eurasian steppe. It is currently part of the People's Republic of China where it covers the northern parts of Hebei, Shanxi, and Shaanxi provinces, most of Gansu and Qinghai, Inner Mongolia and Liaoning, and the western parts of Jilin and Heilongjiang.

Today the area receives an average annual precipitation of five hundred millimeters or less. Most areas in the east receive today 350 to 500 millimeters, and in the west one hundred to four hundred millimeters (Liu 1998). Average temperatures also drop as one moves north and west. In the Chifeng region, which is located in the heart of the eastern part of the Northern Zone, average temperatures in January are minus 9.7 degrees Celsius, and an average of 23.2 degrees in July. In Hohhot, located toward the central-western part of this region, average degrees in January are minus 13.1 and 21.9 Celsius in July (Liu 1998). While climatic conditions during the 2nd and 1st millennia BCE were probably warmer and moister, the area was then, as now, less suitable for agriculture than areas in the main river basins to the south. The soils and natural vegetation of most of the Northern Zone are classified as those of a steppe (*caoyuan*) (Hou 1982). But today large parts of it are also under cultivation, and there is no reason to assume that agriculture was not a viable adaptation option during the prehistory of this region.

Human presence in this area goes back to the Pleistocene, and sedentary village life, probably associated with agriculture, is dated to around 6200 BCE (Shelach 2000). By the late 3rd and early 2nd millennia BCE the local population had multiplied (Drennan et al. 2003), and in different regions within the Northern Zone settlement hierarchies developed (Linduff 1998; Shelach 1999; Tian and Han 2003). Some sites are larger than twenty hectares and show substantial investment in permanent structures, such as stone walls which enclosed sites or parts of a site (known from the eastern part of the Northern Zone) as well as in domestic structures (Liaoning 2001; NMGW-WKGYJS 2000; Shelach 1999). Stone tools, a substantial number of storage pits, as well as the remains of grains and animal bones, suggest that societies throughout the Northern Zone developed heavy reliance on agricultural production (Debaine-Francfort 1995; Huang 2000; Gansu sheng 1990; Li and Gao 1985; Linduff 1995, 138; Shui 2001; Wang 2004; Zhongguo 1996, 362–409). High-quality and complex ceramic vessels and evidence for incipient bronze production (Debaine-Francfort 1995; Li and Han 2000; Li and Shui 2000; Linduff 1998; Shelach 1999, 101–105; Tian and Han 2003; Zhongguo 1996, 188–190) point to at least some degree of craft specialization.

To the south of the Northern Zone, complex state-level polities developed in the Yellow, Wei, and Yangzi river basins by the 2nd and 1st millennia BCE. Although interactions among the regions are evident (Shelach 2005), societies in the north remained politically and culturally independent from Shang and Zhou control at least until around 400 BCE. Recent research suggests that local processes among Northern Zone societies during this period are more complex than was previously thought. Rather than a collapse of the settlement system that flourished during the 3rd and early 2nd millennia BCE, we now recognize, at least in some parts of the Northern Zone, a continuation of high-population densities as well as, perhaps, a settlement hierarchy, well into the 1st millennium BCE (Drennan et al. 2003; Linduff et al. 2004; Shelach forthcoming). Although some aspects of the material culture of these societies suggest a very dramatic change, such as the flourishing bronze industry and the development of a new style of ornamentation (Linduff 1997, 33–73;

Table 5.1.   Percentages of animal bones at sites from the 2nd millennium BCE

	Zhukaigou	Dadianzi	Dashanqian
Pig	33.5	64.1	48.2
Sheep	36.1	0.0	15.3
Cattle	15.5	0.0	24.3
Dog	4.5	35.9	10.9
Wild animals	10.3	0.0	1.3 (including horses)
Total	99.9	100	100

Sources: Data from Huang 2000, 400–421; Wang 2004, 256, Zhongguo 1996, 362–409. Dashanqian: cemetery, Chifeng, eastern part of Northern Zone; Dadianzi: domestic site, Chifeng area; Zhukaigou: cemetery, Ordos area, central part of the Northern Zone.

Table 5.2.   Percentages of animal bones at sites from the 1st millennium BCE

	Dahuazhongzhuang	Maoqinggou (early graves)	Guandongche
Sheep/Goat	64.0	80.3	32.2
Cattle	15.2	14.5	19.2
Horse	20.0	3.9	3.2
Pig	0.19	0.0	25.0
Dog	0.19	1.3	16.2
Wild animals	0.38	0.0	3.2

Sources: Data from Qinghai 1985, 28–33; Tian and Guo 1986, 306–313; Zhu 2004, 433. Dahuazhongzhuang: cemetery, Qinghai, western part of the Northern Zone; Maoqinggou: cemetery, Ordos region, central part of the Northern Zone; Guandongche: habitation, Chifeng region, eastern part of the Northern Zone.

Tian and Guo 1986; Zhu 1987), others, such as ceramic production, suggest the continuation of regional and subregional traditions (Shelach forthcoming; Shui 2001; Tian and Guo 1988).

Most fundamental for this chapter are changes in the economy of Northern Zone societies. Here again, the picture is more varied than previous reconstructions have suggested. Comparing the composition of animal bone collections from sites and cemeteries of the late 3rd and early 2nd millennia BCE to those from sites of the late 2nd and early 1st millennia BCE does suggest that the emphasis on animal husbandry shifted from animals (pigs) raised in pens in or near the habitation during the early period, to herding animals (sheep or goats) during the later period. This transition is more pronounced in the central and western parts of the Northern Zone, and more mixed in the eastern part (tables 5.1 and 5.2).

GIS analysis of the location of sites identified by the Chifeng regional survey in relation to land-use categories supports the conclusion that even during the first half of the 1st millennium BCE societies in the eastern part of the Northern Zone continued to engage in relatively intensive agriculture production (Shelach forthcoming). Storage pits excavated at many sites dated to the same period from the eastern part of the Northern Zone, as well as the type of stone tools that were recovered, also suggest the importance of agriculture production (Liaoning 1983, 1992; Shelach 1999, 143–154; Zhongguo 1974, 1979). While less is known about the continuation of agricultural production in the central and western parts of the Northern Zone, it seems that there as well agriculture production continued throughout the 1st millennium BCE. Recent research conducted at the site of Fengtai, in the eastern part of Qinghai, recovered substantial amounts of domesticated grains of plants such as barley, wheat, and foxtail millet (Zhongguo 2004, 87–88), and other evidence that suggests a relatively advanced level of agriculture practiced by people of the Fengtai community sometime during the 1st millennium BCE (Zhongguo 2004, 89).

So it appears that even by the end of the period addressed here, what emerged was not a purely pastoralist economy but a mixed economy in which agriculture and pastoralism existed side by side, and had a roughly equal importance. Pastoralism, therefore, was adopted by societies in the Northern Zone not to replace the existing economic base but to expand it, and thus improve the reliability of the economic adaptation.

Though economic and social changes among Northern Zone societies were not as dramatic as some previous models have led us to believe, the local trajectory was, nevertheless, quite different from that of societies further to the south. To this period we can date the genesis of a local "Northern Zone identity" that was distinctly different—in real and symbolic terms—from that of their "Chinese" (Zhou) neighbors to the south. It is in this context that I would like to examine the construction of gender identities and gender-related status among Northern Zone societies of the early 1st millennium BCE.

GENDER IDENTITY AND WOMEN'S STATUS IN CEMETERIES OF THE EARLY 1ST MILLENNIUM BCE FROM THE NORTHERN ZONE

In addition to the above-mentioned association between individuals (human skeletons) and artifacts, mortuary data have the advantage of being easily quantifiable, and thus they lend themselves to types of rigorous analysis not always suitable in other archaeological contexts (Shelach 2001). In order to fully utilize this advantage, I choose here to focus on a few relatively well-preserved and fully reported cemeteries, and only occasionally supplement them with data from other graves which were less systematically excavated or reported. Working with coherent data sets, rather than with heterogeneous data collected from many different sources, ensures that the analysis will produce meaningful patterns less affected by different preservation conditions and research biases.

Gideon Shelach

To this end I selected three cemeteries, representing the most complete set of data from their respective regions within the Northern Zone: Xiaobaiyang in northern Hebei in the eastern part of the Northern Zone; Maoqinggou from the Ordos region in the central part, and Dahuazhongzhuang in northeastern Qinghai, located at the western part of this region. The forty-five well-preserved graves at the Xiaobaiyang cemetery are dated to the Upper Xiajiadian (Zhangjiakou 1987, 50–51), making it the largest coherent burial data set of this period. Unfortunately, the skeletons at Xiaobaiyang were not sexed so we cannot associate directly the patterns we identify with the sex of the deceased. The data can, however, be used as a control group to see if patterns we identified at the other two cemeteries appear here as well. From the Maoqinggou cemetery I used data collected from the description and tabulation of the thirty-six well-preserved graves, assigned to periods I and II, dated to about the 8th to the 5th centuries BCE (Tian and Guo 1986, 306–313). From the 117 graves assigned to the Kayue period, dated tentatively to the mid-1st millennium BCE, at the Dahuazhongzhuang cemetery, I analyzed the data pertaining to the ninety-five undisturbed graves (Qinghai 1985, 28–33).

A matrix was prepared for each of the cemeteries containing as much information as possible on the construction and size of each grave, its occupant, and the grave goods and animal offerings placed in it. Searching first for broader patterns of similarities among groups of graves in each cemetery, I clustered the graves in each of the three cemeteries using the K-means clustering method (Euclidean distance) on standardized data. Using this as an exploration method, I tried a number of groups, and it became apparent that four was the optimal number of groups for all three data sets.

Among the four groups produced by the analysis of the Maoqinggou cemetery (table 5.3), group A is the largest. It includes twenty graves with low averages in all the mortuary variables, such as the size of the graves, the number and quality of artifacts placed in them, and the number of sacrificial animals. It would seem that this group includes graves of people of a low overall status. Group B includes seven graves that have a high average number of ceramic vessels and bronze belt parts, and slightly higher than average grave sizes and number of bone artifacts. Group C includes five graves with high average numbers of small bronze ornaments and beads and a slightly higher than average appearance of horse gear and bronze belt parts. Group D includes four graves with high average numbers of artifacts in all categories except for beads. The richer graves have an especially high average number of weapons, animal bones, and horse gear.

It seems that this grouping of the early Maoqinggou graves is based mainly on social and economic status, while most other identities are probably subsumed within this hierarchy. However, groups B and C, which are placed between the "elite" (D) and the "commoners" (A), may suggest other types

Table 5.3. Clustering of graves from the Maoqinggou cemetery

	Group A	Group B	Group C	Group D
Grave numbers	2, 4, 7, 8, 12, 14, 16, 17, 22, 41, 44, 46, 47, 48, 56, 61, 65, 66, 68, 70	9, 39, 42, 43, 45, 58, 60	3, 5, 10, 55, 71	6, 59, 60, 75
Sex ratio	11 male, 4 female (2 child; 3?)	5 male, 2 female	2 male, 3 female	3 male, 1?

of identities which are not as closely related to wealth and prestige. Group D, which seems to represent the highest social strata, is made up of three male graves and one unidentified skeleton. This suggests some overlapping between prestige and gender affiliation. However, the fact that all the other groups are made up from both sexes and that in group A—the poorest graves group—male graves make up more than half of the group, suggests that sex was not a determining factor for awarding personal prestige. The extremely high proportion of weapons found in graves belonging to group D (which on average is 2.5 SD higher than the general average), could suggest a "militaristic" elite (cf. Di Cosmo 2002, 65–68); this notion is more comprehensively tested below.

While we do not know the sex of people buried at graves of the Xiaobaiyang cemetery, the overall patterns are very similar to the data elicited from the Maoqinggou cemetery (table 5.4). Group A, which contains twenty-two graves with low averages in all the mortuary variables, represents the lower socioeconomic stratum. Group B includes five graves that have high averages of grave size, coffins, sacrificial animals, bronze plaques, beads, and stone artifacts. It also has a slightly higher than average occurrence of weapons and bone tools. This group can be seen as comprised of people with a high social and economic status. Group C includes ten graves that have especially high averages of small bronze ornaments, and a higher than average appearance of bronze plaques, beads, ceramic vessels, and animal bones. It would seem to represent people of average sociopolitical status who carried very pronounced identity markers (ornaments, plaques, and beads). Group D includes seven graves with very high percentages of bronze weapons and bone artifacts and somewhat higher than average grave sizes, coffins, and small bronze artifacts. This group represents people with a pronounced "militaristic" identity and of relatively high status. It suggests that although prestige and "militaristic" identities were related to one another, they were not synonymous.

The grouping of the Dahuazhongzhuang graves also seems to be mostly according to the gradations of social and economic prestige, although gender

Table 5.4. Clustering of graves from the Xiaobaiyang cemetery

	Group A	Group B	Group C	Group D
Grave numbers	1, 4, 6, 7, 8, 9, 10, 11, 14, 17, 18, 19, 20, 23, 24, 26, 27, 29, 34, 40, 46, 47	31, 32, 41, 43, 44	2, 3, 13, 16, 21, 25, 33, 35, 36, 38	12, 22, 30, 37, 39, 42, 48

Table 5.5. Clustering of graves from the Dahuazhongzhuang cemetery

	Group A	Group B	Group C	Group D
Grave numbers	2, 8, 10, 11, 12, 16, 17, 18, 20, 21, 22, 26, 28, 29, 31, 34, 35, 36, 37, 40, 44, 46, 47, 51, 55, 58, 59, 62, 63, 68, 69, 70, 71, 73, 74, 75, 76, 77, 80, 81, 82, 84, 85, 86, 88, 89, 93, 94, 100, 101, 106, 107, 108, 109, 110, 111, 112, 113, 114, 117	4, 13, 14, 15, 30, 32, 41, 43, 45, 49, 60, 61, 64, 65, 72, 79, 83, 92, 96, 99, 104, 105, 115	33, 67, 91, 95, 118	6, 39, 42, 53, 57, 87, 90
Sex ratio	18 males, 24 females (18?)	16 males, 5 females (2?)	0 males, 5 females	4 males, 1 female (2?)

identity may also have influenced the results (table 5.5). Group A, which includes sixty graves, is comprised of the poorest graves. The average of all the mortuary variables of the graves in this group is below the cemetery-wide average. Graves in this group have an especially low average of grave size, coffins, ceramic vessels, and animal bones—parameters that seem to be associated with labor investment in the grave.

Group B, which includes twenty-three graves, has a high average of grave size, coffins, ceramic vessels, and animal bones, higher than the cemetery-wide average by less than one SD. Only the average number of stone artifacts is higher by more than one SD than the group average. All the other variables are only slightly higher or lower than the group average. Therefore, it would seem that this group includes graves that are modestly rich, presumably representing persons of middle-high social and economic prestige.

Group C is comprised of five graves. Graves of this group have very high average numbers of bronze beads (3.1 SD above the cemetery-wide average) bronze plaques (higher by 2.4 SD), spindle whorls (by 2.2 SD), and beads (by 1.6 SD). They also have a high average appearance of coffins. This group seems to represent graves in which the externalized identity of the occupants is emphasized through body and dress ornaments. Since all the occupants of graves in this group are female, it would seem that this identity is associated also with gender, or perhaps with the position of women.

Group D includes seven graves that have very high average numbers (more than one SD above the cemetery-wide average) for most variables. The numbers are especially high for bronze mirrors (2.4 SD) but also for all of the variables associated with the investment in graves. It seems that this group represents persons of high social and economic prestige. It is interesting to note that among the graves of this group, four belong to males and only one is of a female (the other two remain unidentified), suggesting that males had better access to higher prestige than females, although they did not have a monopoly on such positions.

While in both cemeteries where the skeletons were sexed there seems to be some correlation between the sex of the deceased and the richness of mortuary treatment, this correlation is by no means straightforward. The above groupings suggest much more complicated associations between the sex of the deceased, the prestige given in death, and the identity or identities with which he or she was affiliated.

From the eastern part of the Northern Zone we have only a few graves in which the sexual identity of the deceased has been determined. Analysis of these graves suggests a relatively high social status of women. In fact, among the five upper Xiajiadian excavated at the Nanshan'gen cemetery the two female graves are much richer in artifacts than the three male graves. While 3 knives (1 in each grave), 168 plaques, and 23 other artifacts were found in the female graves, no bronze artifacts were found in the male graves (Zhongguo 1975). The two female graves at Nanshan'gen each included a spindle whorl but none of the other graves did. This suggests the existence of gender-specific symbols, but the fragmentary information on the sex of the skeletons buried in graves from the eastern part of the Northern Zone prevents further insights and a more thorough analysis. Such an analysis is indeed possible for graves from the central and western parts of the Northern Zone, where the sex of most of the skeletons has been identified.

Among the thirty-six graves in our sample of early graves from Maoqinggou, nine are of females, twenty-one of males, two of children, and four remain unidentified. It seems that gender is not closely associated with wealth or prestige in this cemetery. Variables such as grave size, the number of ceramic vessels, or bronze belt plaques are very similar for both sexes, although

Table 5.6. Distribution of bronze belt parts in male and female graves at Maoqinggou (graves of the early periods only)

	Number of Graves with Tiger Plaques	Number of Tiger Plaques	Number of Graves with Bird Plaques	Number of Bird Plaques	Number of Graves with Other Belt Parts	Number of Other Belt Parts
Male	1 (5%)	1	15 (75%)	169	9 (45%)	17
Female	1 (10%)	2	5 (50%)	50	3 (30%)	5

Table 5.7. Average size of graves and mean numbers of artifacts in male and female graves at Maoqinggou

Graves	Size (m²)	Ceramic	All Bronzes	Bronze Weapons	Belt Plaques	Beads	Animals
Male	2.33	0.7	16.5	1.1	0.9	1.9	2.6
Female	2.34	0.5	22.3	0.0	0.7	13.5	1.2

sacrificial animals are found in higher numbers in the male graves (tables 5.6 and 5.7). However, the distribution of some burial goods among these graves shows clear gender affiliations. Weapons, for example, are exclusively associated with male burials. Seven of the male burials (35%) included at least one weapon, while none of the female graves contained any weapons at all. Beads, on the other hand, are much more commonly found in female than in male graves and may be seen to mark feminine identity.

In contrast to Wu Xiaolong's (2004, 220–221) observation, I found no evidence at Maoqinggou for the symbolization of gender identity by belt ornaments or any other types of bronze plaques. All types of belt plaques were found in both the male and female graves, although the number of male graves in which belt plaques were found as well as the quantity of these artifacts is relatively higher (tables 5.6 and 5.7). Interestingly, the tiger plaques, which are the most elaborate of all the belt ornaments from Maoqinggou, and which Wu Xiaolong (2004, 221) views as one of the markers of male identity, are, in fact, equally distributed among the two sexes.

At the Dahuazhongzhuang cemetery, the occupants of thirty-eight of the graves are male and thirty-five are female.[2] Symbolized social and economic status seems in these cases to be more closely related to the sex of the deceased than in Maoqinggou. As can be seen in table 5.8, male graves are, on average, larger than female graves and more of them contain a coffin and sacrificial animals. As in Maoqinggou, bronze weapons are almost exclusively found in male graves.[3] Bronze mirrors are also predominantly associated with male graves. Only one female grave contained mirrors, as opposed to nine male graves. Female attributes

Table 5.8.   Mean numbers of artifacts in male and female graves at Dahuazhongzhuang

Graves	Size (sq. m)	Percent of Graves with Coffin	Ceramic	All Bronzes	Bronze Weapons	Bronze Plaques	Bronze Mirrors	Bronze Beads	Beads	Shells	Animals
Male	6.43	61.0	0.68	3.79	0.16	2.90	0.50	0.0	15.87	0.26	0.87
Female	2.95	46.0	0.69	7.31	0.06	7.0	0.09	0.14	24.49	1.46	0.51

may be the bronze beads, which are found exclusively in female graves. Spindle whorls may also be associated with female identity although not exclusively so, since they are found in two male graves as well as in six female graves.

As pointed out at the beginning of this chapter, horses are potent symbols of power and prestige among pastoralists. It is therefore interesting to see how they are utilized in the mortuary tradition of societies of the Northern Zone. At both the Maoqinggou and Dahuazhongzhuang cemeteries, horse sacrifices seem to have been a male prerogative. At Maoqinggou horse bones were found only in the male graves. While animal sacrifices were found both in male and female graves (50% and 40% of the graves respectively), sacrificed horses were found in three of the male graves (15%) and in none of the female graves.[4] At Dahuazhongzhuang cattle and sheep bones are found in both male and female graves, but none of the occupants of the nineteen graves in which horse bones were found are female (fourteen are male adults, one is a male child, and four remain unidentified).

It seems that in both cemeteries the sacrifice of a horse during the burial ceremony was clearly a masculine symbol. Since Northern Zone graves of this period, in the above mentioned cemeteries and elsewhere, usually contain only the skulls and hooves of the sacrificed animals but not their entire skeleton (Linduff 1997, 56; NMGWWKG 1989), it is reasonable to assume that the animal's meat was consumed as part of the burial ceremony (or feast) and only parts without meat were placed in the grave as a symbolic gesture. We can conclude then that eating horse meat was a very potent masculine symbol, while eating the meat of sheep or cattle did not carry any gender connotations.

That the horse became a symbol of masculinity is, perhaps, not surprising. However, other aspects associated with the horse, such as evidence for horseback riding, are not as clearly associated with male graves. At Maoqinggou, of the two graves in which horse gear was found, grave M75 is a female grave.[5] This grave is also one of the richest graves found in Maoqinggou, strengthening the observation made above, that at the graves found in the Maoqinggou cemetery symbols of social and economic status cut across gender affiliations. From the eastern part of the Northern Zone comes what may

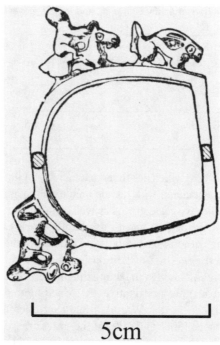

Figure 5.1   Bronze ring with two figures of hunters on horseback chasing a rabbit, tomb 3, Nanshan'gen, Inner Mongolia.

be the strongest association of femininity with horseback riding. Grave M3 at the Nanshan'gen cemetery contains the earliest representation of horseback riding in this region (including all of present-day China): a bronze ring on which are cast two hunters on horseback chasing a rabbit (figure 5.1). The occupant of this grave is a female (Zhongguo 1975, 136–137).

It is interesting to note that Maoqinggou graves in which horse gear was found did not contain horse skulls, and vice versa. In fact, graves M59 and M75 did not contain any sacrificed animals. It is possible that different connotations were associated with horse sacrifice and the ritualistic consumption of horse meat than with the placement of artifacts related to horse riding in graves. While consuming horse meat may have been a symbol of male identity, riding horses does not seem, based on these very partial data, to be associated with such an identity.

THE GENESIS OF GENDER AND OTHER TYPES OF IDENTITY AMONG SOCIETIES OF THE NORTHERN ZONE

In summary, gender identities seem to be an important social marker among societies of the Northern Zone during the late 2nd and early 1st millennia

BCE. We have seen that, although on average wealth and prestige are not closely correlated with the sex of the deceased, access to the highest sociopolitical strata was a male prerogative. Some types of artifacts as well as perhaps the activities they represent were closely associated in my analysis of burial data with the sex of the deceased buried in the grave. This is most clearly seen in the case of weapons, which are predominantly found in male graves. That some weapons are also found in the grave of females, such as M3 and M4 from Nanshan'gen and M95 at Dahuazhongzhuang, could suggest that what they symbolize, probably warrior identity, was not an attribute strictly governed by biological association—many males were buried without them as well—but was socially gendered, so that a few females could also attain this masculine identity (see also Jones-Bley and Rubinson, this volume). The consumption of horse meat was even more restricted to male members of the society, but the fact that horseback riding was not may again suggest social, rather than biological, gender identifications (see also Nelson, this volume).

The analysis and discussion above suggest that during the late 2nd and early 1st millennia BCE, gender became an important component in the construction of personal identity in the societies of the Northern Zone. While some attributes of gender identity already existed in this region during the earlier part of the 2nd millennium, they were much less common and visible than in the late 2nd and early 1st millennia BCE. For example, Wu Jui-man (2004), in her analysis of the mortuary data from the Dadianzi cemetery of northeast China, found some correlations between the sex of the deceased and the quantity and quality of artifacts in the grave. However, these differences are not very significant, and nowhere do we find, during this period, the externalization of symbols associated with gender identity.

Looking at gender identity not in isolation but as part of a more complex pattern of identity mixture is more akin to modern models of personal and group identity. According to such models, individuals will inevitably have different identities which they will emphasize to a different degree according to the social context, the type of interaction, and specific motivations (DiMaggio 1997; Goffman 1969; Howard 2000; Jenkins 1996, 19–28; Meskell 2002; Sokefeld 1999).

Such a socially oriented and multifaceted definition of identity can explain the relative vagueness of the patterns we observe. Because the different identities with which the deceased was associated can all be symbolized in the same grave, it is not easy to separate them from each other. Moreover, while some identities may have been associated with different phases of the death rituals—the preparation of the grave; the process of the funeral, including perhaps the placement of grave goods at different times; the sacrifice of animals, and the consumption of their meat, and so forth—this diachronic process is now combined into one synchronic picture.

One way to unravel this "gestalt" picture is by looking for groups of markers which tend to appear together. It can be assumed that each such "package" marks a certain kind of identity. To explore this idea I use a hierarchical clustering method (with Pearson's *r* correlation coefficient) on the mortuary data set. The advantage of this method over other clustering methods is that the grouping of the variables (not the cases) is relatively rigid and therefore should highlight the discrete identity "packages." Moreover, the number of groups is not predetermined but it, as well as the strength of association among variables in the group, can be seen directly from the results of the analysis.

Experimenting with the Xiaobaiyang data, as can be seen in figure 5.2, the variables seem to be clustered into four groups:[6] Group A includes all types of weapons and bone artifacts, with small bronze artifacts added higher up; group B includes the grave size and coffin, with animal bones and beads added to this group higher up; group C includes stone artifacts and bronze plaques; and group D includes ceramic vessels and small bronze ornaments.

Interestingly, these four groups are clustered into two broader divisions, with groups A and D clustering together and groups B and C clustering together. We can hypothesize that these groups are associated with four different dimensions of identity. Grave size, the construction of the coffin, and the sacrifice of animals are directly associated with expenditure in the burial ceremony. These variables, which are clustered together in group B, may be

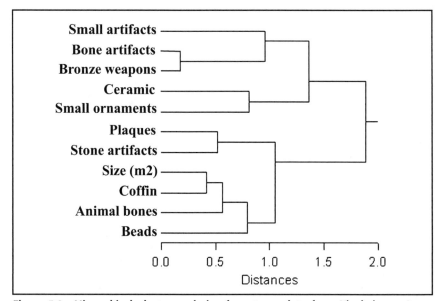

Figure 5.2 Hierarchical cluster analysis of mortuary data from Xiaobaiyang, Inner Mongolia.

seen as signifying social and economic prestige. Weapons and bone artifacts (many of which are bone arrowheads) which are clustered in group A are associated with wars and hunting and may reflect a type of warrior (perhaps masculine) identity. Group C, which includes plaques that were part of clothing and were visible in day-to-day interactions, may be seen as the best expression of personal identity, perhaps associated with ethniclike identity. But the association of group C with the group including the variable of grave size (group B) may suggest that it too is related to prestige. Group D may be associated with lower social and economic prestige.

Clustering the variables of the Maoqinggou cemetery resulted in an interesting grouping of the sacrificial animals (figure 5.3). While sheep and cattle bones are clustered together and are also associated with grave size, similar to the pattern observed in the Xiaobaiyang cemetery, horse bones are clustered with ceramics and more broadly with belt plaques and weapons. This strengthens our previous observation that sacrificing horses carried with it a special symbolic meaning. In more general terms, three main groups are observed. One consists of animal bones, bone artifacts, and grave size, probably representing, like group B at Xiaobaiyang, social and economic prestige. The second group, containing variables of small bronze ornaments, beads, and tiger plaques, is comparable to group C from Xiaobaiyang, suggesting an ethniclike identity, and the third, including weapons, horse gear, plaques, and belt parts and horse bones, is comparable to group A from Xiabaiyang and

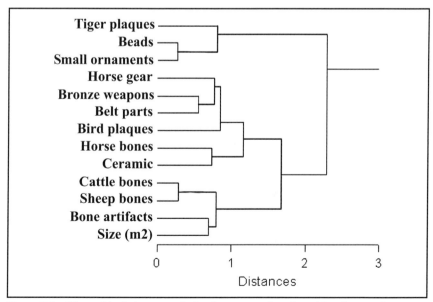

Figure 5.3 **Hierarchical cluster analysis of mortuary data from Maoqinggou Cemetery, Inner Mongolia.**

associated with masculine identity. Very similar results were also found in the analysis of the Dahuazhongzhuang mortuary data.

The "packages" revealed by the hierarchical clustering method seem to confirm our earlier observation about the development, among other things, of a gender-related identity. As pointed out above, gender identity is not synonymous with biologically determined sexes. Indeed, if we were to think of such an identity as being symbolized through "packages" rather than through individual objects, we can understand such an identity as being gradient—with more or less feminine or masculine identity being expressed. Within such a symbolic system it would have been possible for a female to obtain a relatively high masculine identity and vice versa. This may have been the case, for example, for the persons buried in graves M3 and M4 of Nanshan'gen cemetery.

Our analysis suggests that during the late 2nd and especially the early 1st millennia BCE the genesis of gender identity was not an isolated process. Rather, it was part of a much broader phenomenon in which various types of identities were constructed and symbolized. Such processes were partly triggered by local processes and partly due to interactions on regional and interregional scales.

As pointed out at the beginning of this chapter, this was a period of significant sociopolitical changes. The florescence of identity construction and especially the materialization of identities in symbols visible not only in mortuary rituals but during everyday interactions as well, should not be seen as a mere epiphenomenon of those changes but rather as an integral part of them (Shelach forthcoming). The processes which shaped the social and geopolitical landscape of East Asia for the next three millennia were clearly the context for such a need to externalize local and supralocal identities. However, the processes themselves were also affected by the stronger self-identification and commitment of people to those identities. It is interesting to note, therefore, that while gender was an important dimension of identity, gender roles were not yet rigidly fixed during this formative period. It is possible that more rigid gender roles only developed during more stable periods, but such a hypothesis should be tested in further research.

NOTES

1. This name, which in different variations is used by Chinese and non-Chinese scholars (cf. Di Cosmo 1999; Lin 1986; Wu 1985) can be seen as Sinocentric: The "Zone" is "Northern" (Beifang in Chinese) relative, geographically, to China. However, in the absence of a better term I use the Chinese term, without implying any predetermined dependency on areas to the south.

2. Among these graves, several include more than one person buried in them: Three male graves had additional female bones, one female grave had additional male bones, another female grave had additional female bones, and a third female grave had additional bones of unknown sex.

3. The only female grave which contains weapons—M95—is the one in which male bones were also found, so it is possible that the weapons were associated with the male rather than the female occupant.

4. In the contemporaneous Yaozi cemetery, of twenty-two well-preserved graves only grave M5 contained a horse skull, and its occupant was male (NMGWWKG 1989, 79).

5. Wu Xiaolong (2004, 211) identifies the occupant of the second grave that had horse gear in it—M59—as a male, while according to the report its sex could not be identified (Tian and Guo 1986, 310). Wu may have identified the occupant as male because grave M59 contains weapons (one dagger and six arrowheads), however, such identification is based upon circular logic.

6. I did not include shells and spindle whorls because these two variables each appeared in only one grave, so their grouping may be misleading.

Chapter Six

Horses and Gender in Korea

The Legacy of the Steppe on the Edge of Asia

Sarah Milledge Nelson

The sumptuary rules of the early Korean state of Silla (traditional dates 57 BCE–668 CE), in limiting the number of horses and the quality of horse trappings by rank and gender, demonstrate that both women and men, and all ranks, rode horseback (Kim 1965). Although ox carts were also available for women, commoners, and everyone else, the implication of the sumptuary rules is that riding horseback was primary transportation for everyone in the Silla state. It is important to understand the relationship with steppe cultures during the Silla in order to explain why men and the upper classes were not the exclusive users of the horse, as is the case in China at this time (Mair 2003, 163–174).

I will argue that the relationship between people and horses was brought to the southeastern corner of the Korean peninsula by groups who carried the steppe heritage. The similarities between Silla and the steppes demonstrate more than mere borrowing of horses and their accoutrements. Many other items of material culture and ideology also link Silla with the steppes. In addition, both historic documents and archaeological discoveries imply horse ritualism similar to that of some steppe cultures. Finally, ancient Silla documents (see Gardiner 1969; Kim 1965) imply that horses were important in Silla from its founding, for the appearance of a horse guarding a magic egg (Grayson 2001, 92) is part of the justification for accepting the first (possibly mythical) king.[1] This is not to say that all horses were sacred. The horse was essential for warfare and elite displays in some rituals, but at the same time horses which could be ridden by everyone were an indispensable everyday convenience.

The ubiquity of horse riding is related to the gender theme because of the almost automatic association of horse riding with warriors and hunters, wherever horse riding (rather than the traction horse) is found. Thus, the gender

equality of riding horses in the Silla kingdom is notably important for understanding how to interpret horse gear in women's burials. For example, when
women's graves on the steppes contain evidence that they rode horses, the
grave occupants may be interpreted as "warrior-women" (e.g., Davis-Kimball
2002), rather than considering a life on horseback for a variety of purposes.
When the association of horses and weapons is emphasized, other ways that
women might be associated with horses may be left unnoted or unexamined.
I do not reject the possibility that women could be warriors, but I do suggest
that horse-riding women may have a broader meaning beyond fighting or
hunting from horseback.

On the other hand, in emphasizing the role of horses as a means of transportation, I do not mean to imply that horses were not used for warfare.
Generals on horseback appear in the histories and legends of Silla, and horse
armor is depicted in tomb murals, as well as discovered in tombs. Horses
were used for hunting as well as warfare in Korea. Horses and riders are
depicted in a mural in a Goguryeo tomb, estimated to date to the 4th or 5th
century, with bowmen twisted backward to aim at deer and tigers, ready to
deliver the "Parthian shot." However, warfare and hunting were largely, if not
entirely, upper-class male occupations in Korea, insofar as tomb depictions
and later history would indicate. My point is that horses were not exclusively
used for such purposes. Women and the lower classes were not excluded from
horse riding.

Women in the agrarian society of the Silla kingdom probably did not live
their entire lives in the saddle as nomads are purported to do, but when they
needed to venture away from home, horse riding was a basic means of transportation, and it seems that everyone was comfortable on horseback. Since
this is unusual in a society that was based on farming, it is useful to inquire
how this state of affairs came about. First, however, the sumptuary rules,
which demonstrate that everyone in the Silla state was able to own and ride
horses, will be explained and discussed.

SUMPTUARY RULES OF SILLA

The sumptuary rules of Silla[2] are specific and detailed (Kim 1965). They
were recorded in the oldest surviving history of early Korea (Kim 1145;
Shultz 2004). The rules divide the population by rank and gender, including
what could and could not be worn or used by the various "bone ranks" in
Silla society, and further specify distinctions between men and women within
each rank. Since each gender as well as each rank was allowed to display a
different degree of splendor, it follows that the items on the proscribed and
prescribed lists were visible and relevant in the public realm.

The sumptuary rules were based on a system of endogamous ranks unique to Silla. Known as *kolpum* (bone rank), the system mandated endogamous groups with specific rights and privileges in Silla society. Bone is the Korean metaphor for genetic relationships, instead of blood. This metaphor may be related to the Mongol use of "bone" to distinguish the elite (white bone) from the nonelite (black bone) (Kim 1965, 248). The bone ranks were at the same time social, economic, and political (Grayson 1976; Kim 1977; Nelson 1991, 1993a, 2003; Sasse 2001). The highest rank is *Song'gol*, Sacred Bone, which conferred eligibility to rule. Birth into the Sacred Bone rank did not necessarily confer rulership, however, for the ruler was selected by a council of Sacred Bone (Kim 1969). This is a combination of the "nomadic" way of choosing rulers and the limitation of the selection to persons of a particular rank. A rule of hypodescent has been inferred from the list of rulers, their spouses, and their parents. Apparently no one could belong to the rank of Sacred Bone unless both parents were from that rank, and a person took the rank of the lower-ranking parent (Grayson 1976; Sasse 2001). Yi Kidong (1998, 98) suggests that "one condition for holding the songgol rank was maternal lineage originating with the Pak clan." Another way to interpret the same data is that the maternal lineage was provided by the queens, and the kings were those who married them (Nelson 1991). Each rank had its prescribed color. In their official roles, members of the Sacred Bone were distinguished by purple robes, which is relevant in terms of several specific proscriptions for lower ranks, who were not allowed to display anything purple or even purplish.

The second rank is *Chin'gol*, or True Bone. Members of the True Bone rank were also high nobles, who only became eligible to rule following 668 CE, after the pure Song'gol rank died out with two successive queens, the last survivors of the Sacred Bone. A few scholars have used the absence of Sacred Bone in the sumptuary rules to assert that the rules were written after 668 when Silla united the peninsula by conquering the other kingdoms of Baekje and Goguryo (see Grayson 1976; Kim 1965). However, the rules imply the existence of members of Sacred Bone, who presumably are not mentioned because they could flaunt their wealth and status without limits. True Bone members, on the other hand, suffered many restrictions. They were not to wear clothing or decorate houses or horses with precious materials, and they especially were required to avoid purple. Furthermore, the *Samguk Sagi* describes the reinstatement of the rules according to ancient tradition (Kim 1965, 234), demonstrating that these were not new rules.

Below the two highest noble ranks were *Ryuktupum*, *Odupum*, and *Sadupum* (the Sixth, Fifth, and Fourth Head ranks, respectively). Everyone below these ranks was a commoner, ineligible to serve in the court. Sometimes the Fourth Head rank was grouped with commoners in the list of rules.

To begin with horses, their number was not directly regulated, but it is implied by the size of the stables permitted to each rank. No restrictions in stable size are recorded for True Bone. Ryuktupum could maintain a stable containing no more than five horses; Odupum were limited to three horses; and Sadupum and commoners were allowed to stable only two horses. Sizes of houses went along with sizes of stables, becoming progressively smaller and less ornamented for each lower rank. Sacred Bone could build palaces of any size, but True Bone could not build houses larger than twenty-four *chok*. The exact length of the chok is unknown, but a sense of it can be gained because the height of fences was restricted for the Sixth Head rank to eight chok, down to six chok for commoners' fences, which suggests a linear dimension of about one meter. House length restrictions down the line from True Bone were twenty-one chok, eighteen chok, and fifteen chok—each three chok smaller than the rank above, making a visible difference in house sizes.

Other limitations regarding housing related to the costliness of house construction materials. Only the Sacred Bone could roof their houses with Chinese tiles, or build high eaves. Their houses could be decorated with gold, silver, bronze, gems, and the "five colors." Hanging carved wooden fish from the eaves of the house was likewise a privilege of only the highest rank, as inferred from the fact that True Bone were specifically forbidden these flourishes. This apparently odd restriction on wooden fish hung in the eaves suggests that they were gongs to call the spirits, such as are found in Korean Buddhist temples to this day. Korean Buddhism adapted traits of earlier religious traditions, so it is not unreasonable to suggest that the spirit-calling gong could predate the establishment of Buddhism in Silla.

The height of the house platform was also important, being restricted in lesser ranks to two steps or fewer. Additionally, the steps of True Bone and lower ranks' houses had to be unpolished, and could not be made of stones from the mountains, suggesting connections of the Sacred Bone with mountain spirits, important in pre-Buddhist Korea (Lee 2004, 53). The Sacred Bone alone could build fences with a beam and a pillar, which I understand is a gate like a torii, marking off sacred space. Screens inside Sacred Bone houses could be embroidered, and furniture was made of Chinese juniper inlaid with tortoise shells. Their richness was intended to dazzle, inside and out.

The section of the rules pertaining to horse-riding equipment begins with saddles for both genders and all ranks. Also subject to restrictions by rank were saddlecloths and pillows, mudguards, bits, stirrups, and reins. For example, even True Bone men were not permitted to use saddles made of imported wood, especially purple sandalwood and Chinese juniper. Their saddlecloths were forbidden to be made of any kind of fur, raw silk, or brocade. Bits and stirrups could not be decorated with gold, bronze, gems, or jade. The reins were not to be braided or finely knit, nor could they be dyed purple. Mudguards had to be dyed with hemp oil. This last restriction would be inexplicable were it not for the few artifacts identified as mudguards found in royal tombs, made of birch bark and painted with images of white horses. Perhaps the restriction was intended to omit any images on mudguards except on those of the Sacred Bone.

True Bone ladies were prohibited from using saddles inlaid with jewels. Women's saddlecloths and cushions reflect those of the men of their rank, and could not be made of fur or raw silk. Bits and stirrups could not be plated with gold, and the reins could not have gold and silver threaded into them.

The Sixth Head rank was further limited in the wood of which saddles could be made, for in addition to the restrictions for True Bone, the Sixth Head rank was not allowed to use alder, locust, or silkworm oak wood for their saddles, nor decorate their saddles with precious metals, gems, or jade. The saddlecloth had to be leather, but for their saddle cushions the members were permitted padded silk, finely woven ramie cloth, hemp, or leather. No embellished bits or stirrups were allowed, and reins had to be made only of leather or hemp rope.

Women of the Sixth Head rank interestingly had fewer restrictions in wood that could be used for their saddles than men of their rank, but like men they were restricted to plain bits and stirrups and leather mudguards.

Men of the Fifth Head rank had the same restrictions on types of saddle wood as the rank above them. They were specifically enjoined from applying silver or gold inlays or plating to their bits and stirrups. Women of the same rank had similar restrictions, except that tiger skins were also specifically forbidden for their saddlecloths, as well as dusting purple powder on the reins.

Fourth Head and commoner men were required to use mudguards of poplar or bamboo. Bits could be made only of iron, and stirrups of wood and iron. The reins were required to be made of hemp rope. The restrictions on women are fewer, but similar. Women seem to have been allowed a bit more splendor in each rank, but it is impossible to tease out any gender implications from this fact alone. In terms of relationships to the steppes, it is interesting to note that both boots and trousers are mentioned in the sumptuary laws, along with headgear and underwear. For instance, True Bone men could wear a head cloth but not a crown and were not permitted to wear embroidered trousers made of fur, brocade, or silk. True Bone women were forbidden to wear crowns or hairpins inlaid with gems and jades, nor could they wear colored combs made of tortoise shells. Male Sixth Head rank could wear head cloths of coarsely woven wool, but they were forbidden to wear boots made of wrinkled purple reindeer leather, which must have been imported from distant Manchuria. Women of the Sixth Head rank were prohibited from wearing combs with gold inlay, or hairpins of pure gold or silver decorated with gems and jades. They could cover their hair only with gauzy materials such as raw silk or thin silk. Fourth Head rank men likewise were permitted only lesser materials for their head cloths and were restricted to hemp underwear. Their female counterparts could dress their hair only with hairpins of silver or lesser material, and could not wear crowns. Women of the lowest nobility were not allowed to wear underskirts, but they could wear combs of ivory, antler, or wood. Commoners' hairpins were required to be made of bronze, stone, or lesser materials. It is intriguing that antler (presumably reindeer antler) was considered to be more precious than bronze, again suggesting a sacred connotation of antler.

HORSES IN KOREA

Some horses depicted in Three Kingdoms Korea are short and squat, suggesting Mongolian ponies (figure 6.1). Other Korean drawings of horses are more graceful, such as simple line drawings on a Silla stoneware jar (figure 6.2). The larger and more elegant horses are depicted in tombs of royalty.

A great deal more study is needed to tease out the ancestry of East Asian horses in general, and Korean horses in particular. Although some scholars have suggested that the Mongolian pony was separately domesticated, the first

Figure 6.1. Ceramic vessel in the shape of a horseback rider on a Mongolian pony. From the Gold Bell Tomb, Kyongju, Korea. Photo by Sarah Milledge Nelson.

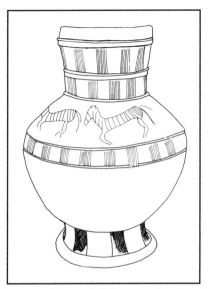

Figure 6.2.   Line drawings on a Silla period stoneware jar from Kyongju, Korea. Illustration by Sarah Milledge Nelson.

evidence of ridden horses is far to the west of Korea (Anthony and Brown 1991; Fitzgerald-Huber 1996). However, horses are found in Paleolithic contexts in northeastern China (Olsen 1984) as well as in the Late Neolithic (Linduff 2003b). Most domesticated horses probably came to the Korean peninsula through the steppes of eastern Eurasia, but the Mongolian pony is so different that it seems worth researching whether it is a domesticated version of wild horses of the northeast. Certainly the tribes of northeastern China were known for their horses and sent large numbers to Han China in tribute. Some are said to be small horses (Gardiner 1969; Parker 1890).

However, as Katheryn M. Linduff (2003b) details, the horse culture included ways to breed and train horses, ways to bridle horses, and attitudes about horses as well as items of material culture. Thus, it seems likely that the stimulus for domesticating horses came from the steppes, even if another breed was available for domesticating in Mongolia and/or points east. The horse culture that reached Korea had many affinities with the steppes, and even if some of the ancestry of specific horses was northeastern, the impetus for domesticating horses, as well as the horse culture, seems to have originated farther away.

SILLA CONNECTIONS WITH THE STEPPES

It is not known precisely how the Silla nobility arose, but both documents and archaeology offer some indications. The Neolithic peoples who populated the peninsula for several millennia may have been gradually forced into a subservient position by newcomers. Immigrants brought with them the tradition of mounded burials, a reverence for white horses, and a preference for gold (Sohn, Kim, and Hong 1970). A Chinese document relates that the old people of "Chinguk" told the scribe that their group had left northeast China to remove themselves from the draconian policies of the conquering Qin dynasty (Parker 1890, 209). It is therefore interesting that crowns and belts almost identical to those of Silla were found near Chaoyang in Liaoning Province, China (observed by the author in the Chaoyang Museum), suggesting that region as a possible former homeland of those who ruled the Silla state, most likely those who formed the Sacred Bone rank. A district of the capital city of Silla is called Choyang, and proto–Three Kingdoms elite graves have been excavated there.

Korean textbooks assert that Korean ancestors came from the Dongbei (northeastern) region of China (Kim 1986), the home of Jurchen, ancestors of the Manchu (Barfield 1989). Several groups named in Chinese documents are said to have migrated into the Korean peninsula during the Bronze Age, beginning no earlier than 1000 BCE according to South Korean archaeologists, although North Korean scholarship would place it earlier (Kim 1978). Archaeological evidence of several kinds, to be delineated below, suggests close ties between the Silla kingdom and the peoples of the Dongbei, and linguistic evidence provides corroboration of the connection of the Korean language with Tungusic languages (Miller 1996). Although a linguistic connection does not provide certainty about Silla forebears, it does suggest that people speaking related languages ancestral to Korean migrated into the Korean peninsula at various times, perhaps between 1000 BCE and 200 CE.

ARTIFACTS RELATED TO THE STEPPES

Artifacts that first appear in Bronze Age Korea include weapons and mirrors echoing those of the Northern Zone of China (Lin 1986). Korean daggers, knives, belts, mirrors, horse equipment, personal ornaments, and clothing all display affinities to the steppes through the Dongbei. Early daggers in Korea, dated as early as 800 BCE (Guo 1995; Liu 1995; Tan et al. 1995) are identical to those found in Liaoning, China, and may be imports. These Liaoning daggers are found in association with horse trappings and sometimes horse-drawn chariots, as depicted at the site of Nanshan'gen (Zhongguo 1975). In the Korean peninsula the shape of the daggers gradually changed from a wide-bladed dagger with edges like curly brackets {} into slender daggers with a vestigial pointed edge, and it is this type of dagger that appears in Yayoi Japan (Seyock 2004).

Mirrors with geometric motifs are found widely in the Northern Zone of China, a region that crosses the steppe zone of Inner Mongolia and includes Liaoning Province and southern Jilin Province (Lin 1986). Common motifs include hatched triangles and rows of slanted, short straight lines. Knobs of early mirrors are placed asymmetrically. Korean mirrors tend to have two strap handles rather than a single handle, but otherwise are reminiscent of Northern Zone mirrors. Within Korea, as the manufacture of bronze became more controlled, mirrors became more refined, but geometric motifs still prevailed. The mirrors have not been found in datable contexts, and are simply reported as Bronze Age.

As early as the 10th century BCE, personal ornaments in Korean elite burials include necklaces made of green or white stone tubular beads. Virtually identical beads have been discovered in Dongbei graves of the same age and earlier, especially in Jilin Province, China. In the Korean peninsula such necklaces often terminated in a curved bead with a suspension hole drilled through the wider top of the bead—a shape called *gogok* in Korean and *magatama* in Japanese. The gogok marked high-status burials even in the Bronze Age and was used as a symbol of power as states formed in Korea and Japan. Gogok are particularly prominent in Silla crowns, which may have as many as eighty gogok amid dangling gold leaf-shaped ornaments. Bronze mirrors and daggers are often found in stone cist graves in both the Northern Zone and Korea. The stone cist graves have been interpreted as the first wave of Bronze Age people from the north (Kim 1986), since similar burials have been found in profusion in the steppes and the forests of northeast China (Liu 1995).

During the Iron Age (300 BCE–300 CE) and Three Kingdoms (300–668) periods, Silla artifacts reflect antecedents in the Dongbei. In particular, gold artifacts, such as the crowns and belts that were associated with royalty, as noted above, are similar to discoveries near Chaoyang in Liaoning Province. Iron Age burials in southern Korea often include decorations for horses and carriages (Seyock 2004). Horse trappings, including gilt-bronze saddlebows with cut-out decoration, are found in Silla burials as well.

Belt plaques were particularly important among the horse riders of the steppes, and they sometimes have dangling chains which hold tools and weapons (Bunker 1995, 23). The royal belts of Silla are constructed of joined plaques with strings of gold pendants, each ending in a symbol, such as fish or gogok, a simple rectangular gold piece, tools, or weapons. While the belts in Korea are made of gold and are not identical to those of the steppes, they are made of joined plaques in a way that is similar to those of the Xiongnu (Bunker 1995). They also sometimes have tools and weapons, such as tweezers and sheathed daggers, attached to the end of the pendant chains. In historical times some shamans wore belts with such pendants.

Figure 6.3. Boots and trousers worn by dancers, Tomb of the Dancers, Goguryeo era, Tongkou, Jilin, People's Republic of China. Illustration by Sarah Milledge Nelson.

The clothing of the northeast included boots and trousers, which are appropriate for horseback riding (figure 6.3). Horse trappings are found along with these clothing styles. Women's clothing as well as men's included baggy trousers in premodern Korea, while boots and shoes had up-turned toes.

The toe style may be related to ancient footwear of Altaic-speaking peoples, such as ancestors of Turkish groups, who also wore footwear with up-turned toes. This suggests the mixing of groups on the steppes and the adoption of each other's material culture.

DESIGNS RELATED TO THE STEPPES

Two types of designs in particular relate Korean artifacts to those of the forest steppe: geometric patterns and the shape of uprights on the circlets of crowns. Fine-lined geometric patterns on mirrors and weapons have already been noted. They have rows of short, straight lines and repeated small triangles, which are quite unlike designs on mirrors from the Chinese Han dynasty and later, but have similarities with the less refined mirrors from Fu Hao's tomb (Linduff 2003a). Guo (1995, 197) characterizes designs on northern bronzes as "chestnut dots, zigzags, and short, slanting lines."

Geometric designs are found not only on mirrors and swords, but also on many other kinds of bronze artifacts. Neolithic pottery in both Korea and the Dongbei was also decorated with similar patterns, and I have previously suggested connections between these regions even in the Neolithic (Nelson 1990). The Bronze Age connection between the peninsula and the Dongbei has long antecedents. Considering the geographic propinquity and similar topography of the two regions, it is not surprising that no boundary existed between them in antiquity.

The tall gold crowns for which the Silla kingdom is best known have no counterparts in China south of the Northern Zone. Furthermore, they are very clearly related to shamanistic ideas (Kim 1998; McCune 1962). The crowns are constructed with a band around the forehead, to which are attached up-rights of two kinds. One shape unmistakably represents antlers. It is notable that in some steppe burials, horses are decked out with headdresses in the form of antlers (Rudenko 1970, pl. 119). The other uprights are more stylized, but they have been interpreted as representing the tree of life, suggesting the shamanism of the forest steppe (Balzer 1997; Kim 1998; McCune 1962).

MATERIALS RELATED TO THE STEPPE

Materials that are related to the Northern Zone and beyond include gold, birch bark, reindeer antler, and reindeer leather. Burials in the vicinity of Beijing feature gold earrings with fan-shaped ends. Gold was never highly valued in China (Bunker 1993), while peoples on the northern borders of China used gold for earrings and other adornments (Sun 2006). Gold was abundant in the Silla kingdom, and was lavishly used for jewelry, crowns, and belts. For example, the queen in Hwangnam Taechong in Kyongju had gold ornaments that together weighed almost five kilos (Kim 1983).

Birch bark appears to have had ritual significance in Silla. The bark must have been imported from the north, since birch trees do not grow in southern Korea, and probably did not grow there in Silla times. Birch-bark containers and a birch-bark lid and other artifacts have been found in various sites in In-ner Mongolia (Linduff 1997, 93). Although bark does not often escape decay, artifacts made of birch bark were exceptionally preserved in royal Silla buri-als. In two instances, white horses were painted on birch-bark artifacts (figure 6.4). One is a circular sun hat and the other consists of flat panels described as mudguards, presumably attached to horse gear, as described in the sumptuary rules. One of the tombs was named by the excavators for a painted horse—it is called the Chonma Chong, the Tomb of the Heavenly Horse.

White horses were particularly prized in Silla. Two legends from the *Samguk Sagi* describe sacrifices of white horses. Reindeer leather for boots is mentioned in the sumptuary laws and must have been imported from the north and highly prized.

IDEOLOGY AND THE STEPPES

Ideology relating the Silla kingdoms to the steppe includes reverence for the horse, especially white horses, as noted above. A horse of unknown color

Figure 6.4. Flying white horse painted on birch bark from the Chonma Chong, Kyongju, Korea. Photo by Sarah Milledge Nelson.

was given a burial of its own in an elite Iron Age burial ground (Kim and Lee 1975). Furthermore, royal tombs feature saddlebows or plates made of gilded bronze in cut-out patterns (Kim 1986, 358). Not only were the members of the Sacred Bone rank displaying their wealth and elite status with these saddlebows, they were also honoring the horse. A saddle was placed near the top of the south mound of Hwangnam Taechong, bringing to mind the suggestion in the *Samguk Sagi* that the spirits of Sacred Bone departed on a heavenly horse (Kim 1998).

Shamanism was important on the steppes and in Siberia. In Silla, it was not merely present, but the ruler may have performed the functions of head shaman. The title of an early Silla ruler translates as shaman (Kim 1965, 147), and the royal headgear implies shamanic rituals, since both kinds of crown uprights (antlers and stylized trees), are references to shamanistic beliefs (Kim 1998). Shamanism continues to be active in Korea to this day (Kendall 1985), so it is not surprising to see indications of shamanism in the Silla kingdom. Current shamanism is conducted almost exclusively by female shamans, and it is possible that women shamans were in the majority even in the Three Kingdoms period (Nelson 1993a). A depiction of a warrior's burial from the Taesong Tombs Museum shows a female shaman performing a burial rite. Shamanism is specifically mentioned in the *Samguk Sagi* in connection with rituals of song and dance. Chinese documents describe early Koreans as performing rituals with singing, dancing, and strong drink (Parker 1890), which is compatible with shamanism.

RELATIONS OF EARLY STATES IN KOREA TO THE DONGBEI

As states began to form within and north of the Korean peninsula, horses are attested both in documents from China and in archaeological discoveries. Two prehistoric states that appear in Korean histories are often considered mythological: Tangun Chosun and Kija Chosun. The earlier of these states was supposedly created by a mythical figure descended from a god and a bear, whose remains (and those of his wife) are reported by the North Korean press to have been recently discovered near Pyongyang, although corroborating details have not been published (Pai 2000). Kija (Qizi) is described in the *Zhou Li* (see Gardiner 1969) as a high official of the defeated Shang dynasty who was allowed to lead five thousand followers into exile in the northeast in about 1000 BCE, to found the state of Chosun (Chaoxian). While Kija might well have existed, no archaeological evidence suggests that a latter-day Shang polity existed in the Korean peninsula (Nelson 1993b). If there was a historic Kija, he and his entourage could have been associated with the state of Yan in the vicinity of Beijing, or perhaps settled farther northeast in the Liaodong peninsula. While the location cannot be verified, this legend suggests connections between the final Shang ruler and the northeast.

In spite of the uncertain nature of Tangun and Kija, the later state of Chosun is attested by both texts and archaeological evidence in the vicinity of modern Pyongyang as early as the 5th century BCE (Gardiner 1969; McCune 1962). The evidence is quite compelling in spite of some skepticism that has been expressed (Barnes 1990). Chinese accounts relate that the state of Chosun, whose ruler was named King Chun, was overthrown by a renegade Chinese from Liaodong named Wiman. Archaeological corroboration of the age of the Chosun state includes a pit grave near Pyongyang of Warring-States age which contains a chariot drawn by two horses (Kim 1978), and another tomb with an inscription dating it to the Qin dynasty (NMK 2001). Tomb 11 near Pyongyang contained an iron horse bit and an iron axle, along with copper horse bells, although no inscribed date was included. Horse and chariot burials from the 2nd century BCE which are earlier than the Chinese commandery of Lelang (called Nangnang in Korean), which was established in 108 BCE, have also been found in the vicinity of Pyongyang and thus would date from the time of Wiman Chosun. But, interestingly for the gender thesis of this volume, since this tomb contained no weapons, it is described as the tomb of a woman (Kim 1978).

Although Wiman was successful in driving out King Chun and establishing himself as ruler, his dynasty only lasted through his grandson Ugo, who lost Chosun to a combined army and navy of Han dynasty China. Descriptions in the *Hou Han Shu*, describing the battles which led to Ugo's defeat, point to a strong city-state centered near Pyongyang (Gardiner 1969). The battles chronicled in the *Shi Ji* between Chinese armies and navies of the former Han and Chosun around Pyongyang suggest equally matched adversaries. According to contemporary Chinese history, huge Han besieging armies required a year to finally conquer Chosun in 108 BCE. Horses were part of Chosun's strength. The *Shi Ji* describes five thousand horses used by Wiman in a single battle. These horses were locally raised, since after the conquest horses became part of the tribute that was owed to China.

As a result of the conquest of Chosun, the northern part of the Korean peninsula was annexed to the Han dynasty and governed as commanderies. A walled city in the vicinity of Pyongyang, with a rectangular shape, a grid pattern, and city gates, is comparable to contemporary Chinese sites (McCune 1962). Some Lelang graves contain chariots drawn by a single horse in Han Chinese style, demonstrating that Chinese fashions followed the establishment of the commandery (Pai 2000).

According to Chinese documents, the unconquered south was called Samhan, the three Han (a different character from the one that designates the Han dynasty), although by other accounts it was called Chinguk, or the state of Chin ruled by the descendants of the defeated King Chun. The polity in the territory that later became Baekje was called Ma Han, or Horse Han. The polity antecedent to Silla was called Chin Han. The *Samguk Sagi* states that King Chun of Chosun fled to the south and ruled Chin Han. It is relevant that the same document recounts that the old men of Silla tell that their ancestors came from northeastern China, but they were driven out by the Qin dynasty's draconian rule (Parker 1890, 213).

Puyo was said to be the predecessor of Goguryo (Kaoguli), the northernmost of the Three Kingdoms. The *Sanguo Ji* describes Puyo specifically as a country that produces horses (Ikeuchi 1930). One Goguryo (Kaoguli) tomb mural depicts headgear in the shape of a horse head, presumably marking the horse clan. The *Sanguo Ji* records that Goguryo clans were named for domesticated animals.

Horse bones were found at a fortress site near Kimhae on the southern coast of Korea, dating to the 1st century BCE (Arimitsu 1996; Sansom 1930). A burial in early Kyongju, where the Silla kingdom arose, consists of an entire articulated horse skeleton in a circular pit lined with white boulders (Kim and Lee 1975). Other than this example, the presence of actual horses in Silla is assumed, although horse bones are as rare as those of humans, because of the acidic soil. While horses may have been the center of some rituals, they

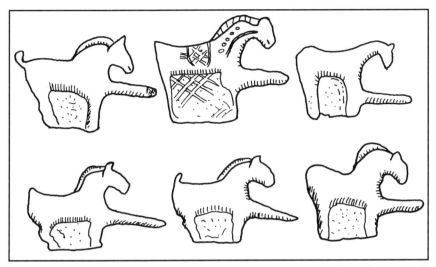

Figure 6.5.   Belt buckles in the shape of horses. Korea, Iron Age. Illustration by Sarah Milledge Nelson.

were not buried with royal tombs. However, bronze belt buckles in the shape of horses are common in southern Korea during the development of the Silla state (figure 6.5).

Nearly every small museum from Pusan to Seoul has a few of these horse buckles on display. Horse statues were found in a 7th-century Silla hilltop fortress above the Han River, possibly indicating horse rituals in which figurines were substituted for real horses (Kim and Shim 1987). Horse figures are also incised into large ritual vessels, and ceramic vessels in the shape of horses and riders have been found in two tombs (see figure 6.2).

WOMEN AS HORSE RIDERS

Saddlebows found in Silla tombs are all similar in shape, although differing in decoration. Usually there are neither bones nor inscriptions to suggest the sex of the interred. However, in the case of tomb 98, an inscription indicates a woman, who has gilded saddlebows. Thus women, like men, rode astride like men. In order to sit comfortably with legs on either side of a horse, trousers are necessary. Traditional Korean women's clothing includes baggy trousers under a skirt, possibly a remnant of a horse-riding past. Kim Chong Sun (1977, 60) remarks that "it is interesting to note that the original pattern of the Korean costume resembled the dress worn by the Mongolian groups of Northeastern Asia, a style which suited their nomadic hunting activities." Boots and trousers are depicted for both men and women on a Goguryo tomb mural, and evidence of boots has been found in the southern part of Korea as well (Daesong Tombs Museum 2003). Trousers and boots certainly were appropriate for horseback riding for any purpose.

Given the archaeological and historic continuities, it seems unlikely that women riding horses was a feature which arose without precedent in the Silla kingdom. Rather, women riding horses must have been acceptable ever since the adoption of the horse and saddle. This event must have occurred before the formation of Silla, because myths of the beginning of the Silla kingdom often refer to horses, including the appearance of a white horse at the founding of the kingdom by the six tribes of Saro in Kyongju (Kim 1145).

Additional evidence of women riding horses comes from the *Samguk Yusa*. For example, in one Silla folktale a woman rides a white horse to the seaside to watch for her husband returning from the Japanese islands (Ilyon the Monk 1972).

CONCLUSION

The sumptuary rules of Silla demonstrate that the fact that women rode horses was taken for granted. Restrictions pertaining to horses were based on rank more than gender. While differences in clothing type marked gender, differences in display of wealth marked rank. All members of the community had access to horses. The upper ranks who formed the Silla nobility in southeastern Korea used many items of material culture that relate them closely to Iron Age peoples in Chaoyang, Liaoning Province, and earlier artifacts connect the Bronze Age elite with eastern Liaoning as well.

Given that polities in the Korean peninsula became ever more Sinicized through time, and that some documents in China at least as early as the Han dynasty were antagonistic to women (Linduff 2002), it is reasonable to suppose that any cultural traditions that treated genders equally were a part of Silla culture before it became inundated with Chinese influence in the 6th and 7th centuries.

Silla became Sinicized more slowly than Baekje and Goguryo. Both of the latter kingdoms adopted Buddhism and Chinese writing at least two centuries earlier than Silla, although at the time of the sumptuary laws, Silla had already adopted China's written language and much of its governance. Buddhism was less gynophobic than Confucianism, and the Confucianizing of Korea was a long, slow process, which was detrimental to both women's freedom of movement and their status within the community (Deuchler 1992).

Gender and rank equality in horse riding shows that horses were never restricted to upper-class men and their activities. The horse culture, inherited from the steppes, must have included women on horseback as well as men. Even before Silla was established as a state, the connection with horses is clear, as is the gender parity that allowed everyone to ride horses, using the splendor of the horse trappings to distinguish primarily by rank rather than gender.

The sumptuary rules of Silla supply a vivid picture of Sacred Bone men and women, riding horses on the streets of Kumsong. Sacred Bone men rode on a purple sandalwood saddle, with a fur saddlecloth and an embroidered brocade saddle cushion. The mudguards, bearing a painting of a heavenly white horse, declared the sacredness of the rider. The metal parts of the horse trappings were embellished with gold and jade, and purple reins emphasized rank. On official occasions the rider might have worn a gold crown. His long-sleeved jacket was made of silk brocade, encircled by a belt decorated with white jade above embroidered and fur-trimmed trousers. His boots of purple reindeer leather carried out the purple theme of his exalted rank.

The lady of the Sacred Bone wore an embroidered silk robe over long-sleeved undergarments of silk. Her socks were embroidered, and her boots were made of fur. Over the whole outfit she wore a fur cape, embellished with gold and silver threads, as well as feathers from peacocks and kingfishers. Colored combs in her hair were made of rare tortoise shells, and her hairpins were inlaid with gold and jade. To top off her coiffure, she wore a gold crown shaped like flowers. Her horse was decked out at least as splendidly as that of her male companion, with jewels inlaid into the sandalwood saddle. The lady's saddlecloth and cushions were made of fur and silk and even tiger skin. Stirrups and bits were plated with gold and decorated with jade, and the reins were braided with gold and silver threads.

The noble ladies and gentlemen were equally gloriously attired. But in spite of all the wealth displayed by those of the highest rank, even the lowliest village woman could sit astride a horse, even if she could only do so wearing plain clothing and with simple horse trappings. Neither gender nor rank deprived a person of the right to ride a horse.

NOTES

1. Silla histories have been lost, but historians assume they were available to the compilers of the oldest histories of Korea, both of which are histories of the Three Kingdoms of Korea: Silla, Goguryo, and Baekje. These are *Samguk Sagi (History of the Three Kingdoms)*, by Kim Pusik in 1145, with a Confucian perspective, and *Samguk Yusa (Memorabilia of the Three Kingdoms)*, compiled by the Buddhist monk Ilyon (1206–1289). *Samguk Yusa* has been translated into English (Ilyon the Monk 1972), and a translation of the *Samguk Sagi* is in process by Edward Shultz and others. Gardiner (1969) discusses the reliability of these and other early sources.

2. The following description of the sumptuary rules were taken from Kim 1965, 234–244.

Part III

MARRIAGE, FAMILIES, AND DEATH ON THE STEPPE

Chapter Seven

Women and Children in the Sargat Culture

Natalia Berseneva

Gender dimensions can be an important part of mortuary analysis. As opposed to biological sex, gender is a social construct, involving the sex-related roles of individuals in society. In addition to the masculine-feminine pairing, nonheterosexual categories may also exist. Also, gender may be patterned by sex in relation to the human biological life cycle so that childhood, adulthood, and old age may constitute different and separate genders. Although the universal importance of gender in the mortuary domain is now known, gender relations in Western Siberian Iron Age societies still remain absolutely unexplored. I hope to correct that omission by examining mortuary practice among a group known as the Sargat.[1]

The Sargat society is known only archaeologically, and neighboring nomadic cultures have a direct impact upon the Sargat. These groups are known from ancient written sources such as Herodotus, Hippocrates, and Strabo. Therefore, we can use these accounts as information.

From the beginning one needs to say a few words about stock breeding. Approaches to stock breeding cannot be classified as one uniform economic strategy without accounting for specific conditions and respective cultural attributes. One population can simultaneously practice economic patterns characterized as fully nomadic, seminomadic (seasonal pastoralism), and sedentary forms of stock breeding. The degree of mobility, herd composition, amplitude, and distance of migration obviously depend on local environment, social and economic levels of development, and the traditions of any given society (Khazanov 1984). By the 6th century BCE the western Siberian forest steppe, which lay on the real crossroads between east and west, south and north, forest and steppe, and in the path of transcontinental movements and migrations, experienced the direct impact of a nomadic population. The new synthesis of cultures is represented by numerous sites displaying a settlement hierarchy and burial grounds which show an almost completely nomadic model of mortuary practice. The Sargat culture was formed through inter-action between these nomads and the local population. The model of such interaction can be understood in relation to the intersection of settled herders, hunters, and pastoral nomads (Koryakova 1994).

Eurasia became more densely populated in the Iron Age. The way of life of ancient stockbreeders was characterized by certain economic instability and high mobility. The active interchange among different cultural traditions took place in both the steppe and forest-steppe zones. In a fully settled, farming mode of life, people's place in society had been fundamentally established by birth and could stay quite stable during their lifetime. The mobile way of life may dictate certain markers of self- (ethnic) identity. For instance, tattoos, artificial cranial deformations, weaponry, decorated metalwork, and clothes served to identify the people anywhere, in life or in death. The "animal-style" tattoos on the bodies preserved in frozen tombs at Pazyryk in the Altai Mountains are a case in point (Polos'mak 2001). The Sarmatians practiced artificial deformation of the head, where a "long head" served as evidence of higher military status. All these markers reflected social hierarchy as well as gender symbolism.

Herodotus writes about "royal Scythian," "Scythian-nomads," and "Scyth-ian-ploughsmen" (IV.120). Some scholars suggest that Scythian women held relatively low status by comparison to Sauromatian and Sarmatian women (Khazanov 1975). This conclusion was based mainly on accounts of ancient authors, such as the famous legend about Amazons, recorded by Herodo-tus (IV.114) and, indirectly, on mortuary data. The Scythian female graves contained small numbers of weapons, whereas Sauromatian and Sarmatian female burials are relatively rich in weaponry. However, this question, un-doubtedly, should be reexamined, in light of the latest large-scale investiga-tions of Scythian mortuary practice conducted twenty years ago (Bunyatyan 1985). Now there are new materials that document the presence of elite Scythian females in tombs with heavy weaponry (Petrenko et al. 2004). Prob-ably, the armed women were part of a group of women in the higher echelons of nomadic society; they could participate in raids on creek-side settlements or other sedentary communities. Female participation in raiding may have included a system of military obligation, such as Hippocrates implies (Taylor 1996, 205; Polos'mak 2001, 276).

Information about "late" nomads is much better known. A hierarchical organization based on a vertical genealogical principle governed social rela-tions that included some number of patronymic groups (patrilineages). The social status of any individual was determined by the status of his lineage and birthright, usually according to the position of this lineage in relation to real or mythical ancestors. According to travelers' and ethnographers' accounts, the nomadic women (both free and slaves) performed the greater part of household and economic activity in medieval societies (Turkic, Kazakh, Mongolian groups) in contrast to men (Klyashtorny and Savinov 2005, 156–158; Polos'mak 2001, 276–277). Free women often had high status and great self-sufficiency, but leadership and certain types of decision making usually belonged to men. Women could completely substitute for men during their absence. Women did not take part in military campaigns, but we cannot extend this pattern of relations directly to prehistoric societies.

Iron Age nomadic societies were rather complex. Scythia is accepted as an early state; the Saka, Sauromatians, and Sarmatians are assessed by scientists as complex chiefdoms (Khazanov 1975; for more details see Koryakova and Epimakhov 2007). The Sargat society was highly hierarchical as well. Its vertical symbolism is clearly displayed in huge royal (leaders') kurgans. Family ties are fundamental for mobile societies, including the Sargat, and both vertical and gendered social roles can be recognized *between* families. The gender distinctions inside one family, perhaps, were less pronounced (or visible) and significant than in sedentary communities of comparable complexity. The connections between women and men are correspondingly distinct because of the mobile mode of life and the different relationship to property. It is possible that early nomadic women had higher status in contrast to agricultural women. In order to understand the Sargat case, these problems must be approached carefully and contextually.

The Iron Age Sargat population occupied the vast area between the Ural Mountains and the Baraba lowlands (the Ural-Siberian forest-steppe zone). Western Siberia is an almost flat plain, and while the river network is not of great density, this is an area of large transit rivers: the Ob, Irtysh, Ishim, and Tobol. Chronologically, the sites cover the period from the early 6th century BCE to the 3–4th centuries CE. Although these people are thought to have been seminomadic with an economy based on stockbreeding, the majority of the population inhabited permanent settlements and fortresses (Koryakova 1996, 243–280; Koryakova and Daire 2000, 63–74). Judging by paleoanthropological observations, the Sargat people, including the women, spent some time on horseback (Razhev 2001).

This study concerns the burials of these Sargat peoples. Their cemeteries in the Trans-Urals and Western Siberia consist of burial mounds (kurgans) that are located on high river terraces. They include one or two big kurgans that are surrounded by smaller ones. The mounds of "elite" kurgans reach five to six meters in present height and from fifty to one hundred meters in diameter. One or more ditches usually surround the kurgan. Each kurgan contains from one to fifteen burials placed both in the sterile soil and in the mound. There was usually a central (primary) grave in the geometric center of the kurgan, and the peripheral graves were grouped around it. Quite often above the central grave was a structure constructed from the subsoil supported by a wooden framework. The primary pits were much larger than those on the periphery and they contained more imposing wooden structures, including large roofed areas. Often the central grave is a paired burial. Cenotaphs are rare in Sargat mortuary practice. Flat grave cemeteries are not found.

The Sargat mortuary ritual was, in general, stable through time although it varied in details. The deceased was placed in a supine position and was oriented in a northerly direction. Usually pots and offerings of food were placed near the head. Clothing, ornaments, and slashing weapons were placed where they would have been worn or used in life. Bows were put at the side of the body. The most constant and distinctive features of the Sargat mortuary practices are:

1. Burials took place in a pit grave under a kurgan.
2. Supine inhumation was used, normally with a northwest–southeast orientation.
3. One or more *hand-formed* ceramic vessels with recognizable Sargat decoration were offered, even in burials of elites that contained bronze and silver vessels.
4. Remains of animal bones, clothing, ornaments, and often weaponry were found.
5. Tools usually are not found as grave goods.

These characteristics are included in every undisturbed Sargat grave and in one way or another can be traced even in graves that had been looted. Exceptions are rare. Quality and quantity of grave goods as well as energy expenditures for grave construction should all be assumed as attributes. Both shallow pit graves with minimum grave goods and rich burials containing a great number of gold and silver artifacts have been found in the same cemetery.[2]

GENDER SYMBOLISM IN ADULT BURIALS

The Sargat kurgans contain burials of males, females, and children. The dead of all ages are represented in mortuary sites, the largest number of which were buried in individual tombs. In this study I analyzed 410 burials (454 skeletons) of 110 Sargat kurgans, which were located in the Middle Irtysh area (Western Siberia). Due to poor bone preservation, only 214 skeletons were biologically sexed (adults) and 313 aged (adults + children), but from this we can see that children and females are underrepresented in burial context in contrast to males (table 7.1).[3]

Table 7.1. Those buried in the Sargat kurgans (Middle Irtysh area)

Adults			Juveniles (0–13 years)	Total Number of Skeletons	Cenotaphs
Males	Females	Nonsexed			
136	78	141	99	454	6
30.0%	17.1%	31.0%	21.8%	100%	

As is well known, the gender distinctions often are not obvious in archaeo-logical contexts. However, male/female/child differences can be recognized from several perspectives: (1) spatial distinctions (localization of burial); (2) structure and orientation of the grave; (3) arrangement of the body and selec-tion of artifacts.

LOCATION OF BURIALS WITHIN A KURGAN

Spatial organization may be the most important means of marking distinc-tions between males and females. In the Sargat kurgans, clear differentiation according to burial location was not observed, nor did male/female burials follow the cardinal directions or other physical structures. All burials were consistently situated within the enclosed kurgan area. There were no graves outside the ditches. Both male/female and children's graves were organized along the same principle, however, the central (primary) tomb usually be-longed to an adult (or adults).

In total, there are 112 primary tombs, because two pits held two separate interments (one over the other). The skeletal remains from seventy central tombs (of 112) were anthropologically sexed and aged (table 7.2). Only three of the central graves contained children. Of the remaining sixty-seven graves, nine individual graves were those of females (12.3%) and twenty-five were those of males (35.7%). In nine cases the central tombs contained two males, and in ten cases—one male and one female. In one case, two females were buried in the center of the kurgan. In three paired burials, only males were distinguishable; in four cases, only one female was discernable (sex of the second skeleton was indeterminate due to the small amount of surviving remains). Thus, in the central tombs sixty-six males and thirty-one females (excluding sixteen nonsexed individuals) were interred.

There are also central graves that were collective, including more than three people. From Bogdanovo I cemetery (kurgan B), the four skeletons are identified as males; from Kokonovka II (kurgan 1), there are four females and one male; at Isakovka I (kurgan 6), of the five deceased, two females and one male were able to be sexed. It is interesting to note that the ages of the de-ceased buried together vary: for example, a young man and an older woman;

Table 7.2. Primary tombs (67 adult graves and 3 subadult graves)

Individual								Paired						Collective (more than 3 skeletons)	Total (pit graves)
Male	Female	Child	M+M	F+F	M+F	M & ?	F & ?								
25	9	3	9	1	10	3	4							6	70
35.7%	12.3%	4.3%	12.3%	1.4%	14.4%	4.3%	5.7%							8.6%	100%

or two men, one young and one old. We cannot say whether the dead were kinsmen, but that could be possible. Judging from anthropological observations, certain multiburial kurgans were linked to specific families (Koryakova 1988, 156; Koryakova and Daire 1997, 165). But these osteological and biological tests were conducted within very restricted limits since complete skeletons from central graves are extremely rare. This problem is common for prehistoric kurgan mortuary sites. One hypothesis suggests that access to the central grave was open until both individuals were buried (Pogodin 1988, 31–32). It is quite possible that in these central tombs members of social or kin groups were buried. L. Pogodin proposes that the central graves belonged to warrior elites (*cataphractaries*) because protective armor fragments have been found almost exclusively in these tombs; exceptions are very rare (Pogodin 1997, 118–19). In any case, the central tombs invariably belonged to major personages.

The *individual* primary tombs of females make up 12.3 percent of the total, and *individual* tombs of males total 35.7 percent; about 30 percent of graves are either male + male or male + female groups. Therefore, male tombs constituted more than twice the number of female tombs. Kurgans, therefore, were constructed most often for men, not for women.

However, in the late Sargat sites (Isakovka I and Sidorovka, 2nd–3rd centuries CE) there are exceptions. In two kurgans, the most wealthy and elaborate "warrior" burials were secondary. They were unique undisturbed tombs. Their peripheral localization can be explained by the intention of the mourners to disorient probable robbers. The primary burials were wealthy as well, but they were looted because of their central place.

One interesting discovery was at Sidorovka, kurgan 1, which had a well-preserved peripheral burial. Its large pit held two interments; the upper grave was destroyed, but a lower burial was well preserved. Its contents were intact and rich (Matyuschenko and Tataurova 1997). In the huge grave (3.1 x 4.95 m, 1.85 m deep) was buried a warrior with a full set of weaponry, including iron armor, a sword, dagger, spearhead, bow and quiver, and beautiful gold and silver ornaments and vessels. Another intact elite burial (grave 6 in kurgan 3) was excavated by L. Pogodin in the Isakovka I cemetery. The grave (3.0 x 4.25 m, 5.0 m deep) was covered with a massive three-layer wooden roof. A wooden bed (2.2 x 1.0 m) held the remains of a man dressed in golden textiles. The burial contained a great variety of grave goods: two silver phials, silver bowls adorned with dolphins and swimming ducks, a large ceramic vessel of Central Asian origin, and many other things. The deccased wore a massive gold torque around his neck and one gold earring. Two gold plaques decorated his wide red belt, to which was attached a lacquer-covered scabbard holding a long iron sword. An iron dagger adorned with stone-inlaid gold plaques hung from the belt as well. In the corner were iron armor and a large iron belt. A small handmade Sargat-type pot was placed near the head of the deceased (Pogodin 1989, 1996, 1998a,b).

These kurgans contained wealthy female secondary burials as well. Isakovka I, grave 3 in kurgan 3, mentioned above, also held a rich female (2.25 x 4.3 m, 1.7 m deep). Unfortunately, it was robbed; nevertheless, surviving grave goods allow us to judge its initial wealth. More than five hundred small gold clothing (or funeral shroud) ornaments (tiny plaques and beads) were found in the infill of the pit. Dozens of colored glass and stone beads, threads of golden embroidery, fragments of glass vessels, and an iron bit and cheek piece were collected. The bone remains belong to a woman, 35 to 40 years old. Secondary burials 5 and 3 (kurgan 5 of the same cemetery) were similarly rich. Central female Sargat burials are also well known, but are less numerous than those of males. It is interesting that the central grave 1 of kurgan 1 (Sidorovka cemetery) was that of a female (20–30 years old), whereas the "golden tomb" of the warrior, mentioned above, was peripheral. Female primary burials are totally looted, with the exception of a few glass beads and fine gold clothing ornaments, but their imposing sizes (2.35 x 3.5 m, 1.85 m deep) and the central location suggest the high status of the deceased.

Underrepresentation of females in burial contexts has commonly been recognized archaeologically—sometimes as much as 75 percent in favor of males (McHugh 1999, 30). The Sargat kurgans contain both male and female graves, but the total number of male burials is greater than that of females (approximately 60%–65% of sexed adult graves are identified as male) so that male burials constitute at least two-thirds of the total number of adult dead (see table 7.1). The same proportion can be observed for the central tombs. It is interesting that a similar proportion was determined for Sauromatian and Early Sarmatian sites (Pokrovka cemetery in the southern Ural steppes, 6th–2nd centuries BCE) whose location and date is very close to the Sargat culture of Western Siberia. From that study of 174 identified skeletons, 69 were females (35%) and 105 were males (65%) (Davis-Kimball 1998, 142). Nevertheless, this proportion can vary in different contexts (sites). Table 7.3 catalogues data from five Sargat cemeteries of different chronological periods. We can see that numbers of males vary within the limits of 31.6 to 58.8 percent; females—11.2 to 31.6 percent; children—11.8 to 44.4 percent. The number of males exceeds

Table 7.3. **The proportion of males, females, and children at some Sargat sites (only identified individuals)**

Cemetery	Date	Males	Females	Children	Number of Individuals
Strizhevo I (8 kurgans)	6th–3rd centuries BCE	6 (31.6%)	6 (31.6%)	7 (36.8%)	19 (100%)
Strizhevo II (9 kurgans)	3rd–1st centuries BCE	14 (43.8%)	9 (28.1%)	9 (28.1%)	36 (100%)
Isakovka III (3 kurgans)	3rd–1st centuries BCE	8 (44.4%)	2 (11.2%)	8 (44.4%)	18 (100%)
Isakovka I (12 kurgans)	2nd–4th centuries CE	25 (45.4%)	15 (27.3%)	15 (27.3%)	55 (100%)
Sidorovka (3 kurgans)	2nd–4th centuries CE	10 (58.8%)	5 (29.4%)	2 (11.8%)	17 (100%)

female skeletons almost everywhere. There is no specific patterning of percentages in relation to the chronological position of the sites.

If a living society had roughly the same number of women as men, this discrepancy in our numbers may indicate deliberate exclusion. It may also be possible that some families could not guarantee an elaborate mound burial for all women. Moreover, the most impressive and wealthy Sargat burials (the so-called golden tombs) are identified as male.

STRUCTURE AND ORIENTATION OF THE GRAVE

The structural features of the grave, such as depth and interior organization, position and orientation of the body, and presence of certain grave markers, may also indicate male/female differences. The internal space of all Sargat burials (male, female, and child) was similarly organized; the position and orientation of the dead, the location of grave goods for males and females, and wooden structures were constant in the majority of tombs. There was no difference in the volume and depth of the grave pits of males and females. But as a rule, adult graves are significantly larger and deeper than those of subadults.

Usually the most impressive sizes are found in primary burials. The size of peripheral graves of both males and females varied significantly. In addition to probable status differences, the plausible reason for this variability may be the cold climate and winter frost in this area. Obviously, it is impossible to dig a deep grave or to erect a high mound during the Siberian winter, and the paleosoil investigations of Sauromatian kurgans demonstrate clearly that all kurgan burials in the Volga region were created in the warm season because of the permafrost conditions and the poor quality of tools (Demkin 1997, 180–181). In addition, the quantity of grave goods to be placed in the grave played a part in determining the size of a tomb.

ARRANGEMENT OF ARTIFACTS

In many societies gender distinctions are marked in burial by artifacts, and they can be traced archaeologically. There are clear examples in modern funerals where sex (gender) is represented by particular items or combinations of them (Ucko 1969; Kulemzin 1994, 334–422; McHugh 1999, 32). As a rule, these artifacts are associated with "femaleness" or "maleness" and may reflect social roles performed by individuals of different sexes. Burial with artifacts typical of the opposite gender, especially the inclusion of "male" items in a female grave, may indicate higher status. It is well known, for instance, that in kurgans of the Eurasian Iron Age nomads, weaponry is often included in female burials.

According to K. Smirnov, 20 percent of Sauromatian female graves contained weapons, mainly arrowheads, but sometimes even swords, daggers, and spearheads (1989, 169). Arrowheads are found in Sarmatian female burials more often as compared with Sauromatian ones (Moshkova 1989, 177–191). Furthermore, among Scythian and Sarmatian female graves even swords and spears can be found, although rarely (Davis-Kimball 1998, 143; Petrenko et al. 2004, 194–210). According to J. Davis-Kimball, 94 percent of male burials and at least 15 percent of female burials contained weapons, including arrowheads, quivers, and, rarely, swords and daggers, at the Pokrovka site (1998, 142–143). According to E. P. Bunyatyan, in 97.4 percent of Scythian male burials and in 50 percent of female ones weapons were present (1985, 91–92). In the latter case, most of the dead have been designated male or female by Bunyatyan on the basis of grave goods and, hence, it is not so precise a proportion. Nevertheless, these designations should not be ignored completely; however, they must be used with caution. Pazyryk Iron Age mounds in the Altai Mountains also included weapons in female graves. The grave of a 16-year-old girl from the site of Ak-Alakha-1 contained a bow, quiver, bronze ritual ax, and dagger (Polos'mak 2001, 58).

In Russian Iron Age archaeology, arrowheads traditionally are accepted as weapons in both the steppe and forest-steppe societies (nomadic and seminomadic). The prevailing view of specialists is that the nomadic bows were for battle rather than hunting due to their constructional characteristics (Khudyakov 1986). Before the 3rd century BCE, Sargat burials contained small bronze arrowheads for bows of the Scythian type and bone armor. In the 3rd century BCE, a big composite (so-called Hunnic) bow first appeared.

This bow usually survives in mortuary contexts only as four or seven bone plaques, which were used for strengthening its central part and two shoulders. Such a bow was about 1.50 meters in length. Iron and long-bone arrowheads, which appeared en masse in the 3rd to the 2nd centuries BCE, were used by this larger bow. As a result of this more powerful weapon, bone armor was replaced by iron. It seems likely that this bow appeared in the Sargat area earlier than in Sarmatian territory (Moshkova 1989, 184). "Undoubtedly, at first the forest-steppe inhabitants adopted many military inventions from the southern nomads. However, in the second half of the first millennium BCE, they made their own contribution to the general development of warfare" (Koryakova and Epimakhov 2007). The bow of the Hunnic type was the most effective bow of the late 1st millennium BCE (Khudyakov 1986).

Furthermore, abundant archaeozoological material, obtained from settlements, clearly testifies to a stock-breeding economic basis of the Sargat society and, judging by bone collections, the hunt played an extremely small part in the economic activity of the Sargat people. At the Pavlinovo fortified settlement, which was systematically studied during the last decade, 98.4 percent of all obtained bones belonged to domestic animals (57.1% horse, 30.4% cow, and 12.5% sheep/goat). Only 1.6 percent of the total number of bones consisted of wild animals—elk, small deer (roe), fox, and beaver (Kosintzev and Borodina 1991; Koryakova et al. 2004). We can see that the highest frequency of identifiable remains relates to the horse species, which is a common pattern for Early Iron Age settlements in the Trans-Ural region.

Sargat burials contain a wide variety of grave goods. Only 5 percent of the dead, including men, women, and children, are not accompanied by any grave goods at all. As mentioned above, tools usually are absent and the majority of ornaments and other luxury goods in the tombs were imported from different territories. According to the results of chemical, technological, and morphological analysis of glass, undertaken by N. Dovgaluk (1995), the Sargat people received glass beads from Egypt (presumably Alexandria), the coast of Syria, southwest Asia, and China. The beads were decorations for the masses; burials contain beads quite often (sometimes up to several hundred). Elite graves in the Isakovka and Sidorovka cemeteries produced rich material, including gold objects decorated with turquoise, silver phaleras, bowls, or phialae (Livshits 2002), probably of Bactrian origin. Imports from China dating from the Han dynasty period were numerous: beautiful bronze kettles and vessels and remains of lacquered objects—about twelve belts and around twenty daggers and swords with lacquer coverings. There are remains of silk fabric with golden stitching; these fabrics are rather numerous in the Sargat graves (Pogodin 1996; 1998a, 38). Some scholars have concluded that the northern periphery of the Silk Road trade system embraced the distant lands of the western Siberian forest-steppe (Koryakova and Epimakhov

2007). Sargat society could have participated in long-distance interactions and trade.

The complex of Sargat elite armament included a bow, dagger, long sword, and in special cases, a shield, helmet, and lamellar armor, initially fashioned from bone and leather, and then later from iron. The complex of elite weaponry recovered from unrobbed graves in Sidorovka and Isakovka I belonged to the catafractarian type of heavily armed mounted warrior, which became widely known in Eurasia from the last centuries BCE (Matyushenko and Tataurova 1997; Pogodin 1998b). There is a direct analogy between Sargat weapon types and those in the Scytho-Sarmatian world. It may seem strange, but the single diagnostic artifact for Sargat identity is pottery: hand-formed vessels with round or slightly sharpened bases with festoons covering the shoulder.

Sargat adult graves *with weaponry*, both male and female, most frequently include arrowheads and parts of bows; swords, daggers, and protective armor are less frequently found and only in male burials. Approximately 20 percent of female graves contained arrowheads and parts of a bow, but we *never* find swords or armor in female and child burials. Another group of artifacts much more rarely found in female graves is horse trappings: harnesses, bits, cheek pieces, buckles, and metal belt plaques. In the Middle Irtysh region, only two female (18–20 years old and 50–55 years old) burials containing daggers have been found, and three female graves contained parts of compound bows and quivers. In the first two cases, the remains belonged to young women (18–25 years old) and in the last case, a more mature woman (35–40 years old). In general, the most usual artifacts buried with females and children are clothing attachments and ornaments, glass and stone beads, earrings, bracelets, mirrors, and pendants. Ceramic spindle whorls are frequently found. Interestingly, big bronze cauldrons, so often considered "male" signifiers, are also included in female graves (for example, Bogdanovo III cemetery, kurgans 1 and 2). The deformed skulls, everywhere recognized as a high-status marker, are known both among Sargat men and women (Kovrigin et al. 2006, 188–204).

The ceramic vessels with food offerings and animal meat (bones of animals), iron knives, individual glass beads, and small clothing ornaments have been found equally in the graves of males, females, and children. As opposed to females and children, more than 60 percent of the male graves contained weapons of various types, and no less than 8 percent of the male burials contained jewelry and 12 percent also contained spindle whorls. Therefore, certain types of artifacts were limited to females, while none were limited only to males, including the mirrors.[4]

It is important to note that at the Sargat cemeteries approximately half the burials do not contain weapons or jewelry at all. The grave goods of such burials appear to be *gender neutral*; they contain ceramic vessels, animal bones, iron knives, and individual beads or ornaments. Moreover, they are primarily peripheral graves. Fifty percent of these burials consist of child graves, 13 percent are adult male, and 22 percent are adult female (another 15% are represented by collective tombs and cenotaphs). Although 20 percent of the women were buried with weapons, the majority of females (at least 50%) were accompanied with gender-neutral items such as pottery, animal bones, "table" knives, and so on.

In total, only 46 percent of the entire number of graves actually conforms to traditional gender stereotypes: Males are buried with weapons and females are buried with jewelry. The explanation for this cannot be ascribed to anthropological errors only. Of course, the assignment of biological sex may be systematically biased (often toward males), but if the validity of some sexing is rejected, then the validity of sexing all burials must also be doubted, including those graves where gender stereotypes are observed in their fullest extent.

There are no items that *always* accompany women, and not men. Not long ago, the spindle whorl was considered such a gendered artifact among archaeologists (Polos'mak 1987, 27; Matveyeva 1993, 143), because spinning and weaving traditionally were accepted as female work. However, if we look more carefully, we can see that spindle whorls are associated not only with female burials but also with male and child burials (Pogodin 1998a, 31; Berseneva 1999, 115–117; 2004, 198–201), and this is not unique to the Sargat data. Apart from the Sargat culture, this practice is typical, for example, in the Iron Age Jetyasar culture of Central Asia (Levina 1994, 69). From the Roman Iron Age in northern Europe over 10 percent of burials with spindle whorls were those of males, while almost 15 percent of burials that included weapons were those of females (Parker Pearson 1999, 108).

Spindle whorls are sometimes found with weapons in the Sargat male graves. The central burial at Strizhevo II cemetery, kurgan 4, contained two males; it was a single-burial kurgan. Despite the looting, the tomb contained the remains of iron armor, iron and bone arrowheads, and two spindle whorls. In the undisturbed "golden tomb" of a warrior at Isakovka I, a spindle whorl was found along with a full set of heavy weaponry (Pogodin 1998a, 31). The primary tomb, kurgan B (Bogdanovo II), contained two males who were accompanied by a bow, arrowheads, and a spindle whorl. Of 136 burials that have been identified as male (including the paired males), at least sixteen contained spindle whorls (11.8%). Even so, spindle whorls are found more often in female graves. Twenty graves out of seventy-eight contained these items (25.6%). Spindle whorls are sometimes found in female burials along with weapons (only arrowheads). Rarely, children's graves contained spindle whorls: nine burials of ninety-eight (9.2%), usually along with jewelry.

Traceological (use-wear) analysis of the Sargat ceramic spindle whorls clearly demonstrates the multifunctionality of these items (Berseneva 2004). In addition to spinning and weaving, spindle whorls could have been used as flywheels on an axis for making fire. It is possible that the presence of spindle whorls in graves was not connected to the sex or gender of the dead. I am sure that this problem needs to be considered as a semantic matter because the meanings of things might be varied along with the context of their usage. What might be the symbolic meaning of spindle whorls? In world mythology there are many stories and myths concerning spindles. In many human cultures, these items usually symbolize life cycles (solar, lunar, annual, and so on) and movement, death and rebirth. In her study of Sarmatian sites J. Davis-Kimball also suggests that "this 'tool' had a magical (or cultic) attribute(s)" and was connected with female burials of the highest status (1998, 143). Sargat ceramic spindle whorls (handmade) often were decorated with concentric rows or festoons that have been associated with solar connotations.[5] Could the deceased men, women, and children have received the spindle whorls as magic protective talismans to show the way to the Otherworld?

SUBADULT SYMBOLISM IN BURIALS

Subadult burials constitute, on average, about a quarter of the total number of dead that I analyzed (see table 7.1). Children of all ages are represented in the Sargat kurgan cemeteries, the largest number of whom were buried in individual tombs. Common characteristics of the funeral rite discussed above were found in the graves of both adults and subadults. Nevertheless, it is possible to find features that distinguish burials of subadult members of the society.

SPATIAL LOCATION OF BURIALS WITHIN A KURGAN

Child tombs are secondary in 97.7 percent of the cases (see table 7.2). They usually were located in sterile soil below or in the mound itself, and in general, the number of child graves in each context is approximately equal to what was observed for adults. Like adult burials, subadults were always situated in the enclosed kurgan area, and there were no child burials outside the ditch.

There are only a few examples of primary (central) burials belonging to subadults. In the Middle Irtysh area two kurgans out of 110 were primary burials containing children. An extremely interesting and unique grave was found at the Strizhevo I cemetery, kurgan 11, which contained three burials:

the primary grave (3) and two secondary ones (1 and 2). The undisturbed central grave contained a child (6–7 years old) inside a boat (Pogodin 1991). The grave had a rectangular pit with a wooden roof, 1 x 2.5 meters and 1.4 meters deep. The child was accompanied by various types of rich grave goods: a bronze mirror, astragali, a green stone pendant in a gold mount, a blue stone pendant, a gold earring, blue glass beads, carnelian or amber beads, and a spindle whorl. This is a unique tomb not only because such a small child was buried in the central place of the kurgan, but also because he or she was deposited within a boat. It is the only example of a boat burial in the Sargat culture. Secondary graves 1 and 2 belonged to adults. Pit grave 1 was situated in the mound, and held a woman (50 years old), who was buried only with an offering of meat. The second peripheral grave (2) held a man (50–55 years old) and a baby (0–3 months old) and lacked grave goods.

The chronology of the central child tombs is also of interest. They are dated generally to the 6th through the 2nd centuries BCE, or the early phase of the Sargat culture. These burials may reflect the attempt of certain families or lineages to make their high status more institutionalized. James Brown notes, "as the hierarchical aspects increase, children will be accorded relatively more elaborate attention in proportion to the decline in the opportunity for replacement of the following generation" (1981, 29). Later, when ascribed status was secured, the necessity to bury children in the central place diminished. In the late Sargat sites primary child graves are absent.

STRUCTURE AND ORIENTATION OF THE GRAVE

The internal space of the child burials was organized much like that of the adults. A wooden frame made of boards usually represents the internal construction of ordinary child tombs. The roof is usually made of boards or birch bark. The position and orientation of the dead were constant; the location of grave goods for adults and subadults is also the same, and wooden structures were found in the majority of tombs in the same manner as in adult graves. However, there were differences in the size of the constructions and depth of the grave pits. As a rule, adult graves are significantly larger and deeper than those of subadults. The majority of child graves, as we would expect, are smaller in size and depth and thus usually correspond to the smaller size of the deceased and smaller quantity of accompanying grave goods.

The majority of child burials are rather modest in terms of grave goods and construction, although "rich" child burials are known. They are distinguished by significantly larger dimensions of the grave, both in complexity of construction and the number and quality of accompanying artifacts. For instance, kurgan 2 in the Isakovka I cemetery, Middle Irtysh area, contained three graves: the central grave (1) and two secondary graves (2 and 3) both of which belonged to children. The kurgan was approximately 3.1 meters high and more than 35 meters in diameter. Ditches surrounded the mound. The central grave (1) was totally destroyed. One of the child tombs (3) was large (2.7 x 1.6 m), with a depth of 0.7 meters below the sterile subsoil level (Mogil'nikov et al. 1977). This grave was secondary, and its construction crosscut the second ditch. The grave pit was furnished with an impressive wooden structure; the roof had four layers of boards, and the bottom was also made from boards. After the child interment in grave 3, the kurgan was surrounded with a third ditch, and the mound was enlarged. Goods in grave 3 included a bronze mirror, a gold pendant, a bronze spindle whorl, four agate beads, a massive gold bracelet, an iron knife, small bronze ornaments for clothes, and two ceramic vessels. The skeletal remains were very poorly preserved, and only the milk teeth remained.

Such child burials are quite rare in the Sargat funeral practice. It is obvious that this tomb is not only very impressive in terms of grave goods but that it also required a great deal of physical expenditure for its construction. Interestingly, grave 2 was much more modest than grave 3, mentioned above. The grave pit was not as large: 1.15 x 0.75 meters, with a depth of 0.5 meters below the sterile soil. The grave goods included only one ceramic vessel, animal bones, and a small bone spoon. This burial, like the central grave, was located within the first ditch.

ARRANGEMENT OF ARTIFACTS

Determining what grave goods regularly accompanied the dead is very difficult because many graves are destroyed. Nevertheless, the known data allow us to make some preliminary conclusions. Only four (no more than 4%) of child burials are not accompanied by grave goods; for adult burials it is 6.5 percent (undisturbed graves). Therefore, the proportion of burials without grave goods for children and adults is nearly identical. Clearly, providing the dead with burial items was not strongly linked to age. But several types of accompanying goods are almost completely absent in child burials, primarily weapons. We usually find only single arrowheads and, even more rarely, daggers, but never swords or armor.

Another group of artifacts not found in child graves is horse trappings. We have only one iron bit found so far in a child's grave in Western Siberia. Nevertheless, ceramic vessels with food and animal meat have been found equally in the graves of subadults and adults, and massive amounts of horse bones are no exception, even in tombs of babies. Still, the basic artifacts of child burials are clothing elements and ornaments like those found in female graves (beads, pendants, small bronze or bone clasps). Ceramic spindle whorls are less frequently found. A nearly unique offering in subadult burials is the sheep astragalus. In the Middle Irtysh area all finds of astragali, with one exception, belong to child burials. However, the total number of burials with astragali is quite small, or fewer than 10 percent of the tombs. Therefore, astragali do not serve as an age marker. I would suggest also that some items could be toys (the big ivory arrowhead in a double child burial at the site of Kartashovo in the Middle Irtysh area, sheep astragali, cowry shells, various beads, and probably spindle whorls) and their choice was completely subjective and left to the discretion of the adult mourners.

The "wealthy" burials belonging to children three years and older *in general* are characterized by a greater complexity of inner constructions and variety of accompanying grave goods. Burials of babies are usually more modest. It is difficult to explain what caused these distinctions, but the treatment of children may indicate the degree of their integration into the community so that sentimental aspects are potentially very powerful. Perhaps the affection and attachment of parents, or other family members, was deeper with older children than with babies.

The mortality rate of children in prehistoric populations was high, and it seems unusual that those children were buried in the same way as adults, with such an intensive investment of labor and wealth. Probably the kurgan burial form was hereditary and was determined by the social status of the deceased or his or her family. Interestingly, some impressive Sargat child burials (for instance, Strizhevo I and Isakovka I, mentioned above) had a nonstandard west-east orientation as opposed to the normal north-south one. Still, it is difficult to explain why certain children would receive more elaborate mortuary treatment than some adults. The elaborate treatment of some children cannot be explained since, among other things, we do not know where and in what way their parents were buried. James Brown notes that the wealth and typicality of subadult burials could be determined by specific demographic circumstances. "If the loss of children to a community or lineage can be argued to be critical to the future of a heritable claim, then children can be expected to be singled out for elaborate treatment when the birth rate is low or the family circle is narrow" (1981, 29). Thus, wealthy child burials may not always be a sign of a hierarchical society and ascribed status. The degree of importance of children for the community also needs to be taken into account.

The subadult category in the Sargat society was limited to 12 to 14 years and as with many ethnographic and historical communities, the juvenile age is extremely underrepresented in burial contexts. The main reason for this is not so much an insufficient presence of this category in the kurgans as in a lack of qualified anthropological identification. The difference between 12- and 14-year-olds and young adults is not always easy to determine. The problem is that small adult individuals are identified by some archaeologists as teenagers and conversely. This fact is evidence of the difficulty in distinguishing teen-aged burial from the adult burial without anthropological identification.

The possibility of determining the sex of the deceased on the basis of accompanying artifacts is very troublesome for adults and, especially, for subadults. Strong gender markers have not been firmly identified. We can only suppose the sex of a child even in "extraordinary" burials with a great number of grave goods. For example, the sex of the child that was buried in the boat (Strizhevo I cemetery, kurgan 11, mentioned above) is impossible to determine in such a way. Another child (1.5 years old) was buried with a dagger and iron arrowheads (Sidorovka cemetery, kurgan 2) (Matyuschenko and Tataurova 1997). Most likely, this was a boy, but it is a very rare case in Sargat mortuary practice.

The Sargat child burials in most cases seem to be gender neutral (70% of graves). Only a very small number of graves included weapons or a lot of jewelry and thus allow us to suppose the sex of a subadult. One may suggest that children were *perhaps* males or females before they reached sexual maturity. It is only in their middle teens that boys and girls start to practice binary, gender-specific roles. Among the Sargat burials, there are juvenile male graves with full sets of weaponry, including a sword and dagger. But in the case of a premature death, a child usually received gender-neutral grave goods.

The age-sex analysis of Anglo-Saxon cemeteries in eastern England high-lights the ways that age-based relations linked children and women; male children were rarely found with male sex-linked artifacts, whereas many children, both male and female, were treated as female in terms of grave goods. Later relationships between the sexes became apparent in the consis-tent associations with sex-related artifacts (Parker Pearson 1999, 103). Rarely in Russian archaeology are child burials a matter of special study. E. P. Bun-yatyan in her study of Scythian burials established on average the high degree of similarity between adult and subadult graves recognized by the observance of basic canons of mortuary ritual. These similarities included an orientation of the dead, arrangement of the grave pit, and a presence of grave goods, in-cluding pottery, a knife, beads, and earrings. The distinction consisted of the spatial location of subadult burials and the absence of child primary burials, the size of the grave pit, and the absence of weapons. Bunyatyan also points out that burials of adults are distinguished by greater variety in artifacts and grave constructions in contrast to subadults (1985, 59–63). These features are typical for Sargat mortuary practice as well.

According to ethnographic surveys, differences in social status in egali-tarian societies often relate to age, sex, and ability, whereas in hierarchical societies, differences in social status can be inherited, thus allowing the presence of wealthy child burials. The Sargat society was, without any doubt, quite complex (Koryakova 1996, 2003). Burial practice was uniform, but it is difficult to say what niche was occupied by children in the social structure. We can, however, suggest that their place was significant. Some wealthy and elaborate child tombs are known, among them the central burial within a boat. Rich, but not primary, child burials are found both on early (Strizhevo I), and late (Isakovka I, Sidorovka) Sargat sites. Central (primary) child burials were absent in the late period.

The archaeology of children is an interesting but not easy subject of study. It is difficult to say what place children occupied in the world of adults. The child burials, noted by some archaeologists, point out to us the gap between those being buried and those doing the burying. As funerary archaeologists, we only see children as manipulated entities within an adult world—they are buried by adults. Thus, we never experience the world of children, only attempts of adults to ascribe meaning to their foreshortened lives and premature deaths (Parker Pearson 1999, 103).

CONCLUSION

It is likely that the Sargat society practiced several different forms of disposing of the dead. There is an evident disparity between the number of buried people and the potential number of people that could be accommodated by settlements (Daire and Koryakova 2002). Additionally, demographic parameters of the buried population are not normal (Razhev 2001). In this case, we have to presume some alternative burial rituals did not leave traces in the archaeological record or at least have not yet been found. Apparently, not all the deceased (adult and subadult) were buried in kurgans, but we do not know what criteria were used for selection of individuals for kurgan interment. We cannot hope to reconstruct the gender and age structure of the ancient Sargat society in full based on the evidence currently available. It is possible that the society was quite complex and probably even more hierarchical than can be seen from the existing evidence.

Gendered symbolism had a significant part in funerary rituals of the Sargat population. A gendered social structure is represented in Sargat mortuary practice through assemblages of artifacts (weapons and jewelry) that accompany certain dead and, to a smaller extent, through a spatial location of burial, such as the *male* predominance among the primary tombs. At least 50 percent of all burials demonstrate unambiguous correlation between the sex of the dead and grave goods. To the greatest extent this concerns men (a minimum 60% of male burials contained one weapon or another), although only about 30 percent of women were buried with a significant amount of jewelry. Approximately

20 percent of female burials contained weapons; the remaining female assemblages seem to be gender neutral (about 50%). Weapons, horse trappings, and jewelry do not appear to be markers of biological sex as such, even though they were often directly related to the sex of those buried. These items can be referred to as markers of social position of a sex—or of gender. The significant number of female graves that include weapons, as well as the number of male/female/child burials with sex-neutral artifacts, confirms this conclusion.

Archaeologists frequently point out that stereotypes such as "weapons equal male burial" and "spindle whorls signify the female" quite often are based on ignorance or depend on analysis of a particular excavated context (Pogodin 1998; McHugh 1999, 33; Parker Pearson 1999, 108; Mortensen 2004, 105). In the Sargat kurgan cemeteries, for example Beshaul II and Beshaul III, it is well known that male burials sometimes contained a great quantity of jewelry—glass and stone beads (up to several hundred) and earrings—and not weapons (Matveyeva 1993, 143). Of course, these graves were relatively small in number. Nevertheless, in this respect the Sargat culture is not unique. Similar examples can be found in cemeteries of other cultures, and many ethnographic examples are known as well. Sometimes it is evidence of the presence in society of particular gender groups, usually small in their number. One should not exclude, however, the possibility of incorrect osteological identification (and certain categories of individual may be biologically indeterminate due to hormonal abnormalities).

Absolute age and gender markers have not been firmly identified. There is no *absolute* distinction between male and female in terms of types of burial goods in the Sargat cemeteries, excluding the swords and armor, but these things are very rare. The clothing, headdresses, or other organic items could help to define the age and gender of the dead. In wealthy intact tombs survived the remains of golden fabrics; leather; belt buckles; gold, silver, or bronze ornaments; and shoe buckles.

Despite the fact that children are underrepresented in the Sargat burial mounds, they obviously were major contributors to the life of the society. Numerically, children were the predominant group of individuals in most past societies, and they clearly were included in adult projects from an early age (Chamberlain 1997, 250). Sociologists argue that the category of "childhood" was constituted to support a particular model of social order and adulthood, and that it is very important for a normal functioning society (Scott 1997, 6). The fact that the subadults are buried in the same manner as adults in the Sargat society may confirm their stable and important place in the social structure.

In summary, it is important to stress a few points:

1. The materials from kurgan cemeteries do not suggest a strong male/female dichotomy in the Sargat society that could be fixed in the mortuary

domain. There are no distinctions in the treatment between males and females, neither in their orientation, position in the grave, nor in spatial location of the accompanying artifacts. There are distinctions in the composition of grave goods—the weapons are mainly connected with males. Undoubtedly, the gendered category of "male-warriors" is represented most clearly in mortuary practice. It is difficult to comment on the existence of "women-warriors" even though females were quite often buried with weapons, since the overwhelming majority of these artifacts are arrowheads, sometimes only one or two. One may suggest more confidently that these women belonged to warrior (elite) clans, and arrowheads may well have been a marker (or sign) of this.

2. The weapons in burials may indicate that there is a vertical hierarchy between the individuals buried with weapons and those without, not just gender division. The circumstances of death (in battle, for example) could be taken into account.

3. The groups of people who were buried with gender-neutral artifacts or without grave goods at all could be identified by not using exclusive material symbols for each biological sex.

4. The children are accompanied by a significant number of artifacts and sometimes were buried in big elaborate tombs; consequently, they must be recognized as quite important social actors. Based on the burials of small children with rather rich personal belongings discovered in the Sidorovka and Isakovka I cemeteries, one may assume social status was inherited. Burials of babies, as a rule, are simply arranged in comparison with tombs of 4- to 5-year-old children or older. Most likely children constituted a separate gender class before they reached sexual maturity. The social status of children was similar to that of women, judging by their gender-neutral set of burial items. Specific gender determinations were not achieved by the children before death.

5. Although there is an almost complete absence of tools as grave goods, we can infer from indirect evidence and from ethnographic analogs that the division of labor was organized along lines of gender and age—but this inference is not evidenced in the graves.

In general, the gender structure and gender relations in past societies (including the Sargat) need further serious study, since previous investigations are clearly insufficient. A rigid binary division into males and females, well-defined in the funerary domain, seems to be too simple. If we suppose that the mortuary treatment reflects a social relationship between sexes, a stable and significant position of women in the Sargat society can be posited, despite the dominant roles that clearly belonged to men. In certain realms of life, including management of craft and food production and war, their roles could be quite comparable if not identical. Although the range of items from female burials is quite wide, male burials display more variety. One may suggest that women's social roles were more restricted, but more stable over time, in contrast to that of men's.

NOTES

I wish to thank the editors for their invitation to publish this chapter. I am very grateful to Ludmila Koryakova and Karlene Jones-Bley for their comments and to Leonid Pogodin for the use of his not-yet-published materials. My gratitude also goes to Karlene Jones-Bley for correcting my English. The work for this article was supported by grant RGNF (project No. 05-01-83104a/Y).

1. In the village Sargatskoe near Omsk (Middle Irtysh area), in the 1920s, kurgans with specific festoon ceramics were excavated for the first time. Since the 1920s, the number of newly discovered cemeteries and settlements has increased greatly. These sites were named "Sargat Culture." Literary sources concerning the Iron Age Western Siberian population are completely absent.

2. It is necessary to note that most of the Sargat kurgans were robbed in the 17th–18th centuries CE at the time of the Russian colonization of Siberia. This problem has been exacerbated by plowing in recent times. Many graves in general are characterized by bad preservation of bone remains and suffer from animal activity. This is especially true when the burials were constructed within the kurgan mound.

3. Of the total of sexed adults, 63.6 percent were male and 36.4 percent were female.

4. In general, the Middle Irtysh Sargat burials contained one silver and fourteen bronze mirrors. Two of all numbers belonged to children, six to women, and three to men. The sex of remaining mirror possessors is undetermined.

5. This ornamentation is typical also for Sargat pottery found in the burials.

Chapter Eight

Sorting Out Men and Women in the Karasuk Culture

Sophie Legrand

The Final Bronze Age in the Minusinsk Basin, a region located in the steppic zone in eastern Eurasia (figure 8.1), is characterized by the Karasuk culture. The Minusinsk Basin takes in the middle valley of the Yenisei River and the upper valley of the river Chulym (figure 8.2). It is surrounded on three sides by wide belts of high mountains—the Kuznetsky Alatau and the Abakan range to the west, the western Sayan to the south, and the eastern Sayan to the east.

The excavations of Karasuk sites, led by Russian archaeologists, started in the second half of the 19th century (Kuznetsov-Krasnojarskij 1889, 11–18) and were carried out on a large scale during the Soviet period (Grjaznov 1965, 1979; Lipskij 1949, 1956, 1957; Maksimenkov 1964, 1974). S. A. Teploukhov is the first archaeologist who identified the Karasuk culture. He established the first chronology of the Bronze Age based on the surface features of tombs (1926, 1927, 1929).

The investigations of the Karasuk period have mostly focused on excavation of funerary sites rather than settlements. Most of the cemeteries are vast clusters of several thousand tombs situated on the edges of rivers and lakes.

During almost a century of excavations, a large quantity of pottery and bronze artifacts (knives, ornamental plaques, awls) has been uncovered. Some artifacts, such as bronze knives, that present typological and iconographic characters similar to the Karasuk ones, have been recovered in a vast zone: Transbaikal, Tuva, Mongolia, Ordos, and northern and central China.

Russian archaeologists used the bronze knives as chronological markers in order to date the Karasuk culture; 900–800 BCE for S. A. Teploukhov (1929), 1500–1300 BCE for S. V. Kiselev (1951), 1200–1000 BCE for N. L. Chlenova (1972).

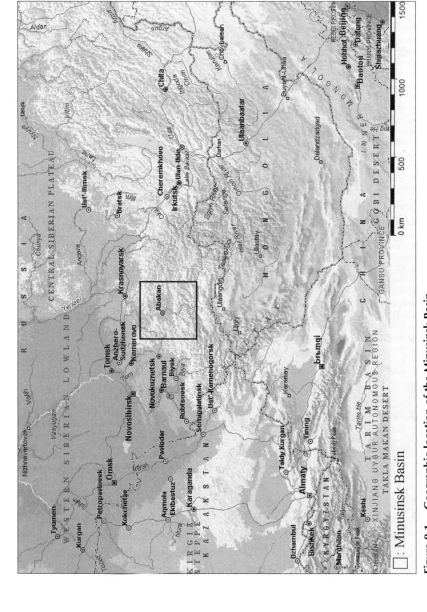

☐ : Minusinsk Basin

Figure 8.1. Geographic location of the Minusinsk Basin.

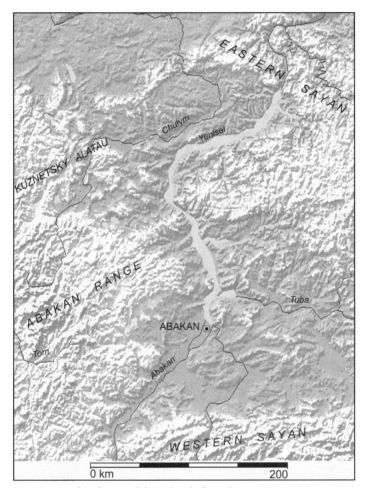

Figure 8.2.   Geographical map of the Minusinsk Basin.

Beginning in 1999, the Institute for Archaeology of St. Petersburg instigated a research program for Bronze Age radiometric analysis. The datation generally set for the Karasuk culture is 1400–1000 BC. However, this evaluation is based on radiocarbon datations obtained from human bone samples recovered at funerary sites that belong to a developed phase of the Karasuk culture. The emergence of Karasuk should thus be placed earlier, but this assumption has still to be confirmed by thorough radiometric datations (Legrand 2004, 139).

Russian scholars who have studied the Karasuk culture focused their research mostly on chronological problems and tried to define the Karasuk by comparing it to other cultures. They did not really explore the culture in terms of its own identity (Teploukhov 1929; Kiselev 1951; Grjaznov 1969;

Khlobystina 1970; Chlenova 1972; Novgorodova 1970; Vadetskaja 1986). Moreover, the extent of their evidence came from scattered reports of mortuary remains and not from the whole Karasuk dataset available.[1]

The Karasuk culture has been defined by S. V. Kiselev, M. P. Grjaznov, and E. A. Novgorodova as an agropastoralist and semimobile society, clustered in villages (Kiselev 1951, 66; Grjaznov 1969, 98, 161; Novgorodova 1989, 126) and under a patriarchal sociopolitical system (Kiselev 1951, 66, 67; Grjaznov 1969), even though this has never been proven or tested archaeologically.

Moreover, practically nothing is known about the family organization of the Karasuk society and its relationship to social organization. In order to consider this point, here I will analyze cemetery arrangement, tomb structure, and grave goods according to sex/gender and age differences; I will see how gender is constructed (through analysis of burial remains, at least we can tell how they viewed their social structure), define the status of individuals and their position in the family, and evaluate the significance of the gender in determining status in the family and the community as a whole.

In this study, only burials sexed from bone analysis are used. Unfortunately, because of mass looting and differing preservation condition of human remains, the quantity of tombs sexed is not very large: four hundred tombs from 120 excavated cemeteries. For better results, statistical tests have been provided for all four hundred tombs from all cemeteries.[2]

CEMETERY ARRANGEMENT

Inside cemeteries, rectangular, square, circular, or oval-shape stone enclosures, including upright slab stones or stone beddings, always surrounded funerary units. They were covered in two ways: a low mound was erected above the funerary unit; or the space inside the surrounding wall was filled with earth and covered with a layer of slab stones. Their shape and manner of construction have no discernable social connotations, but it can be assumed that the differences are related to chronological and as well as local variables.

Cemeteries are mostly organized into compact funerary units of two to twenty enclosures constructed one against one another (clustered funerary units). Isolated funerary units are less common.[3] Most of the clustered and isolated units include a single tomb. They contain, in equal proportion, male and female burials. Child burials are associated more often with clustered funerary units than isolated ones.

Clustered funerary units of adults and child burials contain the following in the central[4] enclosure (figure 8.3):

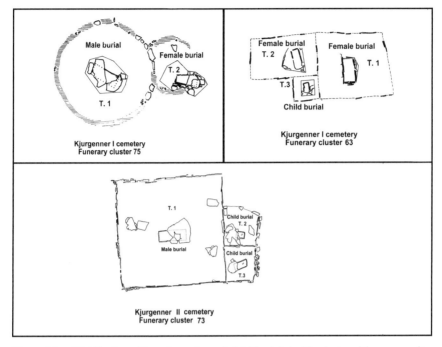

Figure 8.3.   Distribution of female, male, and child burials inside clustered funerary units.

- a female burial, where no males are buried in the clustered funerary units
- a male burial (almost exclusively), where males, females, and children are buried in the clustered funerary units[5]
- subadults interred to the immediate periphery and infants to the external periphery of the central unit

The surface area of the funerary unit is variable according to gender and age (table 8.1).

- Funerary units having a surface area from one to seven square meters mostly contain child burials.
- Funerary units with a surface area from seven to seventeen square meters contain children in a large proportion.
- Funerary units with a surface area from eighteen to thirty-two square meters mostly contain adults and children in smaller numbers.
- Funerary units with a surface area from thirty-three to forty-two square meters contain no children.
- The largest funerary units, from forty-three to 112 square meters, contain only single males.

Table 8.1. Distribution of different sizes of isolated single-tomb funerary units by male, female, and child burials

Size (meter²)	1 (1–7)	2 (8–13)	3 (14–17)	4 (18–22)	5 (23–32)	6 (33–42)	7 (43–62)	8 (63–82)	9 (83–112)	Total
Child	42	43	16	10	10	0	0	0	0	121
Female	5	16	10	10	20	14	0			75
Male	3	10	5	12	21	13	8	4	3	79
Total	50	69	31	32	51	27	8	4	3	275

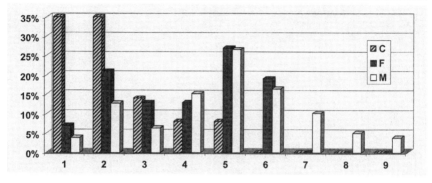

TOMB STRUCTURE

Four types of tombs can be identified:

1. The most widespread type is a cist tomb, with a pit faced with slab stones. These were covered with either a single, or several, slab stones.
2. Less frequent are the cist tombs with slab stone bedding, covered with slab stones piled up in the shape of a circular mound.
3. Simple pits covered mostly with slab stones.
4. Rare are cists with two sides with stone bedding and two faced with slab stones.

The four types of tombs contain females, males, and children in mostly equal proportions.

The tombs are built at a depth of about eighty centimeters; tombs built on the ground surface are almost exclusively child burials. The length of child tombs varies according to age of the deceased (tables 8.2, 8.3). Tombs with a length between 40 and 140 meters are mostly child burials: those with a length from 40 to 80 meters mostly contain an infant to a 1-year-old child; those with a length from 81 to 100 meters mostly contain children from 2 to 4 years; those with a length from 101 to 120 meters mostly contain children from 5 to 9 years;

Table 8.2.   Distribution of different lengths of tombs containing individual male, female, and child burials

Size (meter)	1 (40–60)	2 (61–80)	3 (81–100)	4 (101–120)	5 (121–140)	6 (141–160)	7 (161–180)	8 (181–200)	9 (201–230)	10 (231–290)	Total
Child	63	159	203	120	112	65	27	6	3	3	761
Female		1		3	4	31	91	70	22	8	230
Male	1	1	2	1	2	16	59	66	52	16	216
Total	64	161	205	124	118	112	117	142	77	27	1,207

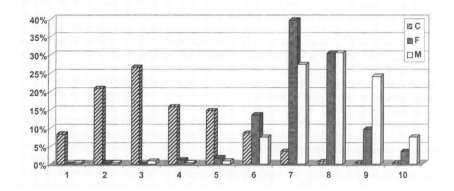

and tombs with a length from 121 to 140 meters or more contain children from 10 to 14 years (table 8.3). The occurrence of children in very long tombs (141 to 290 meters) is mostly associated with adult burials, showing that the length of the child tombs is connected also with the status of the deceased.

The length of adult tombs does not vary much according to age but more with the height[6] of the deceased, gender, and status. Tombs with a length from 141 to 180 meters contain mostly female burials. Those with a length from 181 to 200 meters contain female and male burials in approximately equal proportion, and the longest tombs (from 201 to 290 meters) are associated mostly with male burials.

BURIAL PRACTICES

In the Karasuk period, cemeteries contain only primary burials, mostly of individuals. Only 20 percent are multiple, mostly double, burials[7] associated with interment of an adult (most often a woman) with a child. Double burials of adults usually include male and female bodies, more rarely they contain two male or two female bodies. In double burials of a male and a female, bodies are

Table 8.3.   Distribution of different lengths of individual tombs containing child burials by age

Size (meter) Age	1 (40– 60)	2 (61– 80)	3 (81– 100)	4 (101– 120)	5 (121– 140)	6 (141– 160)	7 (161– 180)	8 (181– 200)	9 (201– 230)	10 (231– 290	Total
1 (0–1 year)	23	32	24	4	3		1				87
2 (2–4 years)	4	18	48	23	8	4		1			106
3 (5–9 years)		1	10	19	15	10	3	1			59
4 (10–14 years)		2	4	15	45	42	20	4	4	3	139
Total	27	53	86	61	71	56	24	6	4	3	391

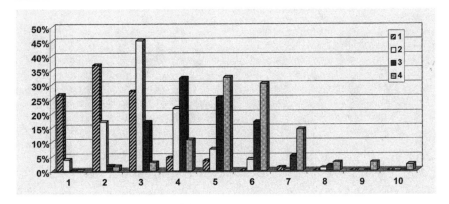

placed side by side: The male is placed with his back against the tomb's wall, and the female is always placed between the male and animal offerings.

Females, males, and children were treated in the same way in the Karasuk burials: The great majority (84%) of the dead were placed with legs slightly drawn up, on their left sides, fewer on the right side. In 9 percent of the total number of burials, the dead are deposited in a stretched position, lying on their backs. The position of the head was mostly oriented to the northeast, east, or east northeast, and less frequently oriented to the southwest, west, or west southwest.

Animal sacrifices were always placed in tombs close to pottery vessels or at the feet of the dead. Most of the time, only one animal sacrifice was placed in the tomb, and less often, two, three, and more rarely four to seven were found. Animal offerings usually included four bones: ribs, scapula, tibia, and humerus. The quantity of animal offerings deposited in the tomb depended on the age, gender, and status of the deceased. In individual tombs of infants or subadults, one animal offering was usual; it is rare to find two animal offerings. In adult individual burials, one animal offering is usually found, but two animal offerings were more frequent than in infant and subadult burials, and they were associated more with male than female burials. In multiple burials, the quantity of animal offerings deposited was, in general, equal to the number of deceased interred. Sheep bones make up the majority of offerings in most Karasuk tombs whether those of infants, subadults, males, or females. Cattle bones are less often included, and horse bones are found even more rarely. Cattle offerings were found in the majority of male tombs, many fewer in female tombs, and rarely in subadult tombs. Unfortunately, horse bones have been found in too small a quantity to make such observations.

POTTERY

Vessels are globular or lentil shaped and of various sizes, seldom carinated, and in most cases have a rounded base. Pottery vessels are undecorated or decorated with motifs only applied to the upper part of the vessel such as double or triple parallel lines, and "dimples" (Novgorodova 1970, 33). The quality of the pottery (well made or not, decorated or undecorated) does not seem to be an indicator of social status, as simple undecorated vases have been found in tombs with high social status markers, and well-shaped deco-rated vases have been found in "common" tombs.

One pottery vessel is generally placed near the head (more rarely two to five pottery vessels are found in the same tomb) of the deceased. We can as-sume that the number of pottery vessels placed in tombs:

- depends on age (the occurrence of more than one pottery vessel in an individual tomb is more connected with adult than with child burials);
- depends on social status of the buried (three, or four to seven pottery vessels are found in approximately the same proportion in individual male, female, and child burials; ones with such numbers of pottery ves-sels are associated with distinctive signs reflecting high social position: very large funerary units, very long tombs, several animal offerings);
- depends less on the number of bodies placed in tombs. Indeed, the number of pottery vessels placed in a tomb with multiple burials is not always equal to the number of bodies placed inside. Likewise, some multiple burials contain only one pottery vessel.

BONE COMBS AND BRONZE ELEMENTS OF HAIRDRESSING

Bone combs and bronze elements of hairdressing (figure 8.4) have been found only in female and child burials (see table 8.4). The seven bone combs found were placed, in all cases, under the skull of the deceased, suggesting that combs were used to fix or to decorate the hair.

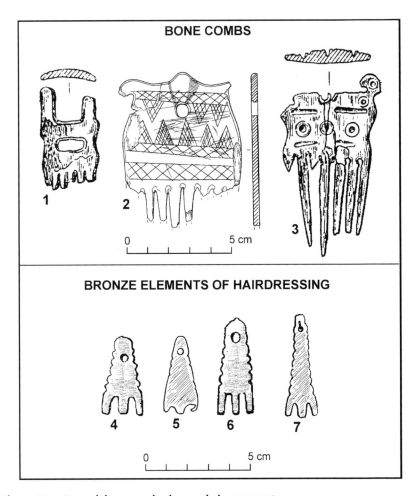

Figure 8.4. Karasuk bone combs; bronze hair ornaments.
Key: 1. Malye Kopjony III cemetery (Zjablin 1977), tomb 40; **2.** Ijuskij cemetery (Bokovenko and Smirnov 1998), tomb 7; **3.** Malye Kopjony III cemetery, tomb 1; **4, 6.** Malye Kopjony III cemetery, enclosure 124, tomb 2; **5.** Tjort Aba cemetery (Pavlov 1999), tomb 12; **7.** Krivinskoe cemetery (Kiselev 1929), tomb 15.

Table 8.4. Distribution of combs and pendants by male, female, and child burials

	Comb	Pendant
Child (510 tombs)	2	19
Female (208 tombs)	5	17
Male (186 tombs)	0	0
Max. quantity found in one tomb	1	10

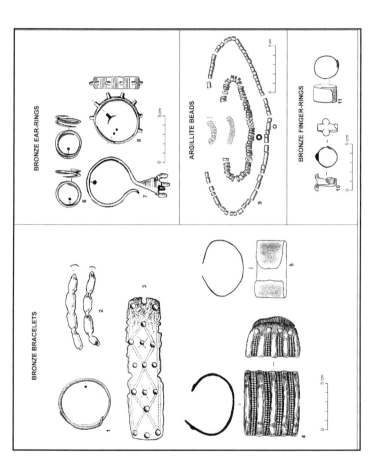

Figure 8.5.   Karasuk jewelry.

Key: 1. Malye Kopjony III (Zjablin 1977), tomb 122; **2.** Bystraja II, enclosure 2, tomb 13; **3.** Malye Kopjony III, tomb 129; **4.** Kuten Buluk; **5.** Tjort Aba (Pavlov 1999), tomb 22; **6.** Arban I (Lazaretov 1995; 2000), tomb 37; **7.** Malye Kopjony III, tomb 48; **8.** Chazy (Pauls 2000), tomb 1; **9.** Sukhoe Ozero II, enclosure 263, tomb 2; **10.** Tjort Aba, tomb 46; **11.** Anchil Chon (Bokovenko and Legrand 2000), kurgan 1, tomb 1.

Table 8.5. Distribution of jewelry by male, female, and child burials

	Circular Wire Earring Fig. 8.5: 6	Cone-shaped Earring Pendant Fig. 8.5: 7	Circular Earring with Heptacylinder Ornaments Fig. 8.5: 8	Chain Bracelet Fig. 8.5: 2	Circular Wire Bracelet Fig. 8.5: 1	Wide Decorated Bracelet Fig. 8.5: 4	Bilobed Finger Ring Fig. 8.5: 10	Wide Finger Ring Fig. 8.5: 11	Bronze Cylindrical Tube Fig. 8.8	Argillite Cylindrical Bead Fig. 8.5: 9	Argillite Circular Bead Fig. 8.5: 9
Child (510 tombs)	144	0	0	1	2	3	2	2	76	24	6
Female (208 tombs)	71	1	3	0	3	6	10	1	50	23	4
Male (186 tombs)	40	0	0	0	1	0	3	0	39	3	0
Max. quantity found in one tomb	10	4	2	1	1	2	4	1	30	25	43

Bronze hair ornaments are flat triangular pendants that end in three "fingers" and are always found near the skull and the neck of the deceased. Ten is the maximum number found in a single tomb. They were used as decorative elements on plaits (Kiselev 1929, 51). The female burial assemblages of intact tombs show that these bronze triangular pendants were not placed in every female burial (see as example figure 8.8).

JEWELRY

Single or double earrings made of bronze wire (figure 8.5: 6) are the most common jewelry found in Karasuk tombs. They are associated with female, male, and child burials. Ten is the maximum quantity found in one tomb (table 8.5). One, two, four, five earrings on each side of the skull were found in unlooted tombs (as examples, see figures 8.8, 8.9, 8.10). The burial assemblages of all the intact tombs revealed that adult burials always contained at least one bronze wire earring, except two female burials where other types of bronze earrings were found instead, and that such jewelry is often absent in burials of infants (1 to 4 years old).

Cone-shaped earring pendants (figure 8.5: 7) and circular earrings with heptacylinder ornaments (figures 8.5: 8, 8.8) have been found only in female tombs (table 8.5). However, the number of burials is not sufficient to say if such earrings are exclusively female jewelry.

Three types of bronze bracelets have been found in Karasuk tombs: chain bracelets (figure 8.5: 2), bracelets of bronze wire (figure 8.5: 1), and wide decorated bracelets (figures 8.5: 4, 8.8). Bracelets of bronze wire and wide decorated ones seem to be more associated with female burials (table 8.5), but again, the number of bracelets recovered is not representative enough to see this as a pattern.

Like bracelets, bronze finger rings, both bilobed (figure 8.5: 10) and wide ones (figure 8.5: 11), have been found in a few burials (table 8.5), mostly those of females and children. Only three bilobed finger rings have been found in male burials.

Bronze cylindrical tubes (one to two centimeters in length and one half centimeter in diameter) are quite widespread and found in roughly the same quantity in female, male, and child burials (table 8.5). Thirty is the largest number found in one tomb. Bronze cylindrical tubes were used in different ways: as elements of hairdressing; as earring pendants in male, female, and child burials (as an example, see figure 8.8: burial of Kolkhoz. Im. M.I. Kalinina cemetery); or as elements of finery that were sewn on the shirt front of clothing of women and children (see figure 8.8: burial 1 of the Karasuk I cemetery, funerary cluster 28).

Argillite cylindrical beads were mostly found in female and child burials (figure 8.5: 9, table 8.5). The maximum number of beads found in one tomb is 250. They were used as elements of finery that were sewn on the shirt front of women's or children's clothes, sometimes along with bronze cylindrical tubes (see figure 8.8: burial of the Karasuk I cemetery, funerary cluster 28) or imitations of cowry shells (see figure 8.10: burial 4 of the Karasuk I cemetery, funerary cluster 48, enclosure 4), or as parts of necklaces (see figure 8.8: burial 4 of the Karasuk I cemetery, funerary unit 25). Argillite circular beads were less frequently found and only in female and child burials as elements of necklaces (table 8.5).

BRONZE CLOTHING ORNAMENTS
AND ARGILLITE IMITATIONS OF COWRY SHELLS

Three types of ornamental bronze plaques of various shapes have been excavated from female, male, and child burials.

The first type consists of bronze oval, circular, and triangular plaques made from thin hammered bronze leaf, perforated in several places to allow them to be stitched onto clothing (figure 8.6: 1–2, 10). Oval ones have been found in female, male, and child burials and are usually placed near the chest of the deceased (figure 8.10: burial from Sabinka II cemetery, funerary cluster 75, tomb 1). Circular and triangular ones have been found in very small numbers (table 8.6), always near the chest of the deceased. We can assume that this first type of plaque was used to decorate the shirt front and that the maximal

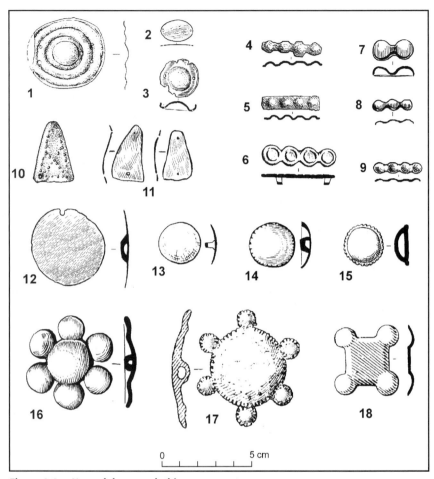

Figure 8.6.   Karasuk bronze clothing ornaments.
Key: 1. Khara Khaja (Kyslasov 1971), tomb 6; **2.** Tjort Aba (Pavlov 1999), tomb 2;
3. Kazanovka II (Bokovenko 1997), enclosure 4, tomb 1; **4, 5.** Sukhoe Ozero II;
6. Chazy (Pauls 2000), tomb 1; **7.** Arban I (Lazaretov 1995; 2000), tomb 44; **8.** Arban I, tomb 46; **9.** Tjort Aba, tomb 26; **10.** Kuten Buluk, enclosure 11, tomb 1;
11. Arban I, tomb 37; **12.** Tjort Aba, tomb 22; **13.** Chazy, tomb 1; **14.** Kazanovka II, enclosure 4, tomb 7; **15.** Anchil Chon (Bokovenko and Legrand 2000) k. 7, tomb 5; **16.** Arban I, tomb 37; **17.** Malye Kopjony III (Zjablin 1977), tomb 129; **18.** Tjort Aba, tomb 55.

quantity of triangular and oval plaques (twelve and five) in one tomb allowed them to be used to form ornamental compositions.

The second type includes cast bronze plaques with no hole and no buckle: bilobed, trilobed, tetralobed (figure 8.6: 7, 8, 4, 9) or square ones (figure 8.6: 18). They were also used as ornaments when sewn on clothing. All of those have rounded parts, probably to allow them to be fixed onto cloth.

Table 8.6.   Distribution of clothing ornaments by male, female, and child burials

	Oval Plaque	Circular Plaque	Triangular Plaque	Bilobed Plaque	Trilobed Plaque	Tetralobed Plaque	Tetracircles Plaque
	Fig. 8.6: 2	Fig. 8.6: 3	Fig. 8.6: 10	Fig. 8.6: 7	Fig. 8.6: 8	Fig. 8.6: 4, 9	Fig. 8.6: 6
Child (510 tombs)	12	1	0	25	3	1	0
Female (208 tombs)	12	1	2	9	10	4	2
Male (186 tombs)	7	0	0	1	1	0	0
Max. quantity found in one tomb	5	1	12	15	15	2	1

	Large Bilobed Plaque	Button	Button Mirror	Rosette-Shaped Plaque	Square Plaque	Nail-Shaped Button	Imitation of Cowry Shell
		Fig. 8.6: 13, 15	Fig. 8.6: 12	Fig. 8.6: 16	Fig. 8.6: 18		
Child (510 tombs)	3	37	4	1	1	16	2
Female (208 tombs)	2	19	11	2	0	23	5
Male (186 tombs)	2	15	0	1	1	4	0
Max. quantity found in one tomb	7	4	1	2	1	22	30

Bilobed, trilobed, and tetralobed plaques have been found most frequently in female burials, less so in child burials, and rarely in male burials (table 8.6). They were found on the chest (figure 8.8: burial 1 from Kolkhoz. Im. M.I. Kalinina cemetery) or on the waist of the deceased in burial, suggesting that such plaques might also have been used as belt ornaments. The number of square plaques found in burials is not significant enough to make such observations.

The third type includes cast bronze plaques with a buckle on the back side: rosette-shaped plaques, button-shaped plaques, button "mirrors," and nail-shaped buttons (figure 8.6: 12–14, 16–17; table 8.6). Rosette-shaped plaques with six petals have been found in a few female, male, and child burials, but never in situ. Button-shaped plaques were also associated with male, female, and child tombs. Those of one to two centimeters in diameter were found in various places inside burials: near the waist, near the feet, and almost behind the skull of the deceased, and were probably used as buttons and also as bronze elements of hairdressing. Button-shaped plaques of four to five centimeters were found on the chest of the deceased and were used as ornamental additions to the necklace (figure 8.9: double burial 1 of Podkuninskie Gory) and could also have been sewn on shirt fronts. Nail-shaped button plaques were most often associated with female and child burials and sometimes were even found in large quantities (a maximum of twenty-two examples in the same tomb). Button "mirrors" are bronze, flat, circular plaques with a reflecting surface of around ten centimeters in diameter. They have been only found in female and child burials and were always placed on the chest of the deceased and used probably as a mirror (Grjaznov 1969, 98; Vadetskaja 1986, 60).

Imitations of cowry shells made of argillite have been found in few tombs, always near the upper part of the chest of the deceased. They were used as elements of finery (thirty examples were found in the same tomb; figure 8.10: burial 4 of the Karasuk I cemetery, enclosure 4), sewn on the collar or on the shirt front of clothing. They were found only in burials of females and children with high social status.

BRONZE KNIVES AND ARGILLITE TOOLS

Bronze knives with slightly arched shape were found in male, female, and child burials (figure 8.7: 1–4, 6; table 8.7). Their morphological character seems to be related to different functions (Legrand 2004, 145). Their funerary context gives some indication of their possible function:

- *Ritual*: when the knife is placed near faunal remains in the tomb. Usually undecorated knifes with ring or lobed pommels were recovered from male and female burials, or more rarely in child burials, where knives with a bronze blade were fitted perpendicularly into a wooden handle.
- *Social*: when the knife is recovered at the body waist (or perhaps on its belt) or near the leg (figure 8.9: double burial 1 from the Podkuninskie Gory cemetery). Longer knives with zoocephalic or ring pommels were richly decorated by comparison to the simple ritual knives mentioned above, and were only found in male burials. These knives must certainly have indicated the prestigious and hierarchical rank of its owner.

Because of the mass looting of burials, the massive bow-shaped bronze artifacts (figure 8.9: 10) were found in very few tombs, and then only in male burials (see table 8.7; figure 8.9: double burial 1 from the Podkuninskie Gory

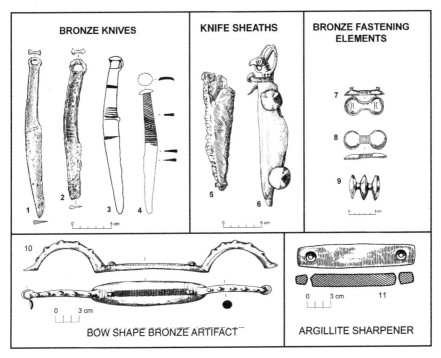

Figure 8.7   Karasuk bronze, leather, and argillite artifacts.
Key: 1. Khara Khaja (Kyslasov 1971), tomb 3.3; **2.** Tjort Aba (Pavlov 1999), tomb 18a;
3. Bejskaja Shakhta, tomb 1; **4.** Bejskaja Shakhta, tomb 2; **5.** Malye Kopjony III (Zjablin 1977), tomb 120; **6.** Podkuninskie Gory (Kotozhekov 2000), tomb 1; **7, 8.** Bejskaja Shakhta, tomb 1, tomb 2; **9.** Podkuninskie Gory, tomb 1; **10.** Podkuninskie Gory, tomb 1; **11.** Kjurgenner I, funerary cluster 71, enclosure 2, tomb 1.

Table 8.7.   Distribution of bronze knives and bronze and argillite tools by male, female, and child burials

	Knife	Bow-Shaped Bronze Artifact	Argillite Sharpener	Socketed Ax (celt)	Awl
	Fig. 8.7: 1–4, 6	*Fig. 8.7: 10*	*Fig. 8.7: 11*		
Child (510 tombs)	28	0	0	0	18
Female (208 tombs)	20	0	0	0	22
Male (186 tombs)	16	3	2	2	4
Max. quantity found in one tomb	2	1	1	2	8

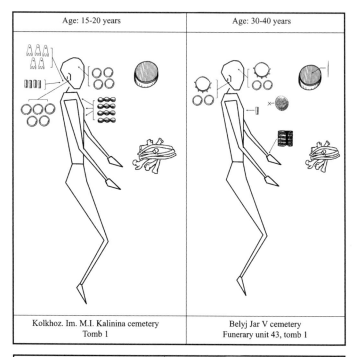

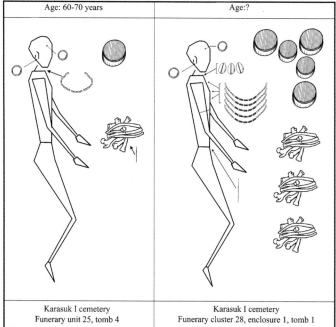

Figure 8.8. Karasuk burial goods in nonlooted female tombs.

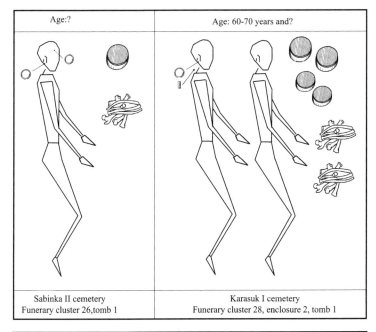

Age:?	Age: 60-70 years and?
Sabinka II cemetery Funerary cluster 26, tomb 1	Karasuk I cemetery Funerary cluster 28, enclosure 2, tomb 1

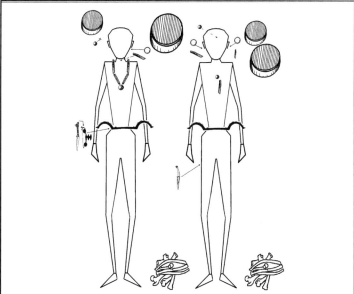

Figure 8.9. Karasuk burial goods in nonlooted male tombs.

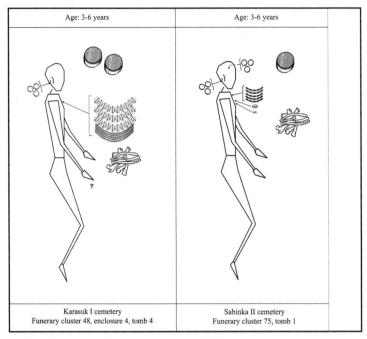

Age: 3-6 years	Age: 3-6 years
Karasuk I cemetery Funerary cluster 48, enclosure 4, tomb 4	Sabinka II cemetery Funerary cluster 75, tomb 1

Figure 8.10.   Karasuk burial goods in looted child burials.

cemetery). They were always placed on the waist of the body. Some archaeologists suppose that this artifact was of use to chariot drivers.[8]

Also because of mass looting, bronze-socketed axes (celts) were found only in two tombs, both male burials. According to the tomb arrangements, such artifacts seem to be associated with men of prestigious rank.

Argillite sharpeners were only found in two male burials (table 8.7; figure 8.7: 11) where they were placed on the body at the waist of the deceased.

Bronze awls were recovered mostly from female, less often in child, and rarely in male burials. As with the knives, their funeral context reflects different functions:

- *Ritual*: The awl is placed near the animal sacrifice (in male and female and child burials; see figure 8.8: burial 4 from Karasuk I cemetery, funerary unit 25) or inside the pottery vessel (only in female burials; see figure 8.8: burial 1 from Belyj Jar V cemetery, funerary unit 43).
- *Social*: The awl is recovered at the waist of the body (only in female burials; see figure 8.8: burial 1 from Karasuk I cemetery, funerary unit 28). Awls found in this context are always associated with burials of a highly ranked individual.

FEMALE, MALE, AND CHILD GRAVE GOODS FROM UNLOOTED TOMBS

The occurrence of a substantial number of unlooted tombs (fifty-one in total) gives us the opportunity to complete our analysis of grave goods of male, female, and child burials and allows us to make some additional observations.

Adult grave goods do not reflect differences according to age. For example, burials of 60-to-69-year-old individuals do not contain more or different artifacts than burials of younger deceased of the same social rank (see figure 8.8).

However, as noted above, some artifacts are gender and social rank markers.

Taken as a whole, female burials contain more jewelry and bronze ornaments for clothing than those of males. Awls (when placed at the waist), imitations of cowry shells, and fineries, including multiple beads and bronze cylindrical tubes, indicate the high social status of the deceased.

Taken as a whole, male burials contain little jewelry and few bronze ornaments for clothing (as examples, see figure 8.9: burial 1 from Sabinka II cemetery, funerary cluster 26; burial 1 from Karasuk I cemetery, funerary cluster 28, enclosure 2). Bronze knives (when placed at the waist), celts, and probably bow-shaped bronze artifacts are associated only with male burials and reflect the high social status of the deceased.

CONCLUSION

The arrangements of burials in cemeteries show that kinship is the base of the Karasuk societal organization. Funerary enclosure clusters built up next to one another formed small family cemeteries. More evidence for this type of organization is provided by the patterns of distribution inside the necropolis: Adults were placed in central funerary units while subadults were placed in funerary units to their immediate periphery and infants to the external periphery. As the analysis of grave goods shows, the place of each member is clearly defined inside the family group according to age and gender, showing that lineage determined status.

The differences observed in distribution of burials by sex inside clustered funerary units, in size of funerary units, in length of tombs, and in quantity of animal offerings deposited in tombs give evidence for hierarchical social order based on a patriarchal system.

Central funerary units from 43 to 112 square meters in area containing cist tombs with a length from 201 to 290 meters with grave goods consisting of several ceramic vessels, several animal offerings, bronze knives, and so on were those of elites and were male burials. In one unusual case—in funerary cluster 28 of the Karasuk I cemetery composed of two enclosures—a female tomb of 220 meters in length was located in the central forty-five-meter enclosure, while two men were buried in a smaller enclosure connected to it. In the female burial were found: five ceramic vessels; three animal offerings; fineries of argillite beads, bronze tubes, imitations of cowry shell; one awl near the waist; and two bronze wire earrings (figure 8.8). The double male burial associated with it contained only four ceramic vessels, two animal offerings, one bronze wire earring, and one bronze tube (placed near the first deceased) (figure 8.9: burial 1 from the Karasuk cemetery, funerary cluster 28, enclosure 2). Only in this case[9] can we suppose that the high social status of this woman is individual, probably achieved, as she did not come from a high-status family and as the double-male burial connected to her central enclosure was a "common" burial, suggesting that the two men belonged to an inferior social rank.

In other cases, female and child burials where a substantial quantity of jewelry and fineries were found, were always located inside enclosures built up next to a large central enclosure (figure 8.8: burials from Kolkhoz. Im. M.I. Kalinina and Belyj Jar V cemeteries; figure 8.10: burial 4 from Karasuk I cemetery, funerary cluster 48, enclosure 4), containing the burial of a male of high social rank. In these cases, we can assume that the women and children "assumed" the social rank of the man with whom they were associated in burial and that their status was ascribed.

NOTES

1. Around 80 percent of the excavations of Karasuk sites were completed between the 1940s and 1970s.

2. The veracity of the results obtained from the general analyses presented in this chapter has been confirmed by comparison with intrasite analyses.

3. Except for the cemeteries of Tjort Aba and Sabinka II, where the isolated enclosures prevail.

4. Central unit means the largest (in surface area) enclosure of the clustered units.

5. In funerary unit 28 of the Karasuk I cemetery, a female is buried in the central enclosure, while two males are buried in a connected enclosure. This is a very rare occurrence that reflects the prestigious rank of the woman buried there.

6. It has been confirmed by a statistical correlation test between the length of tombs and the length of skeletons.

7. Multiple burials of three to seven deceased are rare.

8. The chariot drivers presumably attached the horses' reins to this artifact fixed on the belt in order to keep their hands free (Leont'ev 1980, 82).

9. Although only one case has been identified, it doesn't mean that this situation is unique.

Chapter Nine

The Gender of Luxury and Power among the Xiongnu in Eastern Eurasia

Katheryn M. Linduff

For decades, objects such as the gold belt plaque in figure 9.1, from tomb 2 at a site called Xigoupan, located under the great bend of the Yellow River in a region of central Inner Mongolia called the Ordos, have been taken as diagnostic of the pastoral group known in Chinese historical texts as the Xiongnu (Tian and Guo 1986). In addition, they have been seen as male signifiers as well as indicators of interaction between the Chinese and their northern neighbors. Moreover, because of their lavishness and their association with weapons in burial, they have been assumed to indicate social inequality of privileged men and to underscore male political leadership. But in tomb 4 at the same site, the occurrence of gold and semiprecious stone headgear and necklaces plus gold and carved jade earrings has led to its assessment as a tomb of an elite female leader (figure 9.2). Based on the evidence from the Xigoupan cemetery, where all other tombs (a total of twelve) were modestly outfitted by comparison, it was also proposed that the same social hierarchy and gendered artifacts probably characterized all Xiongnu societies (Tian and Guo 1986).

Although this may properly describe the group buried at Xigoupan, these suppositions can be questioned when examined in light of other sites in the region[1] (figure 9.3).

There are nine sites identified as Xiongnu because of their frontier locations and the steppic contents of their tombs. The cemeteries date from the last three centuries of the 1st millennium BCE and the first two CE. They are located within the borders of present-day China, and all are cemeteries, as no habitation sites are yet located. Information from all of these cemeteries is catalogued in tables 9.1a and 9.1b (see end of the chapter).

Burial patterns revealed there have called attention to a shared lifestyle while also situating local customs.[2] In one cemetery, at Daodunzi, Tongxin

175

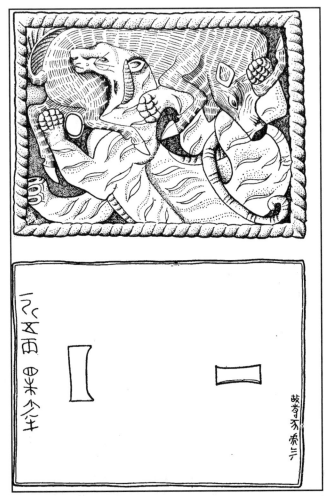

Figure 9.1. Plaque gold, Xigoupan, M2: (top) one of two mirror-image plaques with textile pattern on reverse; (bottom) reverse drawing of plaque with Chinese characters (tomb of male).

County, Hui Ningxia Autonomous Region (NXWWKGYJS 1988a,b, 333–356), the bones of the deceased were systematically sexed and therefore allow a more secure analysis of gender, age, and in this case probably local and/or regional identity, because we can see that the mature females were buried in a special local type of tomb, and the males were all buried in a different type. Cultural uniformity among the Xiongnu has been assumed from the way Chinese texts essentialized their mobile way of life, and because the Xiongnu did not write accounts of themselves. The identification and analysis

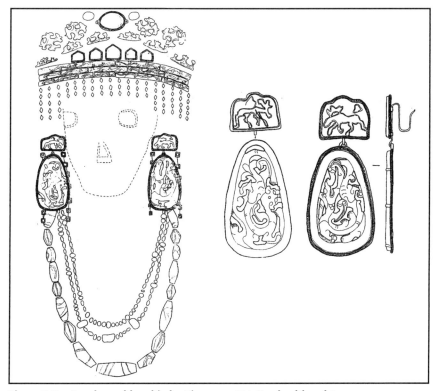

Figure 9.2.   Jewelry, gold and jade, Xigoupan, M4 (tomb of female).

of these excavated cemeteries, therefore, has taken on a very important role in understanding their presence in the region in the late 1st millennium BCE. Just how consistent the Xiongnu lifeways really were across the whole area said to be occupied by them is a question addressed here through study of patterns revealed in display of funerary remains at Daodunzi. (The Xiongnu tomb contents are catalogued in table 9.2, found at the end of the chapter.) My understanding of the patterns is informed as well by noting like habits among living pastoral peoples.

THE EVIDENCE IN CHINA

The Xiongnu were first mentioned in Chinese written records for the year 318 BCE, when they joined with three Chinese states to attack the growing state of Qin. About a century later, in 221 BCE, the Qin unified China and drove the Xiongnu beyond the Yellow River and built the Great Wall to keep them out of Chinese territory, at least symbolically. When the Qin Empire

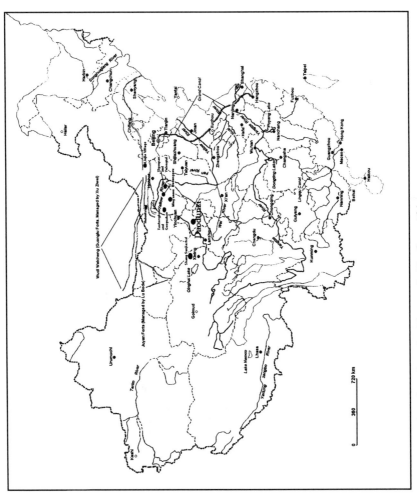

Figure 9.3. Sites thought to be Xiongnu in Northern China.

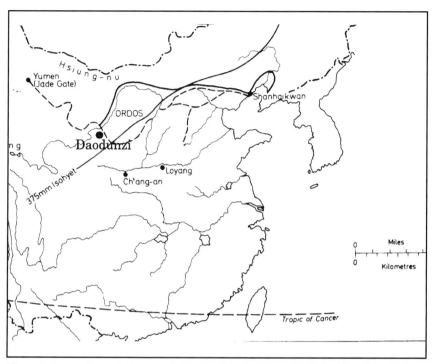

Figure 9.4. Territory of Xiongnu. Solid line delimits Qin wall; dashed line delimits later wall.

crumbled in 209 BCE, the Xiongnu again moved south across the Yellow River to occupy the Ordos region.

Xiongnu is the Chinese name given to the peoples who were led by Maodun (d. 174 BCE), their supratribal leader, or *shanyu*, who had formed an empire on the north Asian steppe.

In 209 BCE Maodun was said to have created a confederacy that gave the Xiongnu control of Inner Asia from present-day Xinjiang to western Manchuria. For many centuries control of the Ordos was thought to have been vital to the stability of the Chinese Empire (Chaliand 2004, 22–23), and for more than seventy years the Han leadership, who succeeded the Qin in 209 BCE, tried to buy off the Xiongnu. These gifts and border trade reduced but did not end the Xiongnu incursions into territory that the Chinese considered their own. Around 130 BCE the Chinese began a more aggressive policy; huge armies were sent against the Xiongnu, sundering their federation, so that in 51 BCE, Huhanxie, one of the several competing shanyu, turned to the Han for assistance. The Chinese recognized him as the legitimate shanyu, and he and his followers temporarily moved within the Chinese pale. The golden age of the Xiongnu had ended (Loewe 1977).

Over the next century, Han-Xiongnu relations varied from amicable to antagonistic. Then in 148 CE the Southern Xiongnu, their population and livestock depleted by calamities, surrendered. Many of them settled in north China and turned to Chinese-style agriculture. Early in the 4th century, descendants of the Southern Xiongnu founded three ephemeral states in north China. The Northern Xiongnu, under pressure from Han and other armies, migrated westward, disappearing from Chinese records after the 2nd century CE. Thus, according to the Chinese records, the Xiongnu lived on the eastern Eurasian steppe at the frontiers of the Chinese Han Empire, between the 3rd century BCE and the 2nd and 3rd centuries CE.

Most of what is known and written about the sociopolitical history of the Xiongnu comes from Chinese written accounts such as that of Sima Qian (1959, 110, 9b–1b) that ideally placed them as indigenous/local tribal leaders at the lowest level by comparison to rankings of Chinese leadership. But since these local leaders were political actors in their own right, they could literally walk away at will. Xiongnu leaders counteracted this low position on the Chinese hierarchy presumably by developing a secure economic base to finance their nomadic state with resources from outside the steppe. From the Chinese *heqin* (exchange) policy they extracted annual payments of silk, wine, grain, and other foodstuffs, and at least one Han princess was given in marriage to a shanyu. When they were a threat, such as in the mid-Han (2nd c. BCE), the Chinese gave the Xiongnu ranks equal to those of their own (Sima Qian 1959, 110, 12b–13a, 18b–19a), allowing the Xiongnu leadership some symbolic equality. Little else is known about the structure of Xiongnu societies.

Many studies in the past have seen the main value of the Han subsidies as a source of luxury goods that the shanyu gave to local leaders (Barfield 1989; Di Cosmo 2002), perhaps such as the persons buried in tombs 2 and 4

Table 9.3. Chronology

BCE 771–220	Eastern Zhou dynasty (Warring-States period 481–220)
318	First mention of the Xiongnu in Chinese texts
221	Qin unifies China into an empire.
209	Qin Empire falls. Xiongnu cross the Yellow River into the Ordos region under the Great Bend. Maodun creates a Xiongnu Confereracy in Inner Asia in the beifang. Han dynasty is founded.
130	Chinese begin a more aggressive foreign affairs policy and send armies against the Xiongnu.
51	Xiongnu shanyu comes under Chinese rule.
CE 148	Southern Xiongnu surrender to the Han.
c. 300	Three states are founded by the Xiongnu by the Southern group. Northern Xiongnu migrate westward out of Chinese purview.

at Xigoupan (figures 9.1, 9.2), in order to extract their fidelity to the Xiongnu nation (Di Cosmo 2002). This description gives only the barest outline of the structure of Xiongnu political hierarchy and activities, and nothing about social organization of the member groups of the confederacy. Moreover, the Chinese written records of official dealings involve men, and practically nothing is documented about the women, yet, as is the case in tomb 4 at Xigoupan, some of their burials are lavishly embellished. My review of available archaeological evidence attributed to the Xiongnu during the period of their initial residence in and adjacent to the Ordos (5th and 4th through the 1st c. BCE), however, has yielded some very interesting preliminary results about the position and background of both men and women, especially in the lower Ordos at the site of Daodunzi.

GENERAL OBSERVATIONS[3]

Archaeological Evidence on the Xiongnu from within the Borders of Present-Day China

The nine cemeteries surveyed in this study date from between the 5th and 4th centuries BCE (one cemetery) and from the 2nd century BCE to the 2nd and early 3rd centuries CE (Tian and Guo 1986). All but six of the seventy-two tombs in the set are rectangular pit tombs of single individuals with the body in supine position and the head pointed toward the northeast (table 9.2; figure 9.5). The one exception to this rule is a group of six catacomb tombs excavated at Daodunzi discussed below (table 9.3).

Size of the tombs in the entire group, including the catacomb tombs, is ranked according to age, with all the oldest of both sexes in the largest tombs. In seven of the nine Xiongnu cemeteries, animal sacrifices were found: horse/bovine/sheep heads and hooves at Taohongbala (c. 350–250 BCE) and Budonggou (c. 100 BCE–100 CE); horses and sheep at Xigoupan (c. 400 BCE–150 BCE: M01, M02, M03, M06) and at Liujia (c. 1–100 CE); bovine and sheep head and hoof combinations at Daodunzi (c. 125–25 BCE); horse skulls or horse, bovine, and sheep combinations at Hulusitai (c. 400–200 BCE: M2) and Ming'anmu (c. 500–400 BCE); and horse/dog combinations at Xigoupan (M09) (table 9.2). Very distinctive combinations (horses, bovine/sheep [2]; horse/sheep [2]; bovine/sheep [1]; horse [2]; sheep and dog [1]) mark the sites, probably reflecting the animals they herded (Barfield 1993). In each of the other two sites, there is only one tomb reported and neither includes animal sacrifice, although each tomb is a rectangular pit with the head pointing northeast, following the shape found in the other seven sites (table 9.2). None of the cemeteries except Daodunzi includes adequate numbers

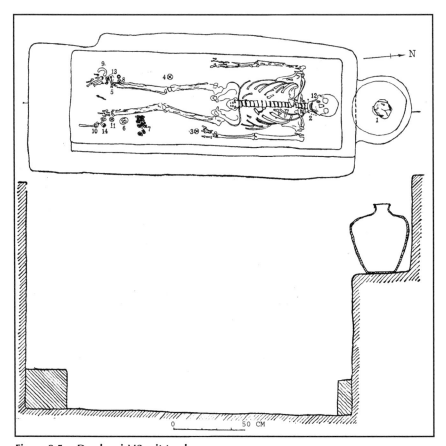

Figure 9.5.   Daodunzi M2, pit tomb.

of excavated tombs to make the data representative of whole populations. For example, the largest set of tombs other than at Daodunzi is at Xigoupan, where there are twelve excavated and reported tombs available for study. Therefore, only the most general statements can be made about each of those cemeteries.

The peoples who commissioned the tombs at these nine sites lived within range of regular trade and communication with their Chinese neighbors (figure 9.3). Their burials are overwhelmingly regular in shape and orientation and are clustered by type of animal sacrifice. It is worth noting at this point that most of these customs do not characterize elite Han Chinese tombs, where for instance the dead were placed in rectangular pit tombs, but with the head pointing to the north and where rank was expressed not according to age, but political position and gender. A closer look at the data from Daodunzi sheds light on many other ways their lifestyle differed from the Chinese.

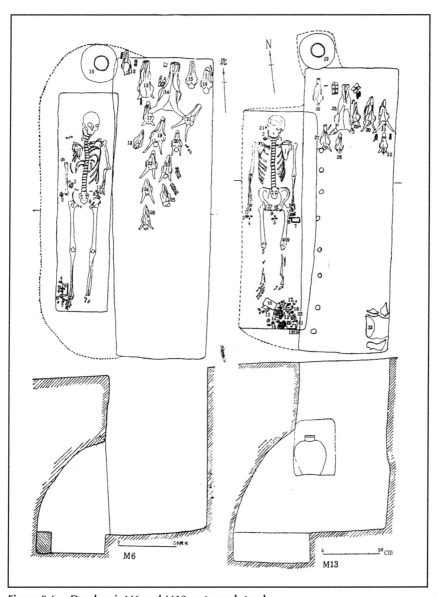

Figure 9.6.   Daodunzi, M6 and M13, catacomb tomb.

Daodunzi, Tongxin County, Ningxia Hui Autonomous Region

The undisturbed cemetery at Daodunzi was excavated in 1985 and reported in 1988 (NXWWKGYZS 1988a,b). The ground plan is shown in figure 9.7; see table 9.4 at the end of the chapter for a summary of the Daodunzi tomb contents. Judging from the *wuzhu* coins[4] found in the tombs, we can date the cemetery from between the mid to late period of the Western Han dynasty, or from 118 BCE through the 1st century BCE, or about fifty years after Maodun established the Xiongnu nation (209–174 BCE). During the latter half of the Western Han period, or by about 75 BCE, the Chinese government established offices to deal with the Xiongnu in the region, and Tongxin County, where Daodunzi is located, was within one of those offices (Linduff 1997, 82). The cemetery dates from just before and during the period when the Han established a military commandery in the region and therefore were struggling for control of the region politically as well.

Twenty of the twenty-seven tombs excavated there are rectangular vertical pits with burial niches at the head of the deceased, six are catacomb tombs with the deceased placed in a chamber to the side of an animal sacrificial pit, and one is a stone pebble-frame pit tomb of an infant (M22). Seven are tombs of adult males (15/35–50 years old), nine are burials of adult females (15/23–50 years old), three are subadults (7–10 years old), five are infants, and age was indeterminable for two (table 9.2). Almost all tombs of adults regardless of type have a small niche in the northern wall containing a large ceramic jar. All have coffins made of wood. All were individuals buried in a supine position, with head pointing to the northeast except one infant (M12), who was buried in a catacomb tomb with its head placed toward the southwest. All are single burials. In all six catacomb tombs were deposited unequal numbers of bovine and sheep skulls and hooves (tables 9.2 and 9.3). Although many tombs in the other cemeteries—at Budonggou, Hulusitai, Liujia, Taohongbala, and Xigoupan—contained animal sacrifice, no other tombs at Daodunzi included animal remains except the catacomb-shaped ones.

In the cemetery there appear to be five clusters running from north to south that are determined by pairs of adults of 40 to 55 years of age (see figure 9.8). Four groupings include one female and one male, and in two of those the females are buried in catacomb tombs. Another group (II) includes two females and a teenage male (17–18 years old) buried in a catacomb tomb. The adult females buried in catacomb tombs are not buried in the same group.

The funerary objects unearthed from these tombs included pottery and bronze, iron, gold, stone, and bone objects. The thirteen excavated clay vessels are all wheel-made, decorated with bowstring, wavy-line, and cord pat-

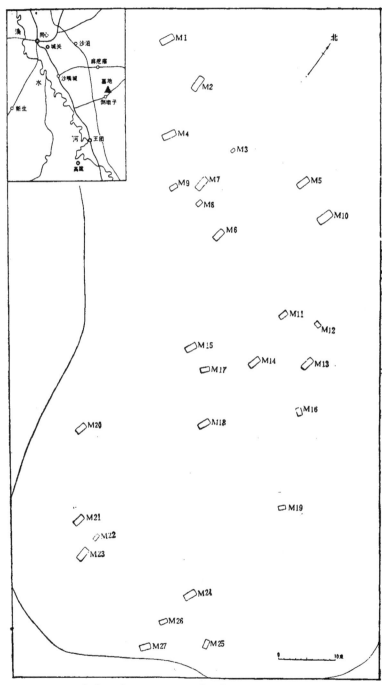

Figure 9.7.   Ground plan of cemetery, Daodunzi.

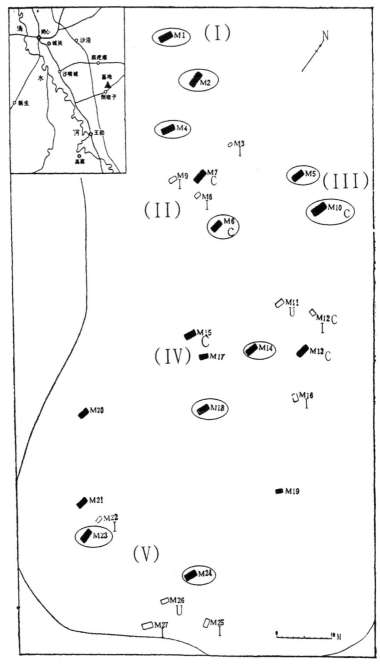

Figure 9.8. Ground plan of Daodunzi, male versus female tombs. Circled tombs are female burials.

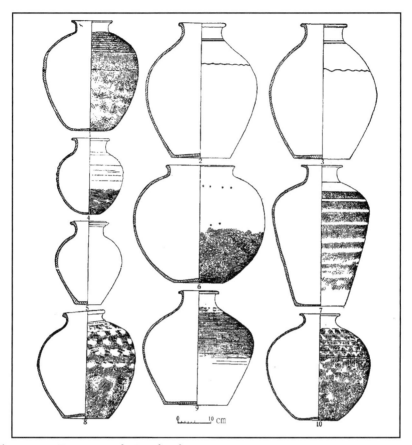

Figure 9.9.   Pottery vessels, Daodunzi.

terns, and were mostly made of black clay (figure 9.9). All were found in the
niche above the head of deceased adults in both catacomb (three vessels) and
pit tombs (ten vessels) (C10F; 07M; 06F; and P02M; 14F; 05M; 04F; 18M;
01M; 20F; 23F; 26U; 19M).

Twenty-one bronze-belt plaques (thirteen illustrated in figure 9.10) were
excavated from ten tombs of both types (C = 02F, 1 infant; P = 7: F[4]/M[2])
(CM22 [infant]; 13F; 10 F [2]; and PM14F; 11U; 05M [2]; 04F [2]; 01F [4];
23F; 19M [3]). In tombs where sex could be determined, all but one were
buried with adults: six were in tombs of females, two with males. All but one
(M22 infant) were found in tombs of adults aged between 40 and 55 (13F;
10 [2]F; and PM14F; 11U; 05M [2]; 04F [2]; 01F [4]; 23F; 19M [3]) and are
variously decorated with openwork or relief double dragons, double camels,
double horses, tigers and deer, tortoise and dragons, sword-wearing warriors,
and horse-drawn carriages with human figures in them. These belt plaques

Figure 9.10.   Daodunzi, bronze belt plaques.

appear to mark age regardless of group affiliation. Intriguingly, the single exception to this pattern is a belt plaque buried in M22 with an infant. This suggests that perhaps the child's natal family was special, not only because of the presence of a plaque in the tomb, but also because this is the only stone-faced rectangular tomb pit in the cemetery.

Excavated iron items include twelve knives from twelve tombs of adults (figure 9.11) (CM13F; 10F; 07F; PM 02M; 14F; 11U; 21M; 04F; 18M; 20F; 26U; 19M), an ax, and circular belt and ornamental pieces. In addition, there are beads made from various stones in most of the tombs of females, a bone plaque (CM07M), and gold earrings only in catacomb tombs of adult females (CM10F; 13F). The only weapon found in the entire cemetery is a bronze pommel found in tomb 18, a pit tomb of an adult male (50 years old). Small, ovoid-shaped bronze bells with a clapper cast in bronze have been found throughout the region from earlier sites and were surely functional as well as ornamental and must have been used by herding peoples of the region for several centuries (Linduff 1997, 41).

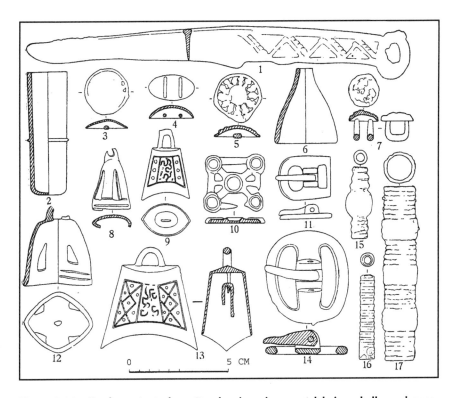

Figure 9.11. Tomb contents from Daodunzi: various metal knives, bells, and ornaments.

The most conspicuous feature, however, of the Daodunzi cemetery is the variety of tomb shapes (figures 9.5, 9.6). Six of the twenty-seven are catacomb tombs (CM06F; 10; 13; 15; 22), the only ones among the seventy-two tombs surveyed from all nine sites thought to be Xiongnu cemeteries (figure 9.3). All of the catacomb tombs included chambers that accommodated hooves and heads of sacrificed bovines and sheep. Four are tombs of adult females (CM06, 13, 10, 15), one of an adolescent male (CM17M), and one of an infant (CM12). Importantly, this catacomb tomb type had been used widely in the region prior to its appearance at Daodunzi (Linduff 1997, 41–42). Burials from sites dating from the 7th to the 3rd century BCE in southern Ningxia and eastern Gansu (figure 9.12) were typically catacomb shaped and included animal sacrifice of heads and hooves of bovines, sheep, and horses (Linduff 1997, 43, 45).

The deceased in the earlier regional tombs, unfortunately, were not sexed but often held bronze or gold belt plaques, short swords of iron or bronze, as well as chariot ornaments and horse gear such as bronze bits, cheek pieces, and crosspieces for bridles suggesting that they were warriors (Linduff 1997, 41, 42). Such finds confirm that domesticated horses were not only available to these peoples, but were also probably highly valued. Horse equipment is

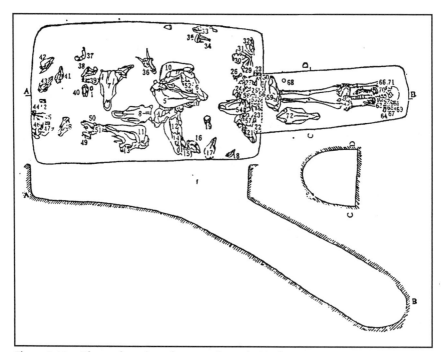

Figure 9.12.   Plan and section of catacomb tomb, Mazhuang.

conspicuously absent from Daodunzi, as were sacrificed horses, suggesting that this group was not military leaders and/or its herding strategies had changed. Nevertheless, other materials such as bells, plaques, and curved knives underscore the long-term dependence on herding as a way of life in the area, as well as the distinctiveness of this burial pattern among communities living in the southern Ordos, to the north and west of the agricultural lands occupied primarily by Han Chinese.

Interestingly at Daodunzi (figure 9.8), four of six of the catacomb tombs were those of females—and their tombs were no less ceremoniously or richly endowed than their male counterparts or the others who lay in the pit tombs. Within this group, animal plaques are found in two female tombs and in one infant tomb (13F; 10 [2]F), as opposed to four in female pit tombs and two in male pit tombs (PM14F; 11U; 05M [2]; 04F [2]; 01F [4]; 23F; 19M [3]). Although cowrie shells were found in almost all tombs at Daodunzi (not in PM03I; PM01F; PM23F; PM25I), the highest numbers in the catacomb tombs were found in female burials (CM13; 10; 15; 07; 06), while the highest numbers found in pit tombs were in those of males (PM18M; PM19M). Is it possible that they were indicators of differentiated wealth within their funerary groups?

DISCUSSION

Because there was a precedent for catacomb tombs in this and no other region in the beifang, I think that we can safely assume that this special burial type indicates some local custom that marks lineage or affiliation. Moreover, four such tombs hold females of various ages, one a male aged 17 or 18, and one an infant, all of whom may be significant individuals of the local lineage or settlement. These six tombs are the only ones in the cemetery that include sacrificed animals (sheep and bovines), presumably ones that they herded, and they probably signify a pastoral lifeway. In addition, the female catacomb tombs are central to at least three burial clusters (figure 9.8: areas II, III, IV). If the presence of clusters around the distinctive "local" females' tombs at Daodunzi can be accepted, then that suggests that the males may have been intrusive. Were they perhaps Xiongnu individuals who returned to this area after the collapse of the Qin, as mentioned in the Chinese historical records? The Daodunzi cemetery is dated at that very time, that is, in the 2nd century BCE and somewhat later. There are no signs of conflict in the archaeological record, which even lacks weapons in the burial remains, to suggest that they dominated the region by force. It appears that these were intercultural families, with both the male and female sides expressed through distinctive burial traditions.

In addition, among the female tombs, those buried in catacomb tombs were also prominent because they included sacrificed animals, as mentioned above. No such display was found in a male tomb of either type (except the tomb of the adolescent in CM07), suggesting that at least at Daodunzi, tomb shape marked one's natal family and animal sacrifice perhaps signified married females or their significant offspring (CM07). Strikingly, almost all mobile pastoral groups (excluding the Tuareg of North Africa) are exclusively patrilineal in kinship organization. In such a case, descent, residence, and inheritance rules pass through the male line, but marriages invariably require bride price, sometimes quite substantial, which transfers wealth from the family of the groom to the bride (Barfield 1993). Is it possible that the catacomb tombs of women at Daodunzi that contained sacrificed bovines and sheep represented, at least symbolically, transferred wealth resulting from bride price?

Differential treatment of males and females based on natal ties has been noted among another, but earlier, pastoral group located about two hundred kilometers to the east of Daodunzi who buried their dead at Maoqinggou in the late 5th–4th century BCE (Wu 2004, 203–236; Shelach, this volume). In that case, for instance, the mortuary goods in women's tombs displayed wealth ascribed through association with their birth families, and grave goods in males' tombs marked accrued wealth. Although social organization of most contemporary pastoral societies is based on segmented lineages and "achieved wealth systems" (Barfield 1991), this was clearly not the case at Maoqinggou (Wu 2004), and perhaps not at Daodunzi. The special treatment of the infant in stone-lined tomb M22 and the presence of a bronze belt buckle in the tomb, make it difficult to argue for achievement as the defining marker of social status and gender at Daodunzi. Rather, males and females are treated differently according to natal associations (females) and perhaps by membership in the larger community of pastoralists (males).

It is not possible without further knowledge of the exact location and the history of its land use to know more precisely about the economic strategies employed over time in the region, but at present it is occupied by agropastoralists, who crop and herd depending on the valley and elevation in which they reside and on their proximity to the river. This location is not one where high-yield agricultural production can be expected, but it is located near good pastureland as well as established trade routes, opened already by the 2nd century CE, to its west. But whatever the explanation, it is noteworthy that the only tombs that received sacrificed animals were those of females, and at least at death females were signified by the item that is often associated with wealth in pastoral, or even agropastoral, societies. In addition, it would seem that residency was determined in this group by the females. Males, on the other hand, were buried with attributes (knives, coins, animal belt plaques) also associated with non-Han pastoral groups, and more particularly with the Xiongnu in type and style (Tian and Guo 1986). Due to the location of this cemetery and suggestions from Chinese historical records that the Xiongnu inhabited it, we can see that the written records generalize about people. We do not know if our group buried at Daodunzi was affiliated with the larger Xiongnu Empire, but only that they themselves were probably formed through a mixing of regional groups. It would seem that our evidence does not support the Chinese view that the Xiongnu were uniform culturally, rather that these were intercultural families.

We know from living nomadic societies that pastoral economic specialization imposed cultural values far beyond job specialization or expertise. And, although the mobile pastoral groups of the Old World have access to a common set of domestic animals, pastoral societies have been divided into distinct zones, each with its own style of animal husbandry and social organization (Barfield 1993, 7). The flat grassland in the region of our nine cemeteries is punctuated or bounded by mountains, the forest and/or deserts, as well as the predominately agricultural regions to the south and east. This eastern Eurasian pastoral, or agropastoral, complex includes today the pasturing of horses, sheep, goats, cattle, and Bactrian camels. A subset of these animals distinguished the cemeteries in this study, and probably defined their region culturally, so that one animal or a specific mix of animals was the key component and central focus of everyone's herd (Barfield 1993, 9). As with East African pastoralists, for instance, exchange of animals may have been required as the glue for all social relationships: marriages, friendships, ceremonies, and conflicts (Barfield 1993, 11). In the case of archaeological evidence of ancient precedent for these parallels, only more sexed burials from ancient tombs in the beifang would show how widespread the use of sacrificial animals was in denoting marriage or other customs of social organization.

Other forms of status or identity are not easily distinguished at Daodunzi. The inclusion of coins and cowry shells, found equally abundant in tombs of adult males and females, shows that both men and women were equally endowed in certain types of grave goods, but not with others (especially sacrificial animals) often associated with status and perhaps power. Both genders were privileged in death by age at Daodunzi where both the large size of tombs and the number and types of burial goods are most conspicuous in tombs of the oldest. By contrast, among Han Chinese communities of the same period, elite women's position in the community relied primarily, if not solely, on the acquired rank of their husbands or fathers, regardless of age. Chinese written records on the Xiongnu say that young men ate the richest food, while the old got what was left over since the tribes honored youth and despised the weak (Sima Qian 1959, 129). The level of nutrition of these pastoralists has not been studied, but the Xiongnu proscription against honoring age reported by the Chinese is contradicted by our evidence at Daodunzi and likewise at the other sites where age was reported.

Because of the patterns of movement inherent in pastoralism, the households are much more autonomous than with sedentary peoples. Organized around (mobile) households rather than individuals, this lifeway involves everyone—men, women, and children—in the various aspects of production. In accordance with this model of economic organization, both the men and women buried at Daodunzi were equally treated at death. And, although we do not know who had political leadership roles at Daodunzi, neither the men nor the women of the group were distinguished as elaborately as those individuals buried in M2 and M4 at Xigoupan with the gold and jade objects. The cemetery at Daodunzi apparently represented a group less powerful (figures 9.8, 9.9) and/or wealthy than that at Xigoupan (figures 9.1, 9.2). Located in the spot where Chinese records tell us that Xiongnu headquarters were, those two at Xigoupan may have been regional notables, but our study points out how diverse the Xiongnu nation was and how distinctive they remained from each other as well as from the Chinese, even if under Chinese command. No essentialized view of the Xiongnu is, therefore, adequate to explain the complex nature of their identity as expressed in burial customs found even at the one site of Daodunzi. Although the Chinese records give us a single view, archaeological research gives us a rich and more nuanced view of the Xiongnu, or whoever these peoples were, including a window on how one's sex and age affected the solemn ritual of burial.

NOTES

1. This is the region that the Chinese call the *beifang*, or Northern Zone. It includes all territories south of present-day Mongolia, from the east coast of Liaoning, across Inner Mongolia and west to Ningxia, Gansu, and Xinjiang.

2. I am deeply grateful to Mandy Jui-man Wu for leading the access brigade and to Ding Xiaolei for inputting the data.

3. In the subsequent discussion the following shorthand is used: C = catacomb tomb; P = pit tomb; M = male; F = female; I = infant; U = Unknown sex; M preceding a number = "tomb"; brackets [] are used to designate the number of items.

4. These are bronze coins cast by the Chinese that can be dated from after 118 BCE, when they were first minted.

Table 9.1a. Tombs from the Spring-Autumn and Warring-States periods in the Northern Frontier

Location	Number of Tombs	Tomb Shape	Orientation	Coffins and Skeletons	Main Grave Goods	Animals	Dates	References
Taohongbala 桃红巴拉	7	rectangular pit grave	north-south	No coffin; single, extended and supine burial, heading north	pottery pot, bowl, bronze dagger, pickax, buckle, animal-mask-shaped ornament, tube-shaped ornament, plaque with animal figure design, curb bit, iron knife, gold earring, etc.	skulls and hooves of horse, bovine and sheep, forty-nine individuals at most in one grave	late Spring-Autumn to early Warring-States period	Tian 1976
Aluchaideng 阿鲁柴登	2				gold crown ornament, plaque with animal-figure design		late Warring-States period	Tian and Guo 1980 NMGWWGZDD 1980
Xigoupan 西沟畔	3	rectangular pit grave	north-south	No coffin; single, extended and supine burial, heading north	gold necklace, ear pendant, finger tube, plaque with animal-figure designs, bronze dagger (sword), knife, arrowhead, silver fitting (jieyue) with inscriptions "Gu-si-shi-hu-san 故寺家虎三" and so on	skulls of horse and sheep	early Warring-States period	
Fanjiayaozi 范家窑子	1				bronze sword, ge-dagger-ax, knife, ring, tube-shaped ornament, plaque with animal-figure design		early Warring-States period	Li 1959
Yulongtai 玉隆太	1				bronze knife, adze, ring, buckle, pearl-string-shaped ornament, horse-shaped plaque, free-standing animal-shaped ornament, iron pickax, curb bit; silver necklace		late Warring-States period	NMGBWG 1977 & NMGWWGZDD 1980

Table 9.1a. (continued)

Location	Number of Tombs	Tomb Shape	Orientation	Coffins and Skeletons	Main Grave Goods	Animals	Dates	References
Sujigou	速机沟1				bronze figures of deer, horse, crane head, and sheep head		late Warring-States period	Gai 1965
Hulusitai	呼鲁斯太 3	rectangular pit grave	north-south	No coffin; single, extended and supine burial, heading north	bronze sword, pickax, knife, adze, button-shaped ornament, tube-shaped ornament, deer-shaped plaque, bell, etc.	skull of horse, twenty-seven individuals at most in one grave	early Warring-States period	Liang and Ta 1980
Maoqinggou	毛庆沟 67	rectangular pit grave	east-west	Most no coffin; some had wood coffin or inner and outer coffins; single, extended and supine burial, heading north or east	early phase: bronze sword, buckle, bird-shaped plaque, plaque with tiger design, tube-shaped ornament, pearl-string-shaped ornament	later phase: iron sword, pickax, and tiger-shaped plaque, increased skulls of horse, bovine and dog, six individuals at most in one grave	late Spring-Autumn to late Warring-States periods	NMGWWGZD 1986
Yinniugou	饮牛沟 15	rectangular pit grave	north-south or east-west	Most no coffin; some had wood coffin or inner and outer coffins; single, extended and supine burial	pottery jar, bronze tube-shaped ornament, animal mask-shaped ornament, plaque with deer design; iron sword, pickax, etc.	sheep, dog, pig, and fox	late Warring-States period	NMGWWZZQGZD 1984
崞县窰子	31	rectangular pit grave	east-west	No coffin; single, extended and supine burial, heading east	pottery double-lugged jar, double-lugged pot, bronze buckle, plaque with bird, tiger and sheep design, pearl-string-shaped ornament, tube-shaped ornament	skulls of horse, bovine, sheep and dog, nineteen individuals at most in one grave	late Spring-Autumn to early Warring-States periods	NMGWWKGYJS 1989

Table 9.1b. Xiongnu tombs in the Western and Eastern Han dynasties, by country

Location	Number of Tombs	Tomb Shape	Orientation	Coffins and Skeletons	Main Grave Goods	Animals	Dates	References
China								
Xigoupan	9	rectangular pit grave	north-south	no coffin; single, extended and supine burial, heading north	pottery jar; pot decorated with wave-shaped pattern, some marked "丹石"; bronze horse; gilt lying-sheep-shaped plaque and belt fittings; gold decorative foils; stone ornaments; etc.	complete heads of sheep or dog	early Western Han or later	YKZMWWGZZ 1981 and NMGWWGZD 1961
Bodonggou	9	rectangular pit grave	north-south	no coffin; most single, extended and supine burial, heading north	pottery jar, iron ding-tripod, fu-cauldron, sword, belt buckle, horse bridle bit, bronze plaque, mirror with TLV patterns, etc.	heads of horse, cattle, and sheep	late Western to early Eastern Han	YKZMWWGZZ 1981
Daodunzi	27	rectangular shaft pit grave (twenty-one), side-chambered catacomb (six)	north-south	wood coffin; extended and supine burial, heading north	pottery jar, bronze knife, belt buckle, bell, tube, belt plaque with animal or human images, iron knife, ax, ring, belt buckle, stone plaque, whetstone, Wuzhu coin, cowry shell, lacquer ware	head and hooves of cattle and cheep, at most fifteen pieces in one tomb	middle and late Western Han	NXWWKGYJS 1988b
Lijiataozi	5	rectangular shaft pit and rectangular brick chamber	north-south	wood coffin, some with wooden chamber, single, extended and supine burial, heading north	pottery jar, bronze axle finial, belt buckle, open-worked ring, open-worked belt plaque with animal images, iron fu-cauldron, ring, Wuzhu and Huoquan coins		early Eastern Han	NXWWKGYJS 1988a
Kexingzhuang M1140	1	rectangular pit grave	north-south	single, extended and supine burial, heading north	open-worked bronze belt plaque with human images, open-worked ring, gold wire ring, iron knife, etc.		early Western Han	ZGKXYKGYJS 1962

Table 9.1b. (continued)

Location	Number of Tombs	Tomb Shape	Orientation	Coffins and Skeletons	Main Grave Goods	Animals	Dates	References
Zaomiao M25	1	rectangular pit grave	east-west		pottery jar, open-worked belt plaque with animal images, etc.		early Western Han	SXKGYJS 1986
Shangsunjia zhai	1	mound on the ground; brick chambers with dome-shaped ceilings and ramp passage	east-west	wood chamber and coffin	pottery silo, well, and oven; bronze mirror, Wuzhu coins and seal with inscription of "汉匈奴归义亲汉长," etc.		late Eastern Han	QHSWWGLCKGD 1979
Mongolia								
Noin-Ula	large 12; small 10; sacrifice pits 8	Large tombs had mounds on the ground; the chambers had three layers of wooden structures and passages. Small tombs were rectangular pit graves with stone slab facing	north-south	Large tombs had inner and outer wood chambers; wood coffins were set in the inner wood chambers. single, extended and supine burial, heading north	pottery jar with wave patterns, bronze lamp, fu-cauldron, bell, curb bit and chain, buckle, Han-styled mirror, silk garments (including shoes, head wear, and hair hood), wool-woven textiles (tapestry and carpet), lacquer and wooden wares, ear cup with "建平五年" (the fifth year of Jianping Era, 2 BCE) and tray, hair braid, etc.		late Western Han to early Eastern Han	Dorzhsuren 1962; Kozlov 1925; Rudenko 1962; Trever 1931; Umehara 1960
Gol Mod	26	rectangular pit graves with stone facing	north-south	N/A	pottery jar, bronze bell, mirror, fu-cauldron with iron ring-foot, iron sword with wooden hilt, hair braid; lacquer wares	horse skull	late Western Han to early Eastern Han	YKZMWWGZZ 1981

Site (Chinese)	No.	Grave structure	Orientation	Burial	Grave goods	Animal remains	Date	Reference
Tebuxi-Ula (特布乌拉 希乌拉)	12	cone-shaped stone mound on the ground; rectangular pit grave with stone facing	north-south	wood coffin; single, extended and supine burial, heading north	pottery jar, iron plaque, lacquer ware cup, etc.	horse, bovine and sheep; eighteen individuals at most in one grave	late Western Han to early Eastern Han	Konovalov 1985
Naimatuolegai (乃玛托勒盖)	5	cone-shaped stone mound on the ground; rectangular pit grave	north-south	no coffin; single, extended and supine burial, heading north	pottery jar, iron curb bit and chain, buckle, etc.	N/A	middle and late phases of Western Han	Konovalov 1985
Chandman-Uul	5	cone-shaped stone mound on the ground; rectangular pit grave	north-south	wood coffin; single, extended and supine burial, heading north or northeast	iron buckle, bone arrowhead, bow grip, etc.	N/A	middle and late phases of Western Han	Konovalov 1985
Nuhejina mu (奴 赫金阿姆)	3	cone-shaped stone mound on the ground; rectangular pit grave	east-west	wood coffin; single, extended and supine burial, heading east or southeast	pottery jar, iron dagger, spearhead, and arrowhead, etc.	N/A	middle and late phases of Western Han	Konovalov 1985
Darhan-Ula	6	rectangular pit grave	north-south	wood coffin, some had wood outer coffin; single, extended and supine burial, heading east or southeast	pottery jar, whetstone, silk textiles	N/A	late Western Han to early Eastern Han	Konovalov 1985
Dulege-Ula (都 勒格乌拉)	15							Konovalov 1985
Hutage-Ula (呼 塔格乌拉)	2							Konovalov 1985; Grishin 1978
Bolexi (伯勒希)	2							Grishin 1978
Halateng-Zhafusaer (哈拉腾-扎夫萨尔)	2							Konovalov 1985
								Konovalov 1985

Table 9.1b. (continued)

Location	Number of Tombs	Tomb Shape	Orientation	Coffins and Skeletons	Main Grave Goods	Animals	Dates	References
Wule Gu-te (乌勒古特)	1							Konovalov 1985
Small Wule Gu-te (小乌勒古特)	1							Konovalov 1985
Salexite (萨勒希特)	6							Konovalov 1985
Trans-Baikal, Russia								
Il'movii	Large 3; Small 57	stone mound on the ground; rectangular pit grave	north-south	wood coffin, some had wood outer coffin; single, extended and supine burial, heading north	pottery jar with wave pattern; iron sword, buckle, ring, curb bit, plaque, brocade with plant pattern, bronze mirrors with four-dragon, epigraph including 日光 (sunshine) and four-nipple designs; lacquer ware cup, etc.	skulls of horse, bovine, sheep and donkey, nineteen individuals at most in one grave	late Western Han to early Eastern Han	Davydova 1985; Konovalov 1976; Sosnovskii 1946; Tal'ko-Gryntsevich 1898
Qieliemu-20 huo-fu 切列姆霍夫		round tone mound on the ground; rectangular pit grave	north-south	wood coffin, some had wood outer coffin; most single, some joint, extended and supine burial, heading north	pottery jar, iron knife, arrowhead, buckle, ring, plaque, bronze bell, ring, mirror, turquoise pendant, birchen ware, lacquer ware	skulls of domestic animals	late Western Han to early Eastern Han	Konovalov 1976
Derestuy	32	rectangular pit grave with stone facing	north-south	wood coffin; single, extended and supine burial, heading north	pottery jar, bronze buckle, ring, bell, plaque, mirror with TLV pattern, Wuzhu coin, iron buckle, curb bit, plaque, gold belt ornament with openwork animal figures, glass beads, silk textiles	N/A	middle Western Han to early Eastern Han	Konovalov 1976

Site		rectangular pit grave	most north-south, some east-west	wood coffin, some had wood outer coffin; most single, extended and supine burial, heading north or east	skulls of domestic animals	pottery jar, bronze fu-cauldron, bell, ring, buckle, belt ornament with openwork animal figures, Wuzhu coins, iron knife, ring, buckle; stone plaque, cowry shell	middle Western Han to early Eastern Han	
Ivolga	216	rectangular pit grave	most north-south, some east-west	wood coffin, some had wood outer coffin; most single, extended and supine burial, heading north or east	skulls of domestic animals	pottery jar, bronze fu-cauldron, bell, ring, buckle, belt ornament with openwork animal figures, Wuzhu coins, iron knife, ring, buckle; stone plaque, cowry shell	middle Western Han to early Eastern Han	Davydova 1985
Ust'-Kyakhta								Hamzina 1982
Suji	苏吉							Hamzina 1982
Buerdong	布尔冬							Hamzina 1982
Tsaraamm								Hamzina 1982
Wuergen	Hun-du-yi 乌尔根~浑都依							Konovalov 1985
Gudejier	Mei-ge 古 德吉尔~梅格							Hamzina 1982
Khara-osso								Konovalov 1985
Halabu-song	哈拉布松							Konovalov 1985
Aoergaiteng	奥尔盖腾							Konovalov 1985
Aidui	爱堆							Konovalov 1985
Suheyi	苏赫依							Konovalov 1985

Table 9.2. Catalog of Xiongnu tomb contents

Tomb ID	Shape	L x W x D = Size of the tomb (cm³)	Bodies	Sex of Master	Age of Master	Head Orientation	Animal	Date	References
Budonggou M1 Dongsheng		270 x 145 x 50 = 1957500	2	1 female, 1 male	unknown	northwest	horse, bovine, and sheep	later Western Han–early Eastern Han	NMGWWKG 1989, pp. 27–33
Budonggou M2 Dongsheng	rectangular pit grave	280 x 90 x 50 = 1260000	1	unknown		northwest		later Western Han–early Eastern Han	NMGWWKG 1989, pp. 27–33
Budonggou M3 Dongsheng	rectangular pit grave	210 x 92 x 110 = 2125200	1	1 unknown		northwest		later Western Han–early Eastern Han	NMGWWKG 1989, pp. 27–33
Budonggou M4 Dongsheng	rectangular pit grave	260 x 110 x 85 = 2431000	1	1 unknown		north		later Western Han–early Eastern Han	NMGWWKG 1989, pp. 27–33
Budonggou M5 Dongsheng	rectangular pit grave	250 x 95 x 80 = 1900000	1	unknown		north		later Western Han–early Eastern Han	NMGWWKG 1989, pp. 27–33
Budonggou M6 Dongsheng	rectangular pit grave	270 x80 x 60 = 1296000	1	unknown		northwest		later Western Han–early Eastern Han	NMGWWKG 1989, pp. 27–33
Budonggou M7 Dongsheng	rectangular pit grave	280 x 100 x 80 = 2240000	1	1 unknown		north		later Western Han–early Eastern Han	NMGWWKG 1989, pp. 27–33
Budonggou M8 Dongsheng	rectangular pit grave	230 x 90 x 60 = 1242000	1	1 unknown		north		later Western Han–early Eastern Han	NMGWWKG 1989, pp. 27–33
Budonggou M9 Dongsheng	rectangular pit grave	230 x 80 x 50 = 920000	1	1 unknown		northwest		later Western Han–early Eastern Han	NMGWWKG 1989, pp. 27–33
Daodunzi M01 Tongxin, Ningxia	rectangular pit grave	287 x 75 x 180 = 3874500	1	1 female	45	northeast		middle and late phases of Western Han	KGXB 1998: 3, pp. 333–355
Daodunzi M02 Tongxin, Ningxia	rectangular pit grave	233 x 98 x 166 = 3790444	1	1 male	50–55	northeast		middle and late phases of Western Han	KGXB 1998: 3, pp. 333–355
Daodunzi M03 Tongxin, Ningxia	rectangular pit grave	98 x 38 x 78 = 290472	1	infant	unknown	northeast		middle and late phases of Western Han	KGXB 1998: 3, pp. 333–355
Daodunzi M04 Tongxin, Ningxia	rectangular pit grave	234 x 85 x 133 = 2645370	1	1 female?	40–45	northeast		middle and late phases of Western Han	KGXB 1998: 3, pp. 333–355

Site/Grave	Grave type	Dimensions	No.	Sex	Age	Orientation	Animal offerings	Date	Reference
Daodunzi M05 Tongxin, Ningxia	rectangular pit grave	255 x 90 x 198 = 4544100	1	1 male	35–40	northeast		middle and late phases of Western Han	KGXB 1998: 3, pp. 333–355
Daodunzi M06 Tongxin, Ningxia	catacomb grave	266 x 61 x 154 = 2498804	1	1 female	50	northeast	bovine and sheep	middle and late phases of Western Han	KGXB 1998: 3, pp. 333–355
Daodunzi M07 Tongxin, Ningxia	catacomb grave	250 x 62 x 151 = 2340500	1	1 male	17–18	northeast	bovine and sheep	middle and late phases of Western Han	KGXB 1998: 3, pp. 333–355
Daodunzi M08 Tongxin, Ningxia	rectangular pit grave	100 x 40 x 59 = 236000	1	infant	unknown	northeast		middle and late phases of Western Han	KGXB 1998: 3, pp. 333–355
Daodunzi M09 Tongxin, Ningxia	rectangular pit grave	120 x 50 x 53 = 318000	1	infant	unknown	northeast		middle and late phases of Western Han	KGXB 1998: 3, pp. 333–355
Daodunzi M10 Tongxin, Ningxia	catacomb grave	220 x 53 x 192 = 2238720	1	1 female	50–55	northeast	bovine and sheep	middle and late phases of Western Han	KGXB 1998: 3, pp. 333–355
Daodunzi M11 Tongxin, Ningxia	rectangular pit grave	125 x 33 x 111 = 457875	1	unknown	unknown	northeast		middle and late phases of Western Han	KGXB 1998: 3, pp. 333–355
Daodunzi M12 Tongxin, Ningxia	catacomb grave	110 x 28 x 58 = 178640	1	infant	unknown	southwest		middle and late phases of Western Han	KGXB 1998: 3, pp. 333–355
Daodunzi M13 Tongxin, Ningxia	catacomb grave	211 x 65 x 175 = 2400125	1	1 female	22–24	northeast	bovine and sheep	middle and late phases of Western Han	KGXB 1998: 3, pp. 333–355
Daodunzi M14 Tongxin, Ningxia	rectangular pit grave	235 x 90 x 162 = 3426300	1	1 female	50	northeast		middle and late phases of Western Han	KGXB 1998: 3, pp. 333–355
Daodunzi M15 Tongxin, Ningxia	catacomb grave	170 x 43 x 123 = 899130	1	1 female?	12–13	northeast	bovine and sheep	middle and late phases of Western Han	KGXB 1998: 3, pp. 333–355

Table 9.2. (continued)

Tomb ID	Shape	Bodies	Sex of Master	Age of Master	Head Orientation	Animal	Date	References
		L x W x D = Size of the tomb (cm³)						
Daodunzi M16 Tongxin, Ningxia	rectangular pit grave	159 x 58 x 58 = 534876	1	infant	8–9	northeast		middle and late phases of Western Han	KGXB 1998: 3, pp. 333–355
Daodunzi M17 Tongxin, Ningxia	rectangular pit grave	218 x 62 x 111 = 1500276	1	1 female	25–30	northeast		middle and late phases of Western Han	KGXB 1998: 3, pp. 333–355
Daodunzi M18 Tongxin, Ningxia	rectangular pit grave	205 x 95 x 176 = 3427600	1	1 male	50	northeast		middle and late phases of Western Han	KGXB 1998: 3, pp. 333–355
Daodunzi M19 Tongxin, Ningxia	rectangular pit grave	234 x 80 x 197 = 3687840	1	1 male	40	northeast		middle and late phases of Western Han	KGXB 1998: 3, pp. 333–355
Daodunzi M20 Tongxin, Ningxia	rectangular pit grave	190 x 70 x 84 = 1117200	1	1 female	15	northeast		middle and late phases of Western Han	KGXB 1998: 3, pp. 333–355
Daodunzi M21 Tongxin, Ningxia	rectangular pit grave	240 x 78 x 65 = 1216800	1	1 male	15–16	northeast		middle and late phases of Western Han	KGXB 1998: 3, pp. 333–355
Daodunzi M22 Tongxin, Ningxia	stone-faced rectangular pit grave	89 x 44 x 65 = 254540	1	infant	unknown	northeast		middle and late phases of Western Han	KGXB 1998: 3, pp. 333–355
Daodunzi M23 Tongxin, Ningxia	rectangular pit grave	220 x 83 x 112 = 2045120	1	1 female	40–45	northeast		middle and late phases of Western Han	KGXB 1998: 3, pp. 333–355
Daodunzi M24 Tongxin, Ningxia	rectangular pit grave	240 x 73 x 162 = 2838240	1	1 male	45–50	northeast		middle and late phases of Western Han	KGXB 1998: 3, pp. 333–355.
Daodunzi M25 Tongxin, Ningxia	rectangular pit grave	160 x 45 x 95 = 684000	1	infant	7–8	northeast		middle and late phases of Western Han	KGXB 1998: 3, pp. 333–355

Site/Tomb	Grave type	Dimensions	Count	Sex	Age	Orientation	Animal sacrifice	Date	Reference
Daodunzi M26 Tongxin, Ningxia	rectangular pit grave	190 x 80 x 94 = 1428800	1	unknown	unknown	northeast		middle and late phases of Western Han	Wu 1989: 3, pp. 333–355
Daodunzi M27 Tongxin, Ningxia	rectangular pit grave	144 x 38 x 66 = 361152	1	infant	10–11	northeast		middle and late phases of Western Han	Wu 1989: 3, pp. 333–355
Gongsuhao M1 Hanggin	rectangular pit grave	210 x 80 x 60 = 1008000	1	unknown	unknown	northeast		early Warring-States period	Tian 1976: 1, pp. 131–143
Hulusitai 79.Hu.M1 Urad	rectangular pit grave	0	1	unknown	unknown			Warring-States period	NMGWWGZDD 1980: 7, pp. 11–12
Hulusitai 79.Hu.M2 Urad	rectangular pit grave	0	1	unknown	unknown	north	27 horse skulls	Warring-States period	NMGWWGZDD 1980: 7, pp. 11–12
Hulusitai 79.Hu.M3 Urad	rectangular pit grave	0	1	unknown	unknown			Warring-States period	NMGWWGZDD 1980: 7, pp. 11–12
Liujia Village Tomb Xinghe	rectangular pit grave	260 x 90 x 130 = 3042000	1	unknown	unknown	northwest	horse and sheep	Warring-States to Han	ZGKXYKGYJSZ 1974: 5, p. 473
Ming'anmu Ejin Horo	unknown	0	1	unknown	unknown	unknown	horse	late Spring-Autumn to early Warring-States	Tian 1992: 5, pp. 79–81
Shang Sunjiazhai Area B M1 Qinghai	brick two-chambered tomb	0	3	male	middle-aged	unknown		late Eastern Han	WW 1979: 4, pp. 49–53
Taohongbala M1 Hanggin	rectangular pit grave	300 x 90 x 50 = 1350000	1	male	35 or so	northeast	horse, bovine, and sheep	early Warring-States period	Tian 1976: 1, pp. 131–143
Taohongbala M2 Hanggin	rectangular pit grave	175 x 120 x 50 = 1050000	1	unknown	3 or so	northeast	horse, bovine, and sheep	early Warring-States period	Tian 1976: 1, pp. 131–143
Taohongbala M3 Hanggin		120 x 80 x 18 = 172800	1	unknown	unknown	northeast		early Warring-States period	Tian 1976: 1, pp. 131–143
Taohongbala M4 Hanggin		0	1	unknown	unknown	unknown		early Warring-States period	Tian 1976: 1, pp. 131–143

Table 9.2. (continued)

Tomb ID	Shape	L x W x D = Size of the tomb (cm³)	Bodies	Sex of Master	Age of Master	Head Orientation	Animal	Date	References
Taohongbala M5 Hanggin		200 x 90 x 0	1	unknown	unknown	northeast		early Warring-States period	KGXB 1976: 1, pp. 131–143
Taohongbala M6 Hanggin		0	1	unknown	unknown	northeast		early Warring-States period	KGXB 1976: 1, pp. 131–143
Xigoupan 79XiM01 Jungar	unknown	0	1	unknown	unknown	unknown	horse and sheep	late Warring-States period	WW 1980: 7, pp. 1–10
Xigoupan 79XiM02 Jungar	unknown		1	male	unknown	25	horse and sheep	late Warring-States period	WW 1980: 7, pp. 1–10
Xigoupan 79XiM03 Jungar	unknown		1				horse and sheep	late Warring-States period	WW 1980: 7, pp. 1–10
Xigoupan 79XiM04 Jungar	rectangular pit grave	0	1	female?	unknown			Han	NMGWWBWG 1986, pp. 15-26
Xigoupan 80XiM05 Jungar	rectangular pit grave	0						Han	NMGWWBWG 1986, pp. 15–26
Xigoupan 80XiM06 Jungar	rectangular pit grave	0					horse and sheep	Han	NMGWWBWG 1986, pp. 15–26.
Xigoupan 80XiM07 Jungar	rectangular pit grave	0						Han	NMGWWBWG 1986, pp. 15–26
Xigoupan 80XiM08 Jungar	rectangular pit grave	0	1	unknown	child			Han	NMGWWBWG 1986, pp. 15–26

Xigoupan 80XiM09 Jungar	rectangular pit grave	0	1	female?	middle-aged	2 sheep, 1 dog skull	Han	NMGWWBWG 1986, pp. 15–26
Xigoupan 80XiM10 Jungar	rectangular pit grave	0	1	unknown	child		Han	NMGWWBWG 1986, pp. 15–26
Xigoupan 80XiM11 Jungar	rectangular pit grave	0	1	male	unknown		Han	NMGWWBWG 1986, pp. 15–26
Xigoupan 80XiM12 Jungar	rectangular pit grave	0	1				Han	NMGWWBWG 1986, pp. 15–26
Yulongtai Tomb Jungar		300 x 500 x 0	1			horse and sheep	Warring-States to Han	NMGBWG 1977: 2, pp. 111–114

Note: Table 9.3 appears on page 180.

Table 9.4. Daodunzi tomb contents

Tomb ID	Shape	L x W x D = Size of the tomb (cm³)	Bodies	Sex of Master	Age of Master	Head Orientation	Animal	Date	Notes
Daodunzi M01 Tongxin, Ningxia	rectangular pit grave	287 x 75 x 180= 3874500	1	1 female	45	northeast		middle and late phases of Western Han	KGXB 1998: 3, pp. 333–355
Daodunzi M02 Tongxin, Ningxia	rectangular pit grave	233 x 98 x 166= 3790444	1	1 male	50–55	northeast		middle and late phases of Western Han	KGXB 1998: 3, pp. 333–355
Daodunzi M03 Tongxin, Ningxia	rectangular pit grave	98 x 38 x 78 = 290472	1	infant	unknown	northeast		middle and late phases of Western Han	KGXB 1998: 3 pp. 333–355
Daodunzi M04 Tongxin, Ningxiax	rectangular pit grave	234 x 85 x 133 = 2645370	1	1 female?	40–45	northeast		middle and late phases of Western Han	KGXB 1998: 3, pp. 333–355
Daodunzi M05 Tongxin, Ningxia	rectangular pit grave	255 x 90 x 198 = 4544100	1	1 male	35–40	northeast		middle and late phases of Western Han	KGXB 1998: 3, pp. 333–355
Daodunzi M06 Tongxin, Ningxia	catacomb grave	266 x 61 x 154 = 2498804	1	1 female	50	northeast	bovine and sheep	middle and late phases of Western Han	KGXB 1998: 3, pp. 333–355
Daodunzi M07 Tongxin, Ningxia	catacomb grave	250 x 62 x 151 = 2340500	1	1 male	17–18	northeast	bovine and sheep	middle and late phases of Western Han	KGXB 1998: 3, pp. 333–355
Daodunzi M08 Tongxin, Ningxia	rectangular pit grave	100 x 40 x 59 = 236000	1	infant	unknown	northeast		middle and late phases of Western Han	KGXB 1998: 3, pp. 333–355

Site	Grave type	Dimensions	No.	Sex	Age	Orientation	Animal bones	Period	Reference
Daodunzi M09 Tongxin, Ningxia	rectangular pit grave	120 x 50 x 53 = 318000	1	infant	unknown	northeast		middle and late phases of Western Han	KGXB 1998: 3, pp. 333–355
Daodunzi M10 Tongxin, Ningxia	catacomb grave	220 x 53 x 192 = 2238720	1	1 female	50–55	northeast	bovine and sheep	middle and late phases of Western Han	KGXB 1998: 3, pp. 333–355
Daodunzi M11 Tongxin, Ningxia	rectangular pit grave	125 x 33 x 111 = 457875	1	unknown	unknown	northeast		middle and late phases of Western Han	KGXB 1998: 3, pp. 333–355
Daodunzi M12 Tongxin, Ningxia	catacomb grave	110 x 28 x 58 = 178640	1	infant	unknown	southwest		middle and late phases of Western Han	KGXB 1998: 3, pp. 333–355
Daodunzi M13 Tongxin, Ningxia	catacomb grave	211 x 65 x 175 = 2400125	1	1 female	22–24	northeast	bovine and sheep	middle and late phases of Western Han	KGXB 1998: 3, pp. 333–355
Daodunzi M14 Tongxin, Ningxia	rectangular pit grave	235 x 90 x 162 = 3426300	1	1 female	50	northeast		middle and late phases of Western Han	KGXB 1998: 3, pp. 333–355
Daodunzi M15 Tongxin, Ningxia	catacomb grave	170 x 43 x 123 = 899130	1	1 female?	12–13	northeast	bovine and sheep	middle and late phases of Western Han	KGXB 1998: 3, pp. 333–355
Daodunzi M16 Tongxin, Ningxia	rectangular pit grave	159 x 58 x 58 = 534876	1	infant	8–9	northeast		middle and late phases of Western Han	KGXB 1998: 3, pp. 333–355

Table 9.4. (continued)

Tomb ID	Shape	L x W x D = Size of the tomb (cm³)	Bodies	Sex of Master	Age of Master	Head Orientation	Animal	Date	Notes
Daodunzi M17 Tongxin, Ningxia	rectangular pit grave	218 x 62 x 111 = 1500276	1	1 female	25–30	northeast		middle and late phases of Western Han	KGXB 1998: 3, pp. 333–355
Daodunzi M18 Tongxin, Ningxia	rectangular pit grave	205 x 95 x 176 = 3427600	1	1 male	50	northeast		middle and late phases of Western Han	KGXB 1998: 3, pp. 333–355
Daodunzi M19 Tongxin, Ningxia	rectangular pit grave	234 x 80 x 197 = 3687840	1	1 male	40	northeast		middle and late phases of Western Han	KGXB 1998: 3, pp. 333–355
Daodunzi M20 Tongxin, Ningxia	rectangular pit grave	190 x 70 x 84 = 1117200	1	1 female	15	northeast		middle and late phases of Western Han	KGXB 1998: 3, pp. 333–355
Daodunzi M21 Tongxin, Ningxia	rectangular pit grave	240 x 78 x 65 = 1216800	1	1 male	15–16	northeast		middle and late phases of Western Han	KGXB 1998: 3, pp. 333–355
Daodunzi M22 Tongxin, Ningxia	stonefaced rectangular pit grave	89 x 44 x 65 = 254540	1	infant	unknown	northeast		middle and late phases of Western Han	KGXB 1998: 3, pp. 333–355
Daodunzi M23 Tongxin, Ningxia	rectangular pit grave	220 x 83 x 112 = 2045120	1	1 female	40–45	northeast		middle and late phases of Western Han	KGXB 1998: 3, pp. 333–355.
Daodunzi M24 Tongxin, Ningxia	rectangular pit grave	240 x 73 x 162 = 2838240	1	1 male	45–50	northeast		middle and late phases of Western Han	KGXB 1998: 3, pp. 333–355.

Site	Grave type	Dimensions	Qty			Orientation	Date	Reference
Daodunzi M25 Tongxin, Ningxia	rectangular pit grave	160 × 45 × 95 = 684000	1	unknown	7–8	northeast	middle and late phases of Western Han	KGXB 1998: 3, pp. 333–355.
Daodunzi M26 Tongxin, Ningxia	rectangular pit grave	190 × 80 × 94 = 1428800	1	unknown	unknown	northeast	middle and late phases of Western Han	KGXB 1998: 3, pp. 333–355.
Daodunzi M27 Tongxin, Ningxia	rectangular pit grave	144 × 38 × 66 = 361152	1	infant	10–11	northeast	middle and late phases of Western Han	KGXB 1998: 3, pp. 333–355.

Glossary of Chinese Terms

beifang 北方
Budonggou 補洞溝
Caoyuan (steppe) 草原
Chifeng 赤峰
Dadianzi 大甸子
Dahuazhongzhuang 大华中庄
Daodunzi, Tongxin County, Ningxia Autonomous Region 宁夏自治区同心县倒墩子 （匈奴墓地）
Dashanqian 大山前
Fengtai 丰台
Gansu 甘肃
Guandongche 关东车
Han Dynasty 汉代
Heqin 和亲
Huhhot 呼和浩特
Hulusitai 葫芦丝台
Liujia 六甲
Maodun 冒頓
Maoqinggou 毛庆沟
Ming'anmudu 明安木獨
Nanshan'gen 南山根
Ordos 鄂尔多斯
Qin Empire 秦朝
Shanyu 单于
Shiji 史记
Sima Qian 司马迁
Taohongbala 桃红巴拉
wuzhu coins 五铢钱

Xiaobaiyang 小白阳
Xigoupan 西沟畔
Xiongnu 匈奴
Zhou 周
Zhukaigou 朱开沟

References

Addyman, P. V. and D. H. Hill. (1969). "Saxon Southampton: A Review of the Evidence." *Proceedings of the Hampshire Field Club and Archaeological Society, Part II* 26:61–96.

Adovasio, James M., Olga Soffer, and Buhuslav Klíma. (1996). "Upper Paleolithic Fibre Technology: Interlaced Woven Finds from Pavlov I, Czech Republic, c. 26,000 Years Ago." *Antiquity* 70 (269):526–534.

Aeschylus. (trans. H. Weir Smyth). (1938) (reprint 1988). *Aeschylus, I, Suppliant Maidens, Persians, Prometheus, Seven against Thebes*. Loeb Classical Library. Cambridge, MA: Harvard University Press.

Akhinzhanov, S. M., L. A. Makarova, and T. N. Nurumev. (1990). *K. Istorii Skotovodstva i Okhoty v Kazakhstane*. Almaty, Kazakhstan: Akademia Nauk Kazakhskoi SSR.

Allaby, R. G., G. W. Peterson, D. A. Merriweather, and Y. B. Fu. (2005). "Evidence of the Domestication History of Flax (Linum usitatissimum L.) from Genetic Diversity of the sad2 Locus." *Theoretical and Applied Genetics* 112 (1):58–65.

Allard, F. and D. Erdenebaatar. (2005). "Khirigsuurs, Ritual and Mobility in the Bronze Age of Mongolia." *Antiquity* 79 (305):547–563.

Almagro Basch, M. J. (1966). "El Idolo de Chillaron y la Tipologia de los Idolos del Bronce i Hispano." *Trabajos de Prehistoria* 22:23–39.

Ammianus Marcellinus. (trans. John C. Rolfe). (1935) (reprint 1982). *Ammianus Marcellinus*. Vol. I. Loeb Classical Library. Cambridge, MA: Harvard University Press.

An Zhimin 安志敏 (1998). "Xin Mang Jin Ming Shi Shi 新莽锦铭试释 (Trial Explanation of the Inscriptions on the Brocade of Wang Mang's Xin Period (8–23 CE))." In *Dong Ya Kao Gu Lun Ji* 东亚考古论集 (In Search of the Past: Archaeology in East Asia), pp. 196–198. Hong Kong: Centre for Chinese Archaeology and Art, Chinese University of Hong Kong.

Anthony, David W. and Dorcas R. Brown (1991). "The Origins of Horseback Riding." *Antiquity* 65:22–38.

Anthony, D. (2003). "Bridling Horse Power: The Domestication of the Horse." In S. L. Olsen (ed.), *Horses through Time*, pp. 57–82. Boulder, CO: Roberts Rinehart Publishers.

Anthony, D. and D. Brown. (1998a). "Bit Wear, Horseback Riding and the Botai Site in Kazakstan." *Journal of Archaeological Science* 25:331–347.

———. (1998b). "Eneolithic Horse Exploitation in the Eurasian Steppes: Diet, Ritual, and Riding." *Antiquity* 74:75–86.

Apollodorus. (trans. Sir James George Frazer). (1921) (reprint 1995). *The Library*. Vol. I. Loeb Classical Library. Cambridge, MA: Harvard University Press.

———. (trans. Sir James George Frazer). (1921) (reprint 1989). *The Library*. Vol. II. Loeb Classical Library. Cambridge, MA: Harvard University Press.

Arimitsu Kyoichi. (1996). "Archaeology and Museums in Korea, 1945–46." *Hanguk Kogo Hakbo* 34:7–27.

Arnold, Bettina. (1988). "Slavery in Late Prehistoric Europe: Recovering the Evidence for Social Structure in Iron Age Society." In M. Geselowitz and D. Gibson (eds.), *Tribe and Polity in Late Prehistoric Europe: Demography, Production and Exchange in the Evolution of Complex Social Systems*, pp. 179–192. New York: Springer.

———. (1991). "The Deposed Princess of Vix: The Need for an Engendered European Prehistory." In Dale Wade and Noreen D. Willows (eds.), *The Archaeology of Gender*, pp. 366–374. Calgary: University of Calgary.

———. (1995). "'Honorary Males' or Women of Substance? Gender, Status, and Power in Iron-Age Europe." *Journal of European Archaeology* 3 (2):155–168.

———. (1999). "Drinking the Feast: Alcohol and the Legitimisation of Power in Celtic Europe." *Cambridge Archaeological Journal* 9 (1):71–93.

———. (2001). "The Limits of Agency in the Analysis of Elite Iron Age Celtic Burials." *Journal of Social Archaeology* 1(2):210–224.

———. (2005). "Mobile Men, Sedentary Women? Material Culture as a Marker of Regional and Supra-Regional Interaction in Iron Age Europe." In H. Dobrzanska, V. Megaw, and P. Poleska (eds.), *Celts on the Margin: Studies in European Cultural Interaction 7th Century BC — 1st Century AD*, pp.17–26. Krakow: Institute of Archaeology and Ethnology of the Polish Academy of Sciences.

Arnold, B. and Wicker N. (eds.) (2001a). *Gender and the Archaeology of Death*. Walnut Creek, CA: AltaMira Press.

———. (2001b). "Introduction." In B. Arnold and N. Wicker (eds.), *Gender and the Archaeology of Death*, pp. vii–xxi.Walnut Creek, CA: AltaMira Press.

Ayala Juan, M. M. (1985). "Aportación al Estudio de los Ídolos Calcolíticos de Murcia." *Anales de Prehistoria y Arqueología* 1:23–32.

Babić, S. (2002). "'Princely Graves' of the Central Balkans: A Critical History Research." *European Journal of Archaeology* 5 (1):70–88.

Bachofen, J. (1861). *Das Mutterecht*. Basel: Benno Schwabe.

Balzer, Marjorie Mandelstam. (ed.) (1997). *Shamanic Worlds: Ritual and Lore of Siberia and Central Asia*. New York: North Castle Books.

Barbarunova, Zoya. A. (1995). "Early Sarmatian Culture." In Jeannine Davis-Kimball (et al.), *Nomads of the Eurasian Steppes in the Early Iron Age*, pp. 121–131. Berkeley: Zinat Press.

Barber, E. J. W. (1991). *Prehistoric Textiles: The Development of Cloth in the Neolithic and Bronze Ages*. Princeton, NJ: Princeton University Press.

Barfield, Thomas J. (1989). *The Perilous Frontier: Nomadic Empires and China 221 B.C. to A.D. 1757*. Cambridge, MA: B. Blackwell.

Barfield, T. J. (1991). "Tribe and State Relations: The Inner Asian Perspective." In *Tribes and State Formation in the Middle East*, Philip Khoury and Joseph Kostiner (eds), pp. 153–185. Berkeley: University of California Press.

———. (1993). *The Nomadic Alternative*. Englewood Cliffs, NJ: Prentice-Hall.

Barnes, Gina Lee. (1990). "Early Korean States: A Review of Historical Interpretations." In *Hoabinhian, Joomon, Yayoi, Early Korean States*. Oxford: Oxbow Books.

Barrett, J. (1994). *Fragments from Antiquity: An Archaeology of Social Life in Britian, 2900–1200 BC*. Oxford: Blackwell.

Bashilov, V. and M. Moshkova. (1996). "Russian-Italian Computer Assisted Investigations in Sarmatian Archaeology." *Ancient Civilizations from Scythia to Siberia: An International Journal of Comparative Studies in History and Archaeology* 3:123–128.

Bell, C. (1997). *Ritual: Perspectives and Dimensions*. Oxford: Oxford University Press.

Bell, Robert E. (1991). *Women of Classical Mythology: A Biographical Dictionary*. New York: Oxford University Press.

Ben-Tor, Amnon. (1992). *The Archaeology of Ancient Israel*. New Haven: Yale University Press.

Bernabei, M., L. Bondioli, and A. Guidi. (1994). "Sotzial'naya Struktura Kochevnikov Savromatskogo Vremeni." In M. Moshkova (ed.), *Statisticheskaya Obrabotka Pogrebal'nykh Pamyatnikov Aziatskoi Sarmatii: Vyp. I. Savromatskaya Epokha*, pp. 159–184. Moscow: Nauka.

Bernard, P. (1994). "The Greek Kingdoms of Central Asia." In János Harmatta, B. N. Puri and G. F. Etemadi (eds.), *History of Civilizations of Central Asia, Volume II: The Development of Sedentary and Nomadic Civilizations: 700 B.C. to A.D. 250*, pp. 99–129. Paris: UNESCO.

Bernard, P. and Abdullaev, K. (1997). "Nomady na Granitse Baktrii: kvoprosu ethicheskoi I kul'turnoi identifikatsii." *Rossiiskaya Arkheologiya* 1:68–86.

Berseneva, Natalia A. (1999). "Keramicheskie pryaslitsa iz pogrebenii sargatskoi kultury po materialam Srednego Priirtysh'ya (Ceramic Spindle-Whorls from Sargat Burials, after Middle Irtysh Materials)." In Stanislav A. Grigor'ev (ed.), *XIV Uralskoe arkheologicheskoe soveshanie: tezisy dokladov*, pp. 115–117. Chelyabinsk: Rifei Press.

———. (2004). "Pryaslitsa i problema *gendera* v sargatskikh pogrebeniyakh po materialam Srednego Priirtysh'ya (Spindle-Whorls and Gender Problems in Sargat Burials, after Middle Irtysh Materials)." In Vladimir I. Matyushenko (ed.), *VI Istoricheskie chteniya pamyati M. P. Gryaznova*, pp. 198–201. Omsk: Omskii Universitet.

———. (2006). "Archaeology of Children: Sub-adult Burials during the Iron Age in the Trans-Urals and Western Siberia." In Chrysanthi Gallou and Merkouris Georgiadis (eds.), *The Archaeology of Cult and Death. Proceedings of the Session Held in the 9th Annual Meeting of the European Association of Archaeologists, St. Petersburg, Russia, 10–14 September 2003*, pp. 179–192. Budapest: Archeolingua.

Binford, Lewis R. (1971). "Mortuary Practices: Their Study and Their Potential." In *An Archaeological Perspective*, pp. 209–243. New York: Seminar Press.

Birtalan, Agnes. (2003). "Ritualistic Use of Livestock Bones in the Mongolian Belief System and Customs." In Alice Sárközi and Attila Rákos (eds), *Altaica Budapestinensia Proceedings of the 45th Permanent International Altaistic Conference (PIAC) Budapest, Hungary, June 23–28, 2002*, pp. 34–62. Budapest: Research Group for Altaic Studies, Hungarian Academy of Sciences, Department of Inner Asian Studies, Eötvös Loránd University.

Blundell, Sue (1995). *Women in Ancient Greece*. Cambridge: Harvard University Press.

Boardman, John. (ed.) (1993). *The Oxford History of Classical Art*. Oxford: Oxford University Press.

———. (2003a). "Three Monsters at Tillya Tepe." *Ancient Civilizations from Scythia to Siberia. An International Journal of Comparative Studies in History and Archaeology* 9 (1–2):133–146.

———. (2003b). "The Tillya Gold: A Closer Look." *Ancient West and East* 2 (2):348–374.

Bobrov, V. V. (1979). "O Bronzovoii poyasnoii plastine iz tagarskogo kurgana (On Bronze Belt Plaque from Tagar Kurgan)." *Sovietskaya Arkheologiya* (Soviet Archaeology) (1):254–256.

Bokovenko, N. A. (1995a). "Tuva during the Scythian Period." In J. Davis-Kimball, V. A. Bashilov, and L. T. Yablonsky (eds.), *Nomads of the Eurasian Steppes in the Early Iron Age*, pp. 265–284. Berkeley: Zinat Press.

———. (1995b). "Scythian Culture in the Altai Mountains." In J. Davis-Kimball, V. A. Bashilov, and L. T. Yablonsky (eds.), *Nomads of the Eurasian Steppes in the Early Iron Age*, pp. 285–295. Berkeley: Zinat Press.

———. (1996). "Asian Influence on European Scythia." *Ancient Civilizations from Scythia to Siberia: An International Journal of Comparative Studies in History and Archaeology* 3 (1):97–122.

———. (1997). "Novyj tip pogrebal'nykh kompleksov karasukskoj kul'tury (New Type of Karasuk Funeral Complexes)." In V. M. Masson (ed.), *Novye Issledovanija Arkheologov Rossii i SNG*, pp. 29–31. Saint Petersburg: Institut Istorii Material'noj Kul'tury RAN.

———. (2006). "The Emergence of the Tagar Culture." *Antiquity* 80 (310):860–879.

Bokovenko, N. A. and S. Legrand. (2000). "Das karasukzeitliche Gräberfeld Anchil Chon in Chakassien (The Karasuk Site of Anchil Chon in Khakassia)." *Eurasia Antiqua* 6:209–248.

Bokovenko, N. A. and Ju. A. Smirnov. (1998). Archeologiceskie pamjatniki doliny Belogo Ijusa na severe Chakasii (Archaeological monuments of the White Iyus valley in north Khakasiya). Saint Petersburg.

Bolomey, A. (1973). "An Outline of the Late Epipaleolithic Economy of the Iron Gates: The Evidence on Bones." *Dacia* n.s. 17:41–52.

Bothmer, Dietrich von. (1957). *Amazons in Greek Art*. London: Oxford University Press.

Bradtmiller, B. (1983). The Effect of Horseback Riding on Arikara Arthritis Patterns. Paper presented to the American Anthropological Association, Chicago.

Bridges, P. S. (1990). "Osteolotical Correlates of Weapon Use." In J. E. Buikstra (ed.), *A Life of Science: Papers in Honor of J. Lawrence Angel, Center for American Archaeology, Scientific Papers* 6:87–98.

Brown, James A. (1981). "The Search for Rank in Prehistoric Burials." In Robert Chapman, Ian Kinnes, and Klavs Randsborg (eds.), *The Archaeology of Death*, pp. 25–37. Cambridge: Cambridge University Press.

———. (1995). "On Mortuary Analysis with Special Reference to the Saxe-Binford Research Program." In Lane A. Beck (ed.), *Regional Approaches to Mortuary Analysis*, pp. 3–26. New York: Plenum Press.

Brumbach, Hetty Jo and Robert Jarvenpa. (2006). "Gender Dynamics in Hunter-Gatherer Society: Archaeological Methods and Perspectives." In S. Nelson, *Handbook of Gender in Archaeology*, pp. 503–536. Lanham, MD: AltaMira Press.

Brumfiel, Elizabeth. (2006). "Methods in Feminist and Gender Archaeology: A Feeling for Difference and Likeness." In S. Nelson, *Handbook of Gender in Archaeology*, pp. 31–58. Lanham, MD: AltaMira Press.

Bunker, Emma C. (1993). "Gold in the Ancient Chinese World: A Cultural Puzzle." *Artibus Asiae* 53:27–50.

———. (1995). "The People, the Land, and the Economy." In J. F. So and E. C. Bunker (eds.), *Traders and Raiders on China's Northern Frontier*, 17–31. Seattle: University of Washington Press.

———. (1997). *Ancient Bronzes of the Eastern Eurasian Steppes from the Arthur M. Sackler Collection*. New York: Arthur M. Sackler Foundation.

Bunker, Emma C., C. Bruce Chatwin, and Ann R. Farkas. (1970). *Animal Style Art from East to West*. New York: Asia Society.

Bunker, Emma C., Trudi Kawami, Katheryn M. Linduff, and Wu En. (1997). *Ancient Bronze of the Eastern Eurasian Steppe from the Arthur M. Sackler Collections*. New York: Abrams.

Bunyatyan, Elena P. (1985). *Metodika Soztialnykh Rekonstruktii V Arkheologii. Na Materiale Skifskikh Mogilnikov IV–III vv. do n.e.* (Methodology of Social Reconstructions in Archaeology. After Scythian Burial Materials IV–III Centuries B.C.). Kiev: Naukova Dumka Press.

Caesar, Julius. (trans. H. J. Edwards). (1917) (reprint 1979). *The Gallic War*. Loeb Classical Library. Cambridge, MA: Harvard University Press.

Calligaro, Thomas F. (2006). "Analyse des matériaus: Tillia tepe, étude des incrustations et de l'or." In Pierre Cambon, Jean-François Jarrige, Paul Bernard, and Véronique Schiltz (eds.), *Afghanistan: Les trésors retrouvés. Collections du musée national de Kaboul*, pp. 292–293. Paris: Musée national des Arts asiatiques-Guimet.

Cambon, Pierre. (2006). "Tillia tepe, la connexion de l'Est." In Pierre Cambon, Jean-François Jarrige, Paul Bernard, and Véronique Schiltz (eds.), *Afghanistan: Les trésors retrouvés. Collections du musée national de Kaboul*, pp. 294–297. Paris: Musée national des Arts asiatiques-Guimet.

Cambon, Pierre, Jean-François Jarrige, Paul Bernard, and Véronique Schiltz. (eds.) (2006). *Afghanistan: Les trésors retrouvés. Collections du musée national de Kaboul.* Paris: Musée national des Arts asiatiques-Guimet.

Camp, Charles L. and Natasha Smith. (1942). "Phylogeny and Functions of the Digital Ligaments of the Horse." *Memoirs of the University of California* 13:69–124.

Cannon, Aubrey. (1989). "The Historical Dimension in Mortuary Expressions of Status and Sentiment." *Current Anthropology* 30 (4):437–458.

Cardoso, J. L. (1995). "Os Idolos Falange do Povodao Pre-historico de Lecei (Oeiras): Estudio Comparado." *Estudios Arqueologicos de Oeiras* 5:213–232.

Carr, Christopher. (1995). "Mortuary Practices: Their Social, Philosophical-Religious, Circumstantial, and Physical Determinants." *Journal of Archaeological Method and Theory* 2:105–200.

Chaliand, Gerard. (trans. A. A. Berrett). (2004). *Nomadic Empires: From Mongolia to the Danube.* New Brunswick, NJ: Transaction Publishers.

Chamberlain, Andrew T. (1997). "Commentary: Missing Stages of Life—Towards the Perception of Children in Archaeology." In Jenny Moore and Eleanor Scott (eds.), *Invisible People and Processes: Writing Gender and Childhood into European Archaeology*, pp. 248–250. London: Leicester University Press.

Chapman, J. (2000). "Tension at Funerals: Social Practices and the Subversion of Community Structure in Later Hungarian Prehistory." In M. A. Dobres and J. Robb (eds.), *Agency in Archaeology.* London: Routledge.

Chard, Chester. (1974). *Northeast Asia in Prehistory.* Madison: University of Wisconsin Press.

Chernykh, Evgenii N. (1992). *Ancient Metallurgy in the USSR: The Early Metal Age.* New York: Cambridge University Press.

Chi Kon-gil. (ed.) (2001). *The Ancient Culture of Nangnang.* Seoul: National Museum of Korea.

Chlenova, N. L. (1972). *Khronologija Pamjatnikov Karasukskoj Epokhi (The Chronology of Sites of the Karasuk Epoch).* Moscow: Nauka.

Chou Lien-K'uan 周连宽. (1956). "Sulian Nan Xiboliya suo Faxian de Zhongguo shi Gongdian Yizhi 苏联南西伯利亚所发现的中国式宫殿遗址 (On the Ruins of a Palace in Chinese Style in Southern Siberia)." *Kaogu Xuebao* 考古学报 (*Acta Archaeologica Sinica*) 4:55–66.

Clarke, D. (1973). "Archaeology: The Loss of Innocence."*Antiquity* 47:6–18.

Coe, Paula Powers. (1997). "Mythic Journey: A New Look at an Old Celtic Pot." *Cosmos* 13:49–68.

Cohen, Beth. (1997). "Divesting the Female Breast of Clothes in Classical Sculpture." In Ann Olga Koloski-Ostrow and Claire L. Lyons (eds.), *Naked Truths: Women, Sexuality, and Gender in Classical Art and Archaeology*, pp. 66–94. London: Routledge.

Conkey, Margaret and Janet Spector. (1984). "Archaeology and the Study of Gender." *Archaeological Method and Theory* 7:1–38.

Coon, Carleton S. (1953). "The Mountains of Giants: A Racial and Cultural Study of the North Albanian Mountain Ghegs." *Papers of the Peabody Museum of American Archaeology and Ethnology*, pp. 23.3. Cambridge, MA: Peabody Museum.

Courtaud, P. and D. Rajev. (1998). "Osteomorphological Features of Nomadic Riders: Some Examples from Iron Age Populations Located in Southwestern Siberia." In M. Pearce and M. Tosi (eds.), *Papers from the EAA Third Annual Meeting at Ravenna, Volume I: Pre- and Protohistory*, pp. 110–113. BAR International Series 717. Oxford: Archaeopress.

Cross, Tom Peete and Clark Harris Slover. (1936). *Ancient Irish Tales*. New York: Barnes and Noble Books.

Daesong Tombs Museum. (2003). *Catalog of the Daesong Tombs Museum*. Busan: Daesong Museum.

Daire, M-Y. and L. Koryakova (eds.) (2002). *Habitats et Nécropoles de L'Eurasie du Fer au Carrefour de L'Eurasie: Fouilles 1993–1994*. Rennes, France: Civilisations atlantiques et archéosciences; Russie: Institut d'histoire et d'archéologie, Académie des sciences, Université d'Oural; Paris: de Boccard.

Davies, J. (1994). *Ritual and Remembrance: Responses to Death in Human Societies*. Sheffield: Sheffield Academic Press.

Davis-Kimball, J. (1997a). "Chieftain or Warrior-priestess?" *Archaeology* (September–October):44–48.

———. (1997b). "Sauro-Sarmatian Nomadic Women: New Gender Identities." *Journal of Indo-European Studies* 25 (3–4):327–343.

———. (1997c). "Warrior Women of the Eurasian Steppes." *Archaeology* 50 (1):44–48.

———. (1997–1998). "Amazon Priestesses and Other Women of Status—Females in Nomadic Societies." *Silk Road Art and Archaeology* 5:1–50.

———. (1998). "Statuses of Eastern Iron Age Nomads." In M. Pearce and M. Tosi (eds.), *Papers from the EAA Third Annual Meeting at Ravenna 1997. Volume I: Pre- and Protohistory*, pp. 142–149. BAR International Series 717. Oxford: Archaeopress.

———. (2000). "Enarees and Women of High Status: Evidence of Ritual at Tillya Tepe (Northern Afghanistan)." In J. Davis-Kimball, L. Koryakova, and L. Yablonsky (eds.), *Kurgans, Ritual Sites, and Settlements: Eurasian and Bronze and Iron Age*, pp. 223–239. BAR International Series 890. Oxford: Archaeopress.

———. (2001). "Warriors and Priestesses of the Eurasian Nomads." In P. Biehl, F. Bertemes, and H. Meller (eds.), *The Archaeology of Cult and Religion*, pp. 243–259. Budapest: Archaeolingua.

Davis-Kimball, Jeannine, with Mona Behan. (2002). *Warrior Women: An Archaeologist's Search for History's Hidden Heroines*. New York: Warner Books.

Davis-Kimball, J., V. Bashilov and L. Yablonsky (eds.) (1995). *Nomads of the Eurasian Steppes in the Early Iron Age*. Berkeley: Zinat Press.

Davis-Kimball, J. and L. Yablonsky (1995). *Kurgans on the Left Bank of the Ilek: Excavations at Pokrovka 1990–1992*. Berkeley: Zinat Press.

Davydova, A. V. (1985). *Ivolginskii Kompleks (Gorodishche i Mogil'nik)—Pamyatnik Khunnu v Zabaikal'e* (Ivolga Complex (Fortresses and Cemetery)—Hun Remains in Trans-Baikal). Leningrad: Leningradskogo Universiteta.

Davydova, A. V. and S. S. Minyaev. (1988). "Poyas s bronzovymi blyashkami iz Dyrestuiskogo mogil'nika (Belt with Bronze Plaques in Derestuy Cemetery)." *Sovietskaya Arkheologiya* 4:230–233.

Debaine-Francfort, C. (1995). *Du Neolithique a l'Age du Bronze en Chine du nord-Ouest: La culture de Qijia et ses connexions.* Paris: Editions Recherche sur les Civilisations.

Demkin, Vladimir A. (1997). *Paleopochvovedenie I Arkheologia: Integratia V Izuchenii Istorii Prirody I Obshestva* (Paleosoil Science and Archaeology: The Integration in Investigation of Natural and Social History). Pushchino: ONTI RAN Press.

Dent, John. (1985). "Three Cart Burials from Wetwang, Yorkshire." *Antiquity* 59 (226):85–92.

Deuchler, Martina. (1992). *The Confucian Transformation of Korea.* Cambridge, MA: Council on East Asian Studies, Harvard University.

Devlet, M. A. (1980). *Sibirskie Poyasnoii Azhurnye Plastiny* (Siberian Openwork Plaques). Moscow: Nauka.

Dexter, Miriam Robbins. (1990). *Whence the Goddesses: A Source Book.* New York: Pergamon Press.

Di Cosmo, Nicola. (1999). "The Northern Frontier in Pre-Imperial China." In Michael Loewe and Edward L. Shaughnessy (eds.), *The Cambridge History of Ancient China*, pp. 885–966. Cambridge: Cambridge University Press.

———. (2002). *Ancient China and Its Enemies: The Rise of Nomadic Power in East Asian History.* Cambridge: Cambridge University Press.

Dietler, M. (1990). "Driven by Drink: The Role of Drinking in the Political Economy and the Case of Early Iron Age France." *Journal of Anthropological Archaeology* 9 (4):352–406.

DiMaggio, Paul. (1997). "Culture and Cognition." *Annual Review of Sociology* 23:263–287.

Diodorus Siculus. (trans. C. H. Oldfather). (1939) (reprint 1970). *Diodorus of Sicily: In Twelve Volumes, Vol. III, Books IV (continued) 59–VIII.* Loeb Classical Library. Cambridge, MA: Harvard University Press.

Dobres, Marcia-Anne. (2000). *Technology and Social Agency.* Oxford: Blackwell.

Dommasnes, L. N. (1982). "Late Iron Age in Western Norway: Female Roles and Ranks as Deduced from an Analysis of Burial Customs." *Norwegian Archaeological Review* 15 (1–2):70–84.

Dorzhsuren, Ts. (1961). *Umard Khunnu (Northern Hun).* Ulaanbaatar, Mongolia.

———. (1962). *Raskopki Mogil Hunnu v gorakh Noin-Ula na reke Khuni-gol* (The Excavation of Hun Tombs in Noin-Ula along Khanuy River). Mongol'skii Arkheologicheskii Sbornik (Mongolian Archaeological Works). Ulaanbaatar, Mongolia.

Dovgaluk, Natalia P. (1995). "Steklyannye ukrasheniya Zapadnoi Sibiri epokhi rannego zheleznogo veka (po materialam sargatskoi kultury (The glass ornaments in Western Siberia in the Early Iron Age [Sargat Culture])." PhD diss.: Moscow.

Drennan, R. D., C. E. Peterson, G. G. Indrisano, Teng Mingyu, G. Shelach, Zhu Yanping, K. M. Linduff, and Guo Zhizhong. (2003). "Approaches to Regional Demographic Reconstruction." In *Chifeng International Collaborative Archaeological Project: Regional Archaeology in Eastern Inner Mongolia: A Methodological Exploration*, pp. 152–165. Beijing: Kexue chubanshe 科学出版社 (Science Press).

Drews, Robert. (2004). *Early Riders: The Beginnings of Mounted Warfare in Asian and Europe.* New York: Routledge.

Durham, Mary Edith. (1909). *High Albania*. London: Edward Arnold.

Duval, Paul-Marie. (1977). *Les Celtes*. Paris: Gallimard.

Ehrenberg, Margaret (1989). *Women in Prehistory*. Norman and London: University of Oklahoma Press.

Ehrenreich, R., C. Crumley, and J. Levy. (eds.) (1995). *Heterarchy and the Analysis of Complex Societies*. Washington, DC: Archaeological Papers of the American Anthropological Association.

Ehrhardt, Kathleen. (2005). *European Metals in Native Hands*. Tuscaloosa: University of Alabama Press.

Enoki, K., G. A. Koshelenko and Z. Haidary (1994). "The Yüeh-chih and Their Migrations." In János Harmatta, B. N. Puri and G. F. Etemadi, *History of Civilizations of Central Asia, Volume II: The Development of Sedentary and Nomadic Civilizations: 700 B.C. to A.D. 250*. Paris: UNESCO.

Evtyukhova, L. A. and V. P. Levasheva. (1946). *Raskopki kitaiiskogo doma bliz Abakana* (The Excavation of the Chinoiserie Palaces near Abakan). KSIIMK No. XII.

Fantham, Elaine, Helene Peet Foley, Natalie Boymel Kampen, Sarah B. Pomeroy and H. A. Shapiro. (1994). *Women in the Classical World: Image and Text*. New York: Oxford University Press.

Ferguson, R. B. and N. L. Whitehead. (1992). *War in the Tribal Zone: Expanding States and Indigenous Warfare*. Santa Fe, NM: School of American Research Press.

Fialko, E. (1991). "Zhenskiye pogrebenya s oruzhiem v skyphskih kurganakh stepnoi Skyphii (The Female Burials with Weapons among the Scythians. Kourgan of the Steppe Scythia)." *Editorial Naukova Dumka*:4–18.

Fitzgerald-Huber, Louisa. (1996). "The First Horses in China's Northwest Border." *Institute for Ancient Equestrian Studies Newsletter* (2):2, 7.

Fowler, C. (2004). *The Archaeology of Personhood: An Anthropological Approach*. London: Routledge.

Fowles, S. (2002). "From Social Type to Social Process: Placing 'Tribe' in a Historical Framework." In W. Parkinson (ed.), *The Archaeology of Tribal Societies*, pp. 13–33. Ann Arbor, MI: International Monographs in Prehistory.

Gai Shanlin (Kai Shan-lin) 盖山林. (1965). "Nei Menggu Zizhiqu Zhunge'er Qi Sujigou Chutu Yipi Tongqi 内蒙古自治区准格尔旗速机沟出土一批铜器 (The Bronze Objects Unearthed at Suchikou, Dzungar Banner, Inner Mongolian Autonomous Region)." *Wenwu* 文物 (Cultural Relics) 2:44–46.

Gansu Sheng Wenwu Kaogu Yanjiusuo 甘肃省文物考古研究所 (Gansu Province Institute of Cultural Relics and Archaeology). (1990). "Gansu sheng wenwu kaogu gongzuo shi nian 甘肃省文物考古工作十年 (Ten Years of Archaeological Work in Gansu Province)." In *Wenwu kaogu gongzuo shi nian* 文物考古工作十年 (Ten Years of Archaeological Work), pp. 316–326. Beijing: Wenwu chubanshe.

Gardiner, K. J. H. (1969). *The Early History of Korea*. Honolulu: University of Hawaii Press.

Gardner, A. (ed.) (2004). *Agency Uncovered: Archaeological Perspectives on Social Agency, Power, and Being Human*. London: UCL Press.

Gifford-Gonzalez, Diane. (1992). "Gaps in Zooarchaeology of Butchery: Is Gender an Issue?" In J. Hudson (ed.), *Bones and Behavior*, pp. 181–199. Carbondale: Southern Illinois University Center of Archaeological Materials.

Gilchrist, Roberta. (1999). *Gender and Archaeology: Contesting the Past*. London: Routledge.

———. (ed.) (2000). "Human Lifecycles." Special Issue of *World Archaeology* 31(3).

Gimbutas, Marija. (1989). *The Language of the Goddess*. San Francisco: Harper & Row.

Goffman, Erving. (1969). *Strategic Interaction*. Philadelphia: University of Pennsylvania Press.

Gokhman I. I. (1958). "Antropologicheskie materialy iz pintochnykh mogil Zabaikal'ya (Anthropological Materials in Stone Slab Tombs of Trans-baikal)." *Sbornik muzeya antropologii i etnografii* (Anthropological and Ethnographical Museum Collections) No. XVIII.

Goldstein, J. S. (2001). *War and Gender: How Gender Shapes the War System and Vice Versa*. Cambridge: Cambridge University Press.

Goldstein, Lynne G. (1981). "One-Dimensional Archaeology and Multidimensional People: Spatial Organization and Mortuary Analysis." In Robert Chapman, Ian Kinnes, and Klavs Randsborg (eds.), *The Archaeology of Death*, pp. 53–69. Cambridge: Cambridge University Press.

Grayson, James H. (1976). "Some Structural Patterns of the Royal Family of Ancient Korea." *Korea Journal* 6 (6):27–32.

———. (2001). *Myths and Legends from Korea*. Richmond, Surrey: Curzon Press.

Green, Miranda Aldhouse. (1996). *Celtic Goddesses: Warriors, Virgins and Mothers*. New York: George Braziller.

Grishin, Yu. S. (1978). *Raskopki gunnskikh pogrebenii u Gory Darkhan* (Excavation of Hun Tombs on Darkhan Mountain). In A. P. Okladnikov (ed.), *Arkheologiya i Etnografiya Mongolii* (Mongolian Archaeology and Ethnography), pp. 95–100. Novosibirsk: Nauka, Sibirskoe otdelenie.

Grjaznov, M. P. (1965). "Raboty Krasnojarskoj ekspeditsii: (1960–1963) (Works of the Krasnoyarsk expedition)." *KSIA 100*: 62–71.

———. (1969). *South Siberia*. Geneva: Nagel Publishers.

———. (1979). *Kompleks arkheologicheskikh pamjatnikov u Gory Tepsej na Enisee* (Archaeological Sites Down the Tepsej Mountains on the Enisej). Novosibirsk: Nauka.

Grjaznov, M. P., B. N. Pjatkin, and G. A. Maksimenkov. (1968). "Karasukskaja kul'tura (Karasuk Culture)." In A. P. Okladnikov (ed.), *Istorija Sibiri, tom 1*, pp.180–187. Leningrad: Nauka.

Gubuev, T. A. (2005). *Alanskii Vsadnik: Sokrovischa kniazei I–XII vekov* (Alanian Rider: Treasures of Princes of the I–XX Centuries). Moscow: State Museum of Oriental Art.

Gugliardo, M. (1982). "Tooth Crown Size Differences between Age Groups: A Possible New Indicator of Stress in Skeletal Samples." *American Journal of Physical Anthropology* 58:383–389.

Guguef, V., I. Ravich, and M. J. Triester. (1991). "Han Mirrors and Their Replicas in the Territory of South and Eastern Europe." 金属博物館紀要 *Kinzoku Hakubutsukan kiyo* (*Bulletin of the Metals Museum*) 16:32–50. (Article in English.)

Guirand, Felix. (ed.) (1959) (reprint 1978). *Larousse Encyclopedia of Mythology*. (new ed.).London: Hamlyn.

Guliaev, V. (2003). "Amazons in the Scythia: New Finds at the Middle Don, Southern Russia." *World Archaeology* 35 (1):112–125.

Guo Dashun. (1995). "Northern Type Bronze Artifacts Unearthed in the Liaoning Region and Related Issues." In S. M. Nelson (ed.), *The Archaeology of Northeast China*, pp. 182–205. London: Routledge.

Guo Suxin 郭素新. (1981). "Shilun handai Xiongnu wenhua de tezheng 试论汉代 匈奴文化的特征 (Trial Analysis on the Features of Xiongnu Culture in the Han Dynasty)." *Nei Menggu Wenwu Kaogu Chuang Kan hao* 内蒙古文物考古创刊号 (Cultural Relics and Archaeology of Inner Mongolia, First Issue) 1:34–37.

Hampe, Roland and Erika Simon. (1981). *The Birth of Greek Art: From the Mycenaean to the Archaic Period*. New York: Oxford University Press.

Hamzina, E. A. (1982). *Arkheologicheskie pamyatniki Buryatii* (Buryat Archaeological Remains). Novosibirsk: Nauka.

———. (1991). "Data Types in Burial Analysis." In Berta Stjernquist (ed.), *Prehistoric Graves as a Source of Information*, pp. 31–39. Vitterhets Historie och Antivitets Akademiens Konferenser 29. Stockholm: Kungl.

———. (2001). "Kurgan Burials of the Eurasian Iron Age—Ideological Constructs and the Process of Rituality." In A. T. Smith and A. Brookes (eds.), *Holy Ground: Theoretical Issues Relating to the Landscape and Material Culture of Ritual Space Objects*, pp. 39–48. Oxford: Archaeopress.

Hanks, B. K. (2000). "Iron Age Nomadic Burials of the Eurasian Steppe: A Discussion Exploring Burial Ritual Complexity." In J. Davis-Kimball, E. M. Murphy, L. N. Koryakova, and L. T. Yablonsky (eds.), *Kurgans, Ritual Sites and Settlements: Eurasian Bronze and Iron Age*, pp. 19–30. BAR International Series 890. Oxford: Archaeopress.

———. (2001). "Kurgan Burials of the Eurasian Iron Age—Ideological Constructs and the Process of Rituality." In A. T. Smith and A. Brookes (eds.), *Holy Ground: Theoretical Issues Relating to the Landscape and Material Culture of Ritual Space Objects*, pp. 39–48. BAR S956. Oxford: Archaeopress.

———. (2002). "The Eurasian Steppe 'Nomadic World' of the First Millennium BC: Inherent Problems within the Study of Iron Age Nomadic Groups." In K. Boyle, C. Renfrew, and M. Levine (eds.), *Ancient Interactions: East and West in Eurasia*, pp. 183–197. Cambridge: McDonald Institute Monographs.

———. (2003a). Human-Animal Relationships in the Eurasian Steppe Iron Age: An Exploration into Social, Economic and Ideological Change. PhD thesis, University of Cambridge.

———. (2003b). "The Eurasian Steppe 'Nomadic World' of the First Millennium BC: Inherent Problems within the Study of Iron Age Nomadic Groups." In K. Boyle, C. Renfrew and M. Levine (eds.), *Ancient Interactions: East and West in Eurasia*, pp. 183–197. Cambridge: McDonald Institute Monographs.

————. (forthcoming). "Constructing the Warrior: Death, Memory and the Art of Warfare." In Dušan Borić (ed.), *Archaeology and Memory*. Oxford: Oxbow Books.

Harding, D. W. (1985). *The Iron Age in Lowland Britain*. London: Routledge and Kegan Paul.

Härke, Heinrich. (1990). "Warrior Graves? The Background of the Anglo-Saxon Weapon Burial Rite." *Past and Present* 126:22–43.

————. (1991). "Data Types in Burial Analysis." In Berta Stjernquist (ed.), *Prehistoric Graves as a Source of Information*, pp. 31–39. Vitterhets Historie och Antivitets Akademiens Konferenser 29.

————. (1992). "Changing Symbols in a Changing Society: The Anglo-Saxon Weapon Burial Rite in the Seventh Century." In M. Carver (ed.), *The Age of Sutton Hoo*, pp. 149–165. Woodbridge: Boydell Press.

————. (1997). "Material Culture as Myth: Weapons in Anglo-Saxon Graves." In C. Jensen and K. Nielsen (eds.), *Burial and Society: The Chronological and Social Analysis of Archaeological Burial Data*, pp. 119–125. Oxford: Alden Press.

Harmatta, János, B. N. Puri and G. F. Etemadi (eds.) (1994). *History of Civilizations of Central Asia, Volume II: The Development of Sedentary and Nomadic Civilizations: 700 B.C. to A.D. 250*. Paris: UNESCO.

Harrison, Jane Ellen. (1903) (reprint 1991). *Prolegomena to the Study of Greek Religion*. 3rd ed., 1992. Cambridge: Cambridge University Press. (1991 reprint by Princeton University Press.)

Hemphill, Brian E., John R. Lukacs, and Kenneth A. R. Kennedy. (1991). "Biological Adaptations and Affinities of Bronze Age Harappans." In Richard H. Meadow (ed.), *Harappan Excavations 1986–1990: A Multidisciplinary Approach to Third Millennium Urbanism*, pp. 137–182. Madison: Prehistory Press.

Herodotus. (trans. A. D. Godley). (1920) (reprint 1990). *Herodotus: Books I and II*. Loeb Classical Library. Cambridge, MA: Harvard University Press.

————. (1921) (reprint 1995). *Herodotus: Books III–IV*. Loeb Classical Library. Cambridge, MA: Harvard University Press.

————. (1922) (reprint 1994). *Herodotus: Books V–VII*. Loeb Classical Library. Cambridge, MA: Harvard University Press.

Hillman, G. (1975). "The Plant Remains from Tell Abu Hureyra: A Preliminary Report." *Proceedings of the Prehistoric Society* 41:70–73.

Hillman, G. C., S. M. Colledge, and D. R. Harris. (1989). "Plantfood Economy during the Epipalaeolithic Period at Tell Abu Hureyra Syria: Dietary Diversity, Seasonality and Modes of Exploitation." In D. R. Harris and G. C. Hillman (eds.), *Foraging and Farming: The Evolution of Plant Exploitation*, pp. 240–268. London: Unwin and Hyman.

Hippocrates. (trans. E. T. Withington). (1928) (reprint 1984). *Hippocrates*. Vol. III. Loeb Classical Library. Cambridge, MA: Harvard University Press.

Hodder, Ian. (1982). *The Present Past*. London: Batsfore.

Hoffman, Christopher R. and Marcia-Anne Dobres. (1999). "Conclusion: Making Material Culture, Making Culture Material." In Marcia-Anne Dobres and Christopher R. Hoffman (eds.), *The Social Dynamics of Technology*, pp. 209–222. Washington, DC: Smithsonian Institution Press.

Hollimon, Sandra E. (2001). "Warfare and Gender in the Northern Plains: Osteological Evidence of Trauma Reconsidered." In B. Arnold and L. Wicker (eds.), *Gender and the Arcaheology of Death*, pp. 179–193. Walnut Creek, CA: AltaMira Press.

Homer. (trans. A. T. Murray). (1978). *Iliad*. 2 vols. Loeb Classical Library. Cambridge, MA: Harvard University Press.

Honeychurch, William and Chunag Amartuvshin. (2005). "States on Horseback: The Rise of Inner Asian Confederations and Empires." In M. T. Stark (ed.), *An Archaeology of Asia*, pp. 255–278. Oxford: Blackwell.

Hosler, Dorothy. (1994). *The Sounds and Colors of Power: The Sacred Metallurgical Technology of Ancient West Mexico*. Cambridge: MIT Press.

Hou Xueyu 候学煜 (ed). (1982). *Zhonghua renmin gongheguo zhibei tu* 中华人民共和国植被图 (Vegetation Coverage Map of the PRC). Beijing: Ditu chubanshe.

Howard, Judith A. (2000). "Social Psychology of Identities." *Annual Review of Sociology* 26:367–393.

Huang Yunping 黄蕴平. (2000). "Zhukaigou yizhi shougu de jianding yu yanjiu 朱开沟遗址兽骨的鉴定与研究 (Identification and Analysis of Animal Bones from the Zhukaigou Site)." In E'erduosi bowuguan 鄂尔多斯博物馆 (The Ordos Museum) and Neimenggu zizhiqu wenwu kaogu yanjiusuo 内蒙古自治区文物考古研究所 (The Inner Mongolian Autonomous Region Archaeological Institute) (eds.), *Zhukaigou: Qingtong shidai zaoqi yizhi fajue baogao* 朱开沟-青铜时代早期遗址发掘报告 (Zhukaigou: A Report on the Excavation of an Early Bronze Age Site), pp. 400–421. Beijing: Wenwu chubanshe 文物出版社 (Cultural Relics Press).

Huld, Martin E. (1997). "The Childhood of Heroes: An Essay on Indo-European Puberty Rites." In *Papers in Memory of Marija Gimbutas: Varia on the Indo-European Past*, pp. 176–193. Journal of Indo-European Studies Monograph Series 19. Washington, DC: Institute for the Study of Man.

———. (2002). "Some Thoughts on Amazons." *Journal of Indo-European Studies* 30 (1–2):93–102.

Humphrey, C. and U. Onon. (1996). *Shamans and Elders: Experience, Knowledge, and Power among the Daur Mongols*. Oxford: Clarendon Press.

Hurley, William M. (1979). *Prehistoric Cordage: Identification of Impressions on Pottery*. Washington, DC: Taraxacum.

Ikeuchi Hiroshi (1929). "The Chinese Expeditions to Manchuria under the Wei Dynasty." *Memoirs of the Research Department of the Toyo Bunko*. 4:71–119.

———. (1930). "A Study on Lo-lang and Tai-feng." *Memoirs of the Research Department of the Toyo Bunko* 5:79–95.

Ilyon the Monk. (trans. T. Ha and G. Mintz). (1972). *Samguk Yusa: Legends of the Three Kingdoms of Ancient Korea*. Seoul: Yonsei University Press.

Jacobson, E. (1987). *Burial Ritual, Gender, and Status in South Siberia in the Late Bronze–Early Iron Age*. Bloomington: Indiana University Research Institute for Inner Asian Studies.

———. (1993). *The Deer Goddess of Ancient Siberia: A Study in the Ecology of Belief*. Leiden: Brill.

James, S. (1999). *The Atlantic Celts: Ancient People or Modern Invention?* Madison: University of Wisconsin Press.

Jenkins, Richard. (1996). *Social Identity*. London: Routledge.

Jettmar, Karl. (1967). *Art of the Steppes*. (rev. ed.). New York: Crown.

Jones, A. (2002). *Archaeological Theory and Scientific Practices*. Cambridge: Cambridge University Press.

Jones, D. E. (1997). *Women Warriors: A History*. Washington, DC: Brassey's.

Jones, S. (1997). *The Archaeology of Ethnicity: Constructing Identities in the Past and the Present*. London: Routledge.

Jones, S. and P. Graves-Brown. (1996). Introduction. In P. Graves Brown, S. Jones, and C. Gamble (eds.), *Cultural Identity and Archaeology: The Construction of European Communities*, pp. 1–24. London: Routledge.

Jones-Bley, Karlene. (1990). "'Fame That Will Live Forever'—The Indo-European Tradition of Burial." *Journal of Indo-European Studies* 18 (1–2):215–224.

———. (1994). "Juvenile Grave Goods in Catacomb Graves from the South Russian Steppe during the Neolithic and Early Bronze Age." *Mankind Quarterly* 34:323–335.

———. (1997). "Defining Indo-European Burial." In *Papers in Memory of Marija Gimbutas: Varia on the Indo-European Past*, pp. 194–221. Journal of Indo-European Studies Monograph Series 19. Washington, DC: Institute for the Study of Man.

———. (2006). "Traveling to the Otherworld: Transport in the Grave." In Marco V. Garcia Quintela, Francisco J. González García, and Felipe Criado Boado (eds.), *Anthropology of the Indo-European World and Material Culture*, pp. 357–368. Budapest: Archaeolingua.

Jones-Bley, Karlene and Angela Della Volpe. (1991). "*SEMOS* and *TUMBOS*—More Than Just Mounds." In Angela Della Volpe (ed.), *Proceedings of the Seventeenth LACUS Forum, 1990*, pp. 399–407. Lake Bluff, IL.

Kalieva, S. S. and V. N. Logvin. (1997). *Skotovody Turgaya v Tret'em Tysyacheletti do Nashei Ery.*, Kazakhstan: Kustanay.

Katō, Kyūzō 加藤九祚 (1991). "Sarmatin (sic) Arts and Their Surroundings." In Kodai Oriento Hakubutsukan 古代オリエント博物館, Kyoto-fu Kyoto Bunka Hakubutsukan 京都府京都文化博物館, Fukuoka Iwataya 福岡岩田屋, and Asahi Shinbunsha 朝日新聞社 (eds.), *Minami roshia kibaminzoku no ihōten: Herenizumu bunka tono deai* 南ロシア騎馬民族の遺宝展: ヘレニズム文明との出会 (The Treasures of Nomadic Tribes in South Russia). Tokyo: Asahi Shinbunsha 朝日新聞社.

Katz, Marilyn A. (1995). "Ideology and 'the status of women' in Ancient Greece." In Richard Hawley and Barbara Levick (eds.), *Women in Antiquity: New Assessments*, pp. 21–43. London and New York: Routledge.

Kehoe, Alice. (1992). "The Muted Class: Unshackling Tradition." In Cheryl Claassen (ed.), *Exploring Gender through Archaeology*, pp. 23–32. Madison, WI: Prehistory Press.

Kelly, Fergus. (1988). *A Guide to Early Irish Law*. Dublin: Dublin Institute for Advanced Studies.

Kelly, Patricia. (1992). "The *Táin* in Literature." In J. P. Mallory (ed.), *Aspects of the Táin*, pp. 9–102. Belfast: December Publications.

Kendall, Laurel. (1985). *Shamans, Housewives, and Other Restless Spirits.* Honolulu: University of Hawaii Press.

Khazanov, Anatoly M. (1975). *Sotsialnaya istoria skifov* (Social History of Scythians). Moscow: Nauka.

Khazanov, A.M., 1983. *Nomads and the Outside World.* Cambridge University Press, Cambridge

————. (1994). *Nomads and the Outside World.* 2nd ed. Madison: University of Wisconsin Press.

Khlobystina, M. D. (1961). "O proiskhozhdenie minusinskikh kolenchatykh nozhej (About the Origin of the Minusinsk Bent Knives)." *Soobshchenija Gosudarstvennogo Ermitaja* (21):44–47.

————. (1970). "Kamenskij mogil'nik na Enisee i Ust'-Erbinskaja gruppa karasukskikh pamjatnikov (Kamenskij Cemetery on the Enisej River and Karasuk Sites from Ust'-Erba)." *Sovietskaja Arkheologija* 1:121–129.

Khudyakov, Yurii S. (1986). *Vooruzhenie srednevekovykh kochevnikov Yuzhnoi Sibiri i Tcentralnoi Asii* (A Weaponry of Medieval Nomads of South Siberia and Central Asia). Novosibirsk: Nauka.

Kim B. and K. Shim (1987). *Isong Sansong Excavation Report.* Seoul: Hanyang University Museum Research Series No. 5.

Kim Byong-mo. (1998). *Kumgwan Bimil* (Gold Crowns Decoded). Seoul: Purun Yoksa.

Kim Chae-kuei and Lee Un-chang. (1975). *Report on the Excavation of Tombs at Hwangnamdong, Kyongju.* Kyongju:Yongnam University Museum.

Kim Chong Sun. (1965). The Emergence of Multi-Centered Despotism in the Silla Kingsom: A Study of Factional Struggles in Korea. PhD diss., University of Washington.

————. (1969). "Sources of Cohesion and Fragmentation in the Silla Kingdom." *Journal of Korean Studies* 1 (1):41–72.

————. (1977). "The Kolpum System: Basis for Sillan Social Stratification." *Journal of Korean Studies* 9 (2):43–69.

Kim Jong Hak. (trans. R. and K. Pearsons). (1978). *The Prehistory of Korea.* Honolulu: University of Hawaii Press.

Kim, Pusik. (1145). *Samguk Sagi* (History of the Three Kingdoms). English translation by Edward Shultz and others. Honolulu: University of Hawaii Press.

Kim Won Yong. (1983). *Recent Archaeological Discoveries in the Republic of Korea.* Tokyo: UNESCO.

————. (1986). *Art and Archaeology of Ancient Korea.* Seoul: Taekwang Publishing.

Kiselev, S. V. (1929). "Materialy arkheologicheskoj ekspeditsii v Minusinskij kraj v 1928 g (Archaeological Finds from Minusinskij Kraj Expeditions in 1928)." *Ezhegodnik Gosudarstvennnogo muzeja im. Mart'janova* 4: 47–81.

————. (1951). *Drevnjaja istorija Juzhnoj Sibiri* (Ancient History of Southern Siberia). Moscow: Nauka.

Klyashtorny, Sergei G. and Dmitrii G. Savinov (2005). *Stepnye imperii drevnei Evrazii* (The Steppe Empires of Ancient Eurasia). Saint Petersburg: St. Petersburgskii Universitet Press.

Kodai Oriento Hakubutsukan 古代オリエント博物館, Kyoto-fu Kyoto Bunka Hakubutsukan 京都府京都文化博物館, Fukuoka Iwataya 福岡岩田屋, and Asahi Shinbunsha 朝日新聞社. (1991). 南ロシア騎馬民族の遺宝展: ヘレニズム文明との出会 (The Treasures of Nomadic Tribes in South Russia). Tokyo: Asahi Shinbunsha 朝日新聞社.

Kohl, Philip L. (1989). "The Use and Abuse of World Systems Theory: The Case of the 'Pristine' West Asian State." In C. C. Lamberg-Karlovsky, *Archaeology in the Americas and Beyond*, pp. 241–267. Cambridge: Cambridge University Press.

———. (2007). *The Making of Bronze Age Eurasia*. Cambridge: Cambridge University Press.

Kohl, P. and C. Fawcett. (eds.). (1995). *Nationalism, Politics and the Practice of Archaeology*. Cambridge: Cambridge University Press.

Komarov, V. L. (1985). *Flora of the U.S.S.R.* Vol. 5. Dehra Dun, India: Bishen Singh Mahendra Pal Singh.

Konovalov, P. B. (1976). *Khunnu V Zabaikal'e* (Huns in Trans-Baikal). Ulan Ude, Transbaïkal: Buriat.

———. (1985). "Nekotorye itogi i zadachi izucheniya Khunnu (Some Conclusions and Commissions of Hun Research)." In Ruslan Sergeevich Vasilevskii (ed.), *Drevnie kul'tury Mongolii* (Mongolian Ancient Cultures). Novosibirsk: Nauka.

Koryakova, Ludmila N. (1988). *Rannii zheleznyi vek Zauralya i Zapadnoi Sibiri* (The Early Iron Age of the Trans-Urals and Western Siberia). Sverdlovsk: Uralskii Universitet.

———. (1994). "Pogrebalnaya obryadnost' lesostepnogo naseleniya Tobolo-Irtyshskogo mezhdurechya (Burial rites of forest-steppe people in the Tobol-Irtysh area)." In V. M. Kulemzin and N. V. Lukina (eds.), *Ocherki kul'turogeneza narodov Zapadnoi Sibiri*, pp. 113–170. Tomsk: Tomskii Universitet.

———. (1996). "Social Trends in Temperate Eurasia during the Second and First Millennia BC." *Journal of European Archaeology* 4:243–280.

———. (2000). "Burials and Settlements at the Eurasian Crossroads: Joint Franco-Russian Project." In Jeannine Davis-Kimball, Eileen M. Murphy, Ludmila Koryakova, and Leonid T. Yablonsky (eds.), *Kurgans, Ritual Sites, and Settlements Eurasian Bronze and Iron Age*, pp. 63–74. BAR International Series 890. Oxford: Archaeopress.

———. (2003). "Between Steppe and Forest: Iron Age Societies of the Urals." In Katie Boyle, Colin Renfrew and Marsha Levine (eds.), *Ancient Interactions: East and West in Eurasia*, pp. 265–292. Cambridge: McDonald Institute.

———. (2007). "On the Northern Periphery of the Nomadic World: Research in the Trans-Ural Region." In J. Aruz, A. Farkas, and E. Valtz Fino (eds.), *The Golden Deer of Eurasia*, pp. 102–113. New York: Metropolitan Museum of Art.

Koryakova, Ludmila N. and Marie-Yvane Daire. (eds.) (1997). *Kultura zauralskikh skotovodov na rubezhe er* (The Culture of Trans-Uralian Cattle and Horse Breeders on the Turn of Erae: The Gayevo Burial Ground of the Sargat Community: Anthropological Research). Ekaterinburg: Ekaterinburg Publishers.

Koryakova, Ludmila N and Marie-Yvane Daire (2000). "Burials and Settlements at the Eurasian Crossroads: Joint Franco-Russian Project." In Jeannine Davis-

Kimball, Eileen M. Murphy, Ludmila Koryakova and Leonid T. Yablonsky (eds.), *Kurgans, Ritual Sites, and Settlements Eurasian Bronze and Iron Age*, pp. 63–74. BAR International Series 890. Oxford: Archaeopress.

Koryakova, Ludmila and Andrej V. Epimakhov. (2007). *The Urals and Western Siberia in the Bronze and Iron Ages.* Cambridge: Cambridge University Press.

Koryakova, Ludmila N., Marie-Yvane Daire, L. Langouet, E. Gonsalez, D. Marguerie, P. Courtaud, P. Kosintsev, A. Kovrigin, D. Razhev, N. Berseneva, S. Panteleyeva, S. Sharapova, B. Hanks, A. Kazdym, O. Mikrukova and E. Efimova (2004). "Iron Age societies and Environment: Multi-Disciplinary Research in the Iset River Valley (Russia)." In H. Dobrzanska, E. Jerem and T. Kalicki (eds.), *The Archaeology of River Valleys*, pp. 185–214. Budapest: Archeolingua.

Kosintsev, Pavel A. and Elena N. Borodina (1991). "Fauna gorodisha Pavlinovo i nekotorye aspekty skotovodstva sargatskoi kultury (Fauna of the Pavlinovo settlement and some aspects of live stockbreeding of the Sargat Culture)." In Vladimir I. Matyushenko (ed.), *Problemy izuchenia sargatskoi kultury*, pp. 45–53. Omsk: Omskii Universitet.

Kovrigin, Andrei A., Ludmila N. Koryakova, P. Courtaud, Dmitrii I. Razhev and Svetlana V. Sharapova (2006). "Aristokraticheskie pogrebeniya iz mogilnika Karas'e 9 (Aristocratic burials of Karas'e 9 cemetery)." In Galina T. Obydennova and Nikita S. Savel'ev (eds.), *Yuzhnyi Ural i sopredelnye territorii v skifo-sarmatskoe vremya*, pp. 188–204. Ufa: Gilem.

Kotozhekov, K. G. (2000). "Spätbronzezeitlicher Grabfund aus der Necropole Podkuninskie (Late Bronze Age Tombs of the Podkuninskie Cemetery)." *Eurasia Antiqua* 6:281–295.

Kozlov, P. K. (1925). *Severnaya Mongoliya. Noin-ulinskie Pamyatniki* (Northern Mongolia. Noin-Ula Remains), *Kratkie Otchety Ekspeditsii po Issledovaniyu Severnoii Mongolii v svyazi s Mongolo-Tibetskoii Ekspeditsieii P. K. Kozlova* (Conclusion of Kozlov's Mongolian-Tibetan Expedition to Northern Mongolia). Leningrad.

Kradin, N. (2002). "Nomadism, Evolution and World-Systems: Pastoral Societies in Theories of Historical Development." *Journal of World-Systems Research* 8 (3):368–388.

Kristiansen, K. (1998). *Europe before History.* Cambridge: Cambridge University Press.

Kroll, A-M. (2000). "Looted Graves or Burials without Bodies?" In J. Davis-Kimball, E. M. Murphy, L. N. Koryakova, and L. T. Yablonsky (eds.), *Kurgans, Ritual Sites and Settlements: Eurasian Bronze and Iron Age*, pp. 215–222. BAR International Series 890. Oxford: Archaeopress.

Kubarev, V. D. (1987). *Kurgany Ulandryka.* Novosibirsk: Academy of Sciences.

Kücher, S. (1999). *The Art of Forgetting.* Oxford: Berg.

Kulemzin, Vladimir M. (1994). "Obryady perevoda iz realnogo mira v potustoronnii u narodov Zapadnoi Sibiri v XVIII–XX vv. (Liminal rituals of Western Siberian Natives in the Fourteenth to Twentieth A.D.)." In *Ocherki kul'turogeneza narodov Zapadnoi Sibiri. V. 2*, pp. 334–422. Tomsk: Tomskii Universitet.

Kuzmina, Elena E. (2003). "Origins of Pastoralism in the Eurasian Steppes." In Marsha Levine, Colin Renfrew, and Katie Boyle (eds.), *Prehistoric Steppe Adaptation and the Horse*, pp. 203–232. Cambridge: McDonald Institute for Archaeological Research, University of Cambridge.

Kuznetsov-Krasnojarskij, I. P. (1889). "Drevnie mogily Minusinskogo okruga. Tomsk (Ancient tombs of the Minusinsk region)." *Minusinskie drevnocti*, t. 8, vyp. I:11–18.

Kyslasov, L. R. (1971). "Karasukskij mogil'nik Khara Khaja (Karasuk Cemetery of Khara Khaja)." *Sovetskaja Arkheologija* 3:170–188.

Lane, Rose Wilder. (1922). *The Peaks of Shala*. London: Chapman and Dodd.

Larick, R. (1985). "Spears, Style and Time among Maa-speaking Pastoralists." *Journal of Anthropological Archaeology* 4 (1):201–215.

———. (1986). "Age Grading and Ethnicity in the Style of Loikop (Samburu) Spears." *World Archaeology* 18 (2):269–283.

Larsen, C. S. (1997). *Bioarchaeology: Interpreting Behaviour from the Human Skeleton*. Cambridge: Cambridge University Press.

Lawrence, Dave. (2004). "A New Pictish Figure from Orkney." In *Papers and Pictures in Honour of Daphne Home Lorimer MBE*. Orkney Archaeological Trust. www.orkneydigs.org.uk/dhl/papers/dl.

Lazaretov, L. P. (1995). "Kamenolozhskie pogrebenija mogil'nika Arban I (K kharakteristike pogrebal'nogo obrjada) (Kamenolozhskie Burials from Arban I Cemetery) (Burial Practices)." In D. G. Savinov (ed.), *Juzhnaja Sibir' v Drevnosti*, pp. 39–46. Saint Petersburg: Rossijskaja Akademija Nauk, Rossijskij Gumanitarnij Fond, Institut Istorii Material'noj Kul'tury Gosudarstvennyj Ermitazh.

———. (2000). "Spätbronzezeitliche Fundstellen in Südchakassien (Late Bronze Age Finds in South Khakassia)." *Eurasia Antiqua* 6:249–280.

Lechtman, Heather. (1977). "Style in Technology—Some Early Thoughts." In Heather Lechtman and R. Merrill (eds.), *Material Culture: Styles, Organization, and Dynamics of Technology*, pp. 3–20. St. Paul, MN: West Publishing.

———. (1994). "The Materials Science of Material Culture: Examples from the Andean Past." In David A. Scott and Pieter Meyers (eds.), *Archaeometry of Pre-Columbian Sites and Artifacts*, pp. 3–12. Los Angeles: Getty Conservation Institute.

Lee, Ki-dong. (2004). "The Indigenous Religions of Silla: Their Diversity and Durability." *Korean Studies* 28:49–74.

Legrand, S. (2004). "Karasuk Metallurgy: Technological Development and Regional Influence." In K. M. Linduff (ed.), *Metallurgy in Ancient Eastern Eurasia from the Urals to the Yellow River*, pp. 139–156. Lewiston, NY: Edwin Mellen Press.

Leont'ev, N. V. (1980). "Kolesnyj transport epokhi bronzy na Enisee (Chariot Transportation in the Bronze Age Epoch in the Enisej Region)." In Ja. I. Sunchugashev (ed.), *Voprocy arkheologii Khakasii*, pp. 65–84. Abakan: Khakasskij Nauchno-Issledovatel'skij Institut Jasika, Literatury I Istorii.

Levasheva, V. P. (1950). "O gorodishakh Sibirskogo Yurta (On Siberian Yurt Fortresses)." *Sovetskaya Arkheologiya* (Soviet Archaeology) 13: 341–350.

Levina, Larisa M. (1994). *Jetyasarskaya cultura. Ch. 3–4. Mogilnik Altynasar 4. (Jetyasar Culture. Chapter 4. Altynasar Cemetery 4). Nizov'ya Syrdar'i v drevnosti*. V. 4. Moscow: IEA RAN Press.

Levine, M. (1999a). "Botai and the Origins of Horse Domestication." *Journal of Anthropological Archaeology* 18 (1):29–78.

———. (1999b). "The Origins of Horse Husbandry on the Eurasian Steppe." In M. Levine, Y. Rassamakin, A. Kislenko, and N. Tatarintseva (eds.), *Late Prehistoric Exploitation of the Eurasian Steppe*, pp. 5–58. Cambridge: McDonald Institute Monographs.

Levine, M. and A. M. Kislenko. (1997). "New Eneolithic and Early Bronze Age Radiocarbon Dates for North Kazakhstan and South Siberia." *Cambridge Archaeological Journal* 7:297–300.

Li Gongdu 李恭笃 and Gao Meixuan 高美璇. (1985). "Xiajiadian xiaceng wenhua ruogan wenti yanjiu 夏家店下层文化若干问题研究 (Research of Certain Questions Concerning the Lower Xiajiadian Culture)." *Liaoning daxue xuebao* 辽宁大学学报 (Liaoning University Journal) (5):154–161.

Li Shuicheng 李水城 and Shui Tao 水涛. (2000). "Siba wenhua tongqi yanjiu 四坝文化铜器研究 (Research of Bronzes form the Siba Culture)." *Wenwu* 文物 (Cultural Relics) (3):36–44.

Li Xiuhui 李秀辉 and Han Rubin 韩汝玢. (2000). "Zhukaoigou Yizhi chutu tongqi de jinxiangxue yanjiu 朱开沟遗址出土铜器的金相学研究 (A Metallurgical Study of Bronze Artifacts from Zhukaigou)." In Neimenggu zizhiqu wenwu kaogu yanjiusuo 内蒙古自治区文物考古研究所 (Inner Mongolia Autonomous Region Archaeological Institute) and E'erduosi bowuguan 鄂尔多斯博物馆 (The Ordos Museum) (eds.), *Zhukaigou: Qingtong shidai zaoqi yizhi fajue baogao* 朱开沟-青铜时代早期遗址发掘报告 (Zhukaigou: A Report on the Excavation of an Early Bronze Age Site), pp. 422–446. Beijing: Wenwu chubanshe.

Li Yiyou 李逸友. (1959). "Neimenggu Horinger xian chutu de tongqi 内蒙古和林格尔县出土的铜器 (The Bronzes Unearthed from Horinger County, Inner Mongolia)." *Wenwu* 文物 (Cultural Relics) (6):inside back cover.

Liang Jingming 梁京明 and Ta La 塔拉. (1980). "Hulusitai Xiongnu mu 呼鲁斯太匈奴墓 (The Xiongnu Tombs at Hulusitai)." *Wenwu* 文物 (Cultural Relics) (7):11–17.

Liaoning sheng bowuguan wenwu gongzuodui 辽宁省博物馆文物工作队 (Archaeological Team of the Liaoning Provincial Museum). (1983). "Liaoning Jianpingxian Kalaqin Hedong yizhi shijue jianbao 辽宁建平县喀喇沁河东遗址试掘简报 (Preliminary Report of the Kalaqin Site in Jianping County, Liaoning)." *Kaogu* 考古 (Archaeology) (11):973–981.

Liaoning sheng wenwu kaogu yanjiusuo 辽宁省文物考古研究所 (Institute of Cultural Relics and Archaeology, Liaoning Province). (1992). "Liaoning Fuxin Pingdingshan shichengzhi fajue baogao 辽宁阜新平顶山石城址发掘报告 (Report on the Excavations of the Pingdingshan Stone Wall Site, Fuxin, Liaoning)." *Kaogu* 考古 (Archaeology) (5):399–417.

———. (2001). "Liaoning Beipiaoshi Kangjiatun chengzhi fajue jianbao 辽宁北票市康家屯城址发掘简报 (Preliminary Report on the Excavations at the Kangjiatun Fortified Site, Beipiao City, Liaoning)." *Kaogu* 考古 (Archaeology) (8):31–44.

Lin Yun. (1986). "A Re-examination of the Relationship between Bronzes of the Shang Culture and of the Northern Zone." In K. C. Chang (ed.), *Studies of Shang Archaeology*, pp. 237–273. New Haven: Yale University Press.

Linduff, Katheryn M. (1979). "Epona: A Celt among the Romans." *Latomus Revue d'Études Latines* 38 (4):817–837.

———. (1995). "Zhukaigou: Steppe Culture and the Rise of Chinese Civilization." *Antiquity* 69:133–145.

———. (1997). "Archaeological Overview." In Emma Bunker, Trudi Kawami, Katheryn M. Linduff, and Wu En, *Ancient Bronzes of the Eastern Eurasian Steppe from the Arthur M. Sackler Collections*, pp. 11–97. New York: Abrams.

———. (1998). "The Emergence and Demise of Bronze-Producing Cultures Outside the Central Plain of China." In Victor H. Mair (ed.), *The Bronze Age and Early Iron Age Peoples of Eastern Central Asia*, pp. 619–643. Philadelphia: University of Pennsylvania Museum Publications.

———. (2002). "Women's Lives Memorialized in Burial in Ancient China at Anyang." In Sarah Milledge Nelson and Myriam Rosen-Ayalon (eds.), *In Pursuit of Gender: Worldwide Archaeological Perspectives*, pp. 257–87. Walnut Creek, CA: AltaMira Press.

———. (2003a). "Many Wives, One Queen, in Shang China." In S. M. Nelson (ed.), *Ancient Queens: Archaeological Explorations*, pp. 59–76. Walnut Creek, CA: AltaMira Press.

———. (2003b). "A Walk on the Wild Side: Late Shang Appropriation of Horses in China." In M. Levine, C. Renfrew, and K. Boyle (eds.), *Prehistoric Steppe Adaptation and the Horse*, pp. 113–162. Cambridge: McDonald Institute.

Linduff, Katheryn M. and Sun Yan. (eds.) (2004). *Gender and Chinese Archaeology*. Walnut Creek, CA: AltaMira Press.

Linduff, Katheryn M., R. Drennan, and G. Shelach. (2004). "Early Complex Societies in NE China: The Chifeng International Collaborative Archaeological Research Project." *Journal of Field Archaeology* 29 (1–2):45–73.

Lipskij, A. N. (1949). "Raskopki drevnikh pogrebenij v Abakane (Excavations of Ancient Burials in Abakan)." *KSIIMK* (25):75–86.

———. (1956). "Arkheologicheskie raskopki v Khakassii (Archaeological Excavations in Khakassia)." *KSIIMK* (64):116–129.

———. (1957). "Raskopki 1953 g. v Khakassii (Excavations in 1953 in Khakassia)." *KSIIMK* (70):72–77.

Liu Jing-wen. (1995). "Bronze Culture in Jilin Privince." In S. M. Nelson (ed.), *The Archaeology of Northeast China*, pp. 206–224. London: Routledge.

Liu Mingguang 刘明光. (ed.) (1998). *Zhongguo ziran dili tuji* 中国自然地理图集 (Atlas of Chinese Natural Georgraphy). 2nd ed. Beijing: Zhongguo ditu chubanshe.

Livshits, V.A. (2002). "Three silver bowls from the first burial ground of Isakovka." *Vestnik Drevnei Istoriyi* 2:43–56.

Loewe, Michael. (1977). *Crisis and Conflict in Han China*. London: Allen & Unwin.

Loth, S. and M. Henneberg. (2001). "Sexually Dimorphic Mandibular Morphology in the First Few Years of Life." *American Journal of Physical Anthropology* 115:179–186.

Lovell, Nancy C. (1994). "Spinal Arthritis and Physical Stress in Bronze Age Harappans." *American Journal of Physical Anthropology* 93:149–164.

————. (1997). "Anaemia in the Ancient Indus Valley." *International Journal of Osteoarchaeology* 7:115–123.

Lucy, Sam. (1997). "Housewives, Warriors and Slaves? Sex and Gender in Anglo-Saxon Burials." In J. Moore and E. Scott (eds.), *Invisible People and Processes*, pp. 150–168. London: Leicester University Press.

————. (2005). "Ethnic and Cultural Identities." In Margarita Diaz-Andreu, Sam Lucy, Staša Babić, and David N. Edwards (eds.), *The Archaeology of Identity: Approaches to Gender, Age, Status, Ethnicity and Religion*, pp. 86–109.Oxford: Routledge.

Lukacs, John. (1993). *Dental Anthropology*. Weston, CT: Pictures of Record.

————. (1996). "Sex Differences in Dental Caries Rates with the Origin of Agriculture in South Asia." *Current Anthropology* 37:147–153.

Lysias. (trans. W. R. M. Lamb). (1988) (reprint 1992). *Lysias*. Loeb Classical Library. Cambridge, MA: Harvard University Press.

MacGregor, A. (1972–1974). "The Broch of Burrian, North Ronaldsay, Orkney." *Proceedings of the Society of Antiquaries of Scotland* 105:63–118.

————. (1985). *Bone, Antler, Ivory and Horn: The Technology of Skeletal Materials since the Roman Period*. London: Croom Helm.

Mair, Victor H. (2003). "The Horse in Late Prehistoric China: Wresting Culture and Control from the 'Barbarians.'" In M. Levine, C. Renfrew, and K. Boyle (eds.), *Prehistoric Steppe Adaptation and the Horse*, pp. 163–187. Cambridge: McDonald Institute.

Maksimenkov, G. A. (1964). "Novye dannye ob epokhe bronzy v Minusinskoj kotlovine (New Data on the Bronze Age Epoch in the Minusinsk Basin)." *KSIA* 101:19–23.

————. (1974). "Karasukskij mogil'nik na rechke Chernovoj (The Karasuk cemetery on the Chernovoy river)." *Izvestija Laboratorii Arkheologicheskikh Issledovanij* 5:15–20.

Mallory, J. P. and D. Q. Adams. (eds.) (1997). *Encyclopedia of Indo-European Culture*. Chicago: Fitzroy Dearborn Publishers.

Mamontov, V. I. (1990). *Otchet: O Rabote Privolzhskogo otryada LOEA AN SSSR i Donskoy ekspedetsii VGPE v 1990 godu*. Unpublished.

————. (1991). *Otchet: O Rabote Privolzhskogo otryada LOEA AN SSSR i Donskoy ekspedetsii VGPE v 1991 godu*. Unpublished.

Mandelstam, M. (ed.) (1997). *Shamanic Worlds: Ritual and Lore of Siberia and Central Asia*. New York: North Castle Books.

Marazov, Ivan. (1996). *The Rogozen Treasure*. Sofia: Sekor.

Marcus, M. I. (1993). "Dressed to Kill: Women and Pins in Early Iron Age Assyria." *Oxford Art Journal* 17:3–15.

Martinuk, O. I. (1985). "Keramika Poseleniya Botai." In V. F. Zaibert, S. Zdanovich, N. O. Ivanova, N. Merpert, and A. D. Tairov (eds.), *Eneolit i Bronzovyi Vek Uralo-Irtyshskovo Mezhdurechya*, pp. 59–72. Chelyabinsk, Russia: Chelyabinskii Gosudarstvennyi Universitet.

Maslowski, Robert F. (1996). "Cordage Twist and Ethnicity." In James B. Petersen (ed.), *A Most Indispensable Art: Native Fiber Industries from Eastern North America*, pp. 88–100. Knoxville: University of Tennessee Press.

Matveyeva, Natalia P. (1993). *Sargatskaya kultura na Srednem Tobole (The Sargat Culture in the Middle Tobol Area)*. Novosibirsk: Nauka.

———. (1994). *Rannii zhelezhyi vek Priishimya (Early Iron Age of the Ishim Area)*. Novosibirsk: Nauka.

Matyushenko, Vladimir I. and Tataurova, Larisa V. (1997). *Mogilnik Sidorovka v Omskom Priirtysh'e (Sidorovka Burial Ground in the Omsk Area of the Irtysh Basin)*. Novosibirsk: Nauka.

Mays, S. (1998). *The Archaeology of Human Bones*. London: Routledge.

McCune, Evelyn. (1962). *The Arts of Korea: An Illustrated History*. Tokyo: Tuttle.

McHugh, Feldore. (1999). *Theoretical and Quantitative Approaches to the Study of Mortuary Practice*. BAR International Series 785. Oxford: Archaeopress.

McIntosh, S. (ed.) (1999). *Beyond Chiefdoms: Pathways to Complexity in Africa*. Cambridge: Cambridge University Press.

Meadow, Richard. (1996). "The Origins and Spread of Agriculture and Pastoralism in Northwestern South Asia." In D. R. Harris (ed.), *The Origins and Spread of Agriculture and Pastoralism in Eurasia*, pp. 390–412. Washington, DC: Smithsonian Institution Press.

Megaw, Ruth and Vincent Megaw. (1989). *Celtic Art: From Its Beginnings to the Book of Kells*. New York: Thames and Hudson.

Meindl, R., C. Lovejoy, R. Mensforth, and L. Carlos. (1985). "Accuracy and Direction of Error in the Sexing of the Skeleton." *American Journal of Physical Anthropology* 68:79–85.

Melyukova, Anna I. (1995). "Scythians of Southeastern Europe." In Jeannine Davis-Kimball, Vladimir A. Bashilov and Leonid T. Yablonsky (eds.), *Nomads of the Eurasian Steppes in the Early Iron Age*, pp. 27–62. Berkeley: Zinat Press.

Merlin, Mark David. (1972). *Man and Marijuana: Some Aspects of Their Ancient Relationship*. Rutherford, NJ: Barnes.

Meskell, Lynn. (2002). "The Intersections of Identity and Politics in Archaeology." *Annual Review of Anthropology* 31:279–301.

Meskell, Lynn. (ed.) (1998). *Archaeology Under Fire*. New York: Routledge.

Miller, D. and C.Tilley. (eds.) (1984). *Ideology, Power and Prehistory*. Cambridge: Cambridge University Press.

Miller, Roy Andrew. (1996). *Languages and History: Korean and Altaic*. Bangkok: Orchid Press.

Minar, Jill C. (2000). "Spinning and Plying: Anthropological Directions." In Penelope Ballard Drooker and Laurie D. Webster (eds.), *Beyond Cloth and Cordage: Archaeological Textile Research in the Americas*, pp. 85–99. Salt Lake City: University of Utah Press.

Minns, Ellis H. (1913). *Scythians and Greeks*. Cambridge, England: Cambridge University Press.

———. (1944). *The Art of the Northern Nomads*. London: Milford.

Mogil'nikov, Vyacheslav A., Alexander D. Kolesnikov, and Alexandr V. Kuibyshev. (1977). *Raboty v Priirtysh'e (The Works in Middle Irtysh Area)*. Moscow: Nauka.

Molleson, Theya. (1993). "The Human Remains." In D. Farwell and T. Molleson (eds.), *Excavations at Poundbury 1966–80. Volume II: The Cemeteries*, pp. 142–

214. Dorset Natural History & Archaeology Society Monograph Series 11. Dorset: Dorset Natural History and Archaeology Society.

———. (1994). "The Eloquent Bones of Abu Hureyra." *Scientific American* 271 (2):70–75.

Molleson, T. and M. Cox. (1993). *The Spitalfields Project. Volume 2: The Anthropology.* CBA Research Report 86. York: Council for British Archaeology.

Mortensen, Lena. (2004). "The 'Marauding Pagan Warrior' Woman." In K. Anne Pyburn (ed.), *Ungendering Civilization*, pp. 94–116. New York: Routledge.

Moshkova, Marina G. (1989). "Srednesarmatskaya kultura (Middlesarmatian Culture)." In Anna I. Melyukova (ed.), *Stepi evropeiskoi chasti SSSR v skifo-sarmatskoe vremya. Arkheologiya SSSR*, pp. 177–191. Moscow: Nauka.

———. (1995). "Middle Sarmatian Culture." In Jeannine Davis-Kimball, Vladimir A. Bashilov and Leonid T. Yablonsky (eds.), *Nomads of the Eurasian Steppes in the Early Iron Age*, pp. 137–147. Berkeley: Zinat Press.

Moshkova, M. (ed.) (1997). *Statisticheskaya Obrabotka Pogrebal'nykh Pamyatnikov Aziatskoi Sarmatii: II. Rannesarmatskaya Kul'tura.* Moskva: Nauka.

———. (1994). *Statisticheskaya Obrabotka Pogrebal'nykh Pamyatnikov Aziatskoi Sarmatii: Vyp. I. Savromatskaya Epokha.* Moscow: Nauka.

———. (ed.) (1997). *Statisticheskaya Obrabotka Pogrebal'nykh Pamyatnikov Aziatskoi Sarmatii: II. Rannesarmatskaya Kul'tura.* Moscow: Nauka.

———. (2002). *Statisticheskaya Obrabotka Pogrebal'nykh Pamyatnikov Aziatskoi Sarmatii: Vyp. III. Srednesarmatskaya Kul'tura.* Moscow: Nauka.

Müller, S. 2003. "Chin-straps of the Early Northern Wei: New Perspectives in the Trans-Asiatic Diffusion of Funerary Practices." *Journal of East Asian Archaeology* 5 (1–4):27–71.

Munro, R. (1889). "Notes of a visit to a terp mound at Aalzum, in North Friesland, Holland." In Proceedings of the Society of Antiquaries of Scotland 23, pp. 98–105.

Murphy, E. (1998). An Osteological and Palaeopathological Study of the Scythian and Hunno-Sarmatian Period Populations from the Cemetery Complex of Aymyrlyg, Tuva, South Siberia. PhD thesis, Queen's University, Belfast.

———. (2003). *Iron Age Archaeology and Trauma from Aymyrlyg, South Siberia.* BAR International Series 1152. Oxford: Archaeopress.

NMGBWG [Nei Menggu Buowuguan, Nei Menggu Wenwu Gongzuodui] 内蒙古博物馆　内蒙古文物工作队 (Museum of Inner Mongolia and the Archaeological Team of Inner Mongolia). (1977). "Nei Menggu Zhunge'er Qi Yulongtai de Xiongnu yiwu 内蒙古准格尔旗玉隆太的匈奴遗物 (The Hsiung Nu Tomb at Yü-lung-t'ai in Tsungar Banner, Inner Mongolia)." *Kaogu* 考古 (Archaeology) (2):111–114.

———. (1965). "Nei Menggu Chen Ba'erhu Qi Wangong gumu qingli jianbao 内蒙古陈巴尔虎旗完工古墓清理简报 (Excavations of Ancient Tombs at Wankung in the Old Barga Banner, Inner Mongolia)." *Kaogu* 考古 (Archaeology) (6):273–283.

———. (1986). "Maoqinggou Mudi 毛庆沟墓地 (Maoqinggou Grave)." In *E'erduosi shi Qiongtongqi* 鄂尔多斯式青铜器 (Ordos Bronzeware), pp. 227–315. Beijing 北京: Wenwu chubanshe 文物出版社 (Cultural Relics Press).

NMGWWGZD [Nei Menggu Wenwu Gongzuodui] 内蒙古工作队 (The Archaeological Team of Inner Mongolia Autonomous Region). (1961). "Nei Menggu Zhalai Nuo'er Gumuqun Fajue Jianbao 内蒙古扎赉诺尔古墓群发掘简报 (Ancient Tombs at Chalai Nor, Inner Mongolia)." *Kaogu* 考古 (Archaeology) (12):673–680.

NMGWWGZDD [Nei Menggu Wenwu Gongzuodui Deng] 内蒙古文物工作队等 (CPAM Inner Mongolia and Others). (1980). "Xigoupan Xiongnu Mu 西沟畔匈奴墓 (The Xiongnu Tombs at Xigou)." *Wenwu* 文物 (Cultural Relics) (7):1–10.

NMGWWGZZ [Nei Menggu Wenwu Gongzuozu] 内蒙古文物工作组 (Cultural Relics Work Group of Inner Mongolia). (1955). "Baotoushi Xijiao Hanmu Qingli Jianbao 包头市西郊汉墓清理简报 (Preliminary Report of the Excavation of Han Tombs in Eastern Suburb of Baotou City)." *Wenwu Cankao Ziliao* 文物参考资料 (References of Cultural Relics) (10):59–62.

NMGWWKG [Nei Menggu Wenwu Kaogu Yanjiusuo] 内蒙古文物考古研究所 (The Institute of Archaeology, Inner Mongolia). (1989). "Liangcheng Xian Guoxianyaozi Mudi 凉城县国县窑子墓地 (The Guoxianyaozi Cemetery in Liangcheng County)." *Kaogu Xuebao* 考古学报 (*Acta Archaeologica Sinica*) (1):57–82.

NMGWWGZD [Nei Menggu Wenwu Zizhiqu Gongzuodui] 内蒙古自治区文物工作队 (The Archaeological Team of the Inner Mongolian Autonomous Region). (1984). "Liangcheng Yinniugou muzang qingli jianbao 凉城饮牛沟墓葬清理简报 (Excavation and Description of the Ancient Tomb in Yinniugou, Liangcheng County)." *Nei Menggu Wenwu Kaogu* 内蒙古文物考古 (Cultural Relics and Archaeology of Inner Mongolia) 3:26–32.

NMGWWKGYJS [Nei Menggu Zizhiqu Wenwu Kaogu Yanjiusuo] 内蒙古自治区文物考古研究所 (Inner Mongolia Autonomous Region Archaeological Institute) and E'erduosi bowuguan 鄂尔多斯博物馆 (The Ordos Museum). (eds.) (2000). *Zhukaigou: Qingtong shidai zaoqi yizhi fajue baogao* 朱开沟-青铜时代早期遗址发掘报告 (Zhukaigou: A Report on the Excavation of an Early Bronze Age Site). Beijing: Wenwu chubanshe 文物出版社 (Cultural Relics Press).

Nelson, Sarah Milledge. (1990). "The Neolithic of Northeastern China and Korea." *Antiquity* 64 (243):234–248.

———. (1991). "The Statuses of Women in Ko-Shilla: Evidence from Archaeology and Historic Documents." *Korea Journal* 31 (2):101–107.

———. (1993a). "Gender Hierarchy and the Queens of Silla." In B. D. Miller (ed.), *Sex and Gender Hierarchies*. Cambridge: Cambridge University Press.

———. (1993b). *The Archaeology of Korea*. Cambridge: Cambridge University Press.

———. (1997). *Gender in Archaeology: Analyzing Power and Prestige*. Walnut Creek, CA: AltaMira Press.

———. (1999). "Megalithic Monuments and the Introduction of Rice into Korea." In C. Gosden and J. Hather (eds.), *The Prehistory of Food*. London: Routledge.

———. (2001). "The Question of Agricultural Impact on Sociopolitical Development in Prehistoric Korea." In *Origin of Prehistoric Rice Agriculture in Korea*.

———. (2003). "The Queens of Silla: Power and Connections to the Spirit World." In S. M. Nelson (ed.), *Ancient Queens, Archaeological Explorations*, pp. 77–92. Walnut Creek, CA: AltaMira Press.

————. (2006). "Archaeology in the Two Koreas." In M. T. Stark (ed.), *Archaeology of Asia*. Oxford: Blackwell.

————. (2006). "Introduction: Archaeological Perspectives in Gender." In S. Nelson (ed.), *Handbook of Gender in Archaeology*, pp. 1–27. Lanham, MD: AltaMira Press.

————. (ed.) (2006). *A Handbook of Gender in Archaeology*. Lanham, MD: AltaMira Press.

Nelson, Sarah Milledge and Myriam Rosen-Ayalon. (eds.) (2002). *In Pursuit of Gender: Worldwide Archaeological Approaches*. Walnut Creek, CA: AltaMira.

NXWWKGYJS [Ningxia Wenwu Kaogu Yangjiusuo] 宁夏文物考古研究所 (Ningxia Institute of Archaeology). (1988a). "Ningxia Tongxin xian Lijiataozi Xiongnu mu qingli jianbao 宁夏同心县李家套子匈奴墓清理简报 (Excavation of Xiongnu Tombs in Lijiataozi, Tongxin County, Ningxia)." *Kaogu yu Wenwu* 考古与文物 (Archaeology and Cultural Relics) (3):17–20.

————. (1988b). "Ningxia Tongxin Daodunzi Xiongnu mudi 宁夏同心倒墩子匈奴墓地 (Xiongnu (Hun) Cemetery at Daodunzi in Tongxin County, Ningxia)." *Kaogu Xuebao* 考古学报 (*Acta Archaeologica Sinica*) (3):333–356.

NMK [National Museum of Korea] (2001). *Nangnang*. Seoul: National Museum of Korea.

Novgorodova, E. A. (1970). *Tsentral'naja Azia i Karasukskaja Problema* (Central Asia and the Karasuk Problem). Moscow: Nauka.

————. (1989). *Drevnjaja Mongolija* (Ancient Mongolia). Moscow: Nauka.

Obladen-Kauder, Julia. (1996). "Die Kleinfunde aus Ton, Knochen und Metall." In Ayse Baykal-Seeher and Julia Obladen-Kauder (eds.), *Demircihüyük, Band IV. Die Kleinfunde,* pp. 287–312, taf. 137–155. Mainz, Germany: Verlag Philipp von Zabern, Gegründet 1785.

O'Connor, Frank. (1967). *The Backward Look: A Survey of Irish Literature*. London: Macmillan.

Okauchi Mitsuzane. (1979). *Chariots in Ancient Korea*. Korea: Chindan Hakbo.

Okladnikov, A. P. and Y. A. I. Sunchugashev (1969). "Zamechatel'nyi pamiatnik karasukskoi kul'tury v Khakasii (Notable Monuments of the Karasuk Culture in Khakasy)." *Izvestia sibirskogo otdeleniya AN SSSR* 1 (1):79–82.

Olsen, Stanley J. (1984). "The Early Domestication of the Horse in North China." *Archaeology* (January–February):62–63, 77.

Olsen, S. L. (1996). "Prehistoric Adaptation to the Kazak Steppes." In G. Afanas'ev, S. Cleuziou, J. Lukacs, and M. Tosi (eds.), *The Colloquia of the XIII International Congress of Prehistoric and Protohistoric Sciences, Vol. 16: The Prehistory of Asia and Oceania*, pp. 49–60. Forlì, Italy: A.B.A.C.O. Edizioni.

————. (2000a). "Expressions of Ritual Behavior at Botai, Kazakhstan." In K. Jones-Bley, M. Huld, and D. Volpe (eds.), *Proceedings of the Eleventh Annual UCLA Indo-European Conference*, pp. 183–207. Journal of Indo-European Studies Monograph Series 35. Washington, DC: Institute for the Study of Man.

————. (2000b). "The Sacred and Secular Roles of Dogs at Botai, North Kazakhstan." In S. Crockford (ed.), *Dogs through Time: An Archaeological Perspective*, pp. 71–92. BAR International Series 889. Oxford: Archaeopress.

————. (2001). "The Importance of Thong-Smoothers at Botai, Kazakhstan." In A. Choyke and L. Bartosiewicz (eds.), *Crafting Bone: Skeletal Technologies through Time and Space*, pp. 197–206. BAR International Series 937. Oxford: Archaeopress.

————. (2003). "The Exploitation of Horses at Botai, Kazakhstan." In M. Levine, C. Renfrew, and K. Boyle (eds.), *Prehistoric Steppe Adaptation and the Horse*, pp. 83–104. Cambridge: McDonald Institute Monographs.

————. (2006). "Early Horse Domestication on the Eurasian Steppe." In Melinda A. Zeder, Daniel G. Bradley, Eve Emshwiller, and Bruce Smith (eds.), *Documenting Domestication: New Genetic and Archaeological Paradigms*, pp. 245–273. Berkeley: University of California Press.

————. (2007). "Conclusions: Bone Artifacts and Their Importance to Archaeology." In Christian Gates-St. Pierre and Renee B. Walker (eds.), *Bones as Tools: Current Methods and Interpretations in Worked Bone Studies*, pp. 175–182. BAR International Series 1622. Oxford: Archaeopress.

Olsen, S. L., B. Bradley, D. Maki, and A. Outram. (2006). "Community Organisation among Copper Age Sedentary Horse Pastoralists of Kazakhstan." In D. Peterson, L. M. Popova, and A. T. Smith (eds.), *Proceedings of the 2002 University of Chicago Conference on Eurasian Archaeology*, pp. 89–111. Monograph Series of *Colloquia Pontica* 13. Leiden: Brill Academic Publishers.

Pader, E. (1982). *Symbolism, Social Relations and the Interpretation of Mortuary Remains*. BAR Supplementary Series 130. Oxford.

Pai, Hyung Il. (2000). *Constructing "Korean" Origins*. Cambridge, MA: Harvard University Asia Center.

Pan Qifeng 潘其风 and Han Kangxin 韩康信. (1984). "Nei Menggu Taohongbala he Qinghai Datong Xiongnu mu rengu de yanjiu 内蒙古桃红巴拉和青海大通匈奴墓人骨的研究 (Studies on the Ancient Tombs at Taohongbala in Nei Mongol and the Skeletal Remains from the Xiongnu Tombs at Datong in Qinghai)." *Kaogu* 考古 (Archaeology) 4:367–375.

Parker, E. H. (1890). "On Race Struggles in Korea." *Transactions of the Asiatic Society of Japan* 23:137–228.

Parker Pearson, M. (1982). "Mortuary Practices, Society and Ideology: An Ethnoarchaeological Study." In I. Hodder (ed.), *Symbolic and Structural Archaeology*, pp. 99–113. Cambridge: Cambridge University Press.

————. (1993). "The Powerful Dead: Relationships between the Living and the Dead." *Cambridge Archaeological Journal* 3:203–229.

————. (1999) [2002]. *The Archaeology of Death and Burial*. Stroud, UK: Sutton Publishing.

Parpola, A. (2005). "The Nasatyas, the Chariot and Proto-Aryan Religion." *Journal of Indological Studies* (16–17):1–63.

Paton, W. R. (trans.) (1916) (reprint 1960). *The Greek Anthology*. Vol. I. Loeb Classical Library. Cambridge, MA: Harvard University Press.

Pauls, E. D. (2000). "Mogil'niki Chazy i Mara na severe Minusinskoj Kotloviny (k voprosu izuchenija karasukskoj kul'tury) (The Chazy and Mara cemeteries in the Northern Part of the Minusinsk Basin) (Questions on the study of the Karasuk

Culture)." In A. B. Nikitin (ed.), *Mirovozzrenie Arkheologija Ritual Kul'tura*, pp. 104–118. Saint Petersburg: Mir Knigi.

Pavlov, P. G. (1999). *Karasukskij Mogil'nik Tjort Aba* (The Karasuk Cemetery of Tjort Aba). Saint Petersburg: Avery Press.

Perlee, Kh. (1957). *Khun Naryn gurvan khermiin uldech* (Remains of Three Hun Fortresses). Ulaanbaatar, Mongolia: Shinzhlekh Ukhaany Khureelengiin Khevlel.

Perzigian, A. (1976). "The Dentition of the Indian Knoll Skeletal Population: Odontometrics and Cusp Number." *American Journal of Physical Anthropology* 44:113–121.

Petersen, James B. and Nathan D. Hamilton. (1984). "Early Woodland Ceramic and Perishable Fiber Industries from the Northeast: A Summary and Interpretation." *Annals of Carnegie Museum* 53 (14):413–445.

Petrenko, Vladimir G. (1995). "Scythian Culture in the North Caucasus." In Jeannine Davis-Kimball (ed.), *Nomads of the Eurasian Steppes in the Early Iron Age*, pp. 5–26. Berkeley: Zinat Press.

Petrenko, V. G., V. E. Maslov, and A. R. Kantorovich. (2004). "Pogrebenie znatnoi skifyanki iz mogilnika Novozavedennoe-II (predvaritelnaya publikatia) (Burial of a Noble Scythian Woman from Novozavedennoe-II Cemetery (preliminary publication))." In Leonid T. Yablonsky (ed.), *Arkheologicheskie pamyatniki rannego zheleznogo veka Uga Rossii*, pp. 179–210. Moscow: IA RAN-Press.

Plutarch. (trans. Bernadotte Perrin). (1920) (reprint 2002). *Plutarch, Lives: Demetrius and Antony; Pyrrhus and Caius Marius*. Loeb Classical Library. Cambridge, MA: Harvard University Press.

Pogodin, Leonid I. (1988). "K kharakteristike pogrebalnogo obryada sargatskoi kultury (About Mortuary Practice of the Sargat Culture)." In Vladimir I. Matyushenko (ed.), *Istochniki i istoriografia. Arkheologiya i istoriya*, pp. 27–37. Omsk: Omskii Universitet.

———. (1989), *Otchet ob arkheologicheskikh isslidovanijakh v Nizhneomskom i Gor'kovskom raionakh Omskoi oblasti v 1989 g.* (The Report about archaeological research in Nizhneomsk and Gor'kovo districts of Omsk region in 1989). Omsk.

———. (1991). *Otchet ob arkheologicheskikh isslidovanijakh u b.d. Strizhevo Nizhneomskogo raiona Omskoi oblasti v 1991 g.* (The Report about archaeological research near Strizhevo village in Nizhneomsk district of Omsk region in 1991). Omsk.

———. (1996). "Zolotnoye shity'e Zapadnoi Sibiri (Golden stitching of western Siberia)." In *Istoricheskii ezhegodnik*, pp. 123–34. Omsk: Omskii Universitet.

———. (1997). "K kharakteristike voennoi struktury sargatskoi obtshnosti (About the Military Stucture of the Sargat Cultural Community)." In Vladimir I. Matyushenko (ed.), *IV, Istoricheskie chteniya pamyati M.P. Gryaznova*, pp. 116–121. Omsk: Omskii Universitet.

———. (1998a). "Lakovye izdeliya iz pamyatnikov Zapadnoi Sibiri rannego zheleznogo veka (Lacquered objects from Iron Age western Siberian sites)." In Leonid I. Pogodin (ed.), *Vzaimodeistviye sargatskikh plemen s vneshnim mirom*, pp. 26–38. Omsk: Omskii Universitet.

————. (1998b). *Vooruzhenie naseleniya Zapadnoi Sibiri rannego zheleznogo veka (Weaponry of Western Siberian population in the Early Iron Age)*. Omsk: Omskii Universitet.

Pogodin, Leonid I. and Alexandr Ya. Trufanov. (1991). "Mogilnik sargatskoi kultury Isakovka III (Sargat Cemetery Isakovka III)." In Vladimir I. Matyushenko (ed.), *Drevnie pogrebeniya Ob-Irtysh'ya*, pp. 98–127. Omsk: Omskii Universitet.

Polos'mak, N. V. (1987). *Baraba v epokhu rannego zheleza (The Early Iron Age in Baraba Lowland)*. Novosibirsk: Nauka .

————. (1992). "Excavations of a Rich Burial of the Pazyryk Culture." *Altaica* 1:35–42.

————. (1994a). "The Ak–Alakh 'Frozen Grave' Barrow." *Ancient Civilizations from Scythia to Siberia* 1 (3):346–354.

————. (1994b). *Griffins Watching over Gold (the Ak-Alakha Kurgans) Steregyshchie zoloto grify (ak-alakhinskie kurgany)*. Novosibirsk: Nauka.

————. (2001). *Vsadniki Ukoka (Horsemen of Ukok)*. Novosibirsk: INFOLIO-Press.

Pomeroy, Sarah, B. (2002). *Spartan Women*. Oxford: Oxford University Press.

Popescu, Grigore Arbore, Chiara Silvi Antonini, and Karl Baipakov. (1998). *L'uomo d'oro*. Milan: Electra.

Pringle, Heather (2001). "Gladiatrix." *Discover* 22 (12):48–55.

Pugachenkova, G. A. and L. I. Rempel (1991). "Gold from Tillia-tepe." *Bulletin of the Asia Institute*. New Series/Volume 5:11–25.

Pugachenkova, G. A., S. R. Dar, R. C. Sharma and M. A. Joyenda, in collaboration with H. Siddiqi (1994). "Kushan Art." In Harmatta, János, B. N. Puri and G. F. Etemadi (eds.), *History of Civilizations of Central Asia, Volume II: The Development of Sedentary and Nomadic Civilizations: 700 B.C. to A.D. 250*, pp. 331–395. Paris: UNESCO.

Puhvel, Jaan. (1987). *Comparative Mythology*. Baltimore, MD: Johns Hopkins University Press.

QHSWWGLCKGD [Qinghai Sheng Wenwu Guanlichu Kaogudui] 青海省文物管理处考古队 (Archaeological Team of CPAM (Committee on Preservation of Ancient Monuments), Qinghai Province). (1979). "Qinghai Datong Shangsunjiazhai de Xiongnu mu 青海大通上孙家寨的匈奴墓 (Excavation of a Xiongnu Tomb at Datong County in Qinghai Province)." *Wenwu* 文物 (Cultural Relics) (4):49–53.

QHSHYXBWG [Qinghai Sheng Huangyuan Xian Bowuguan] 青海省湟源县博物馆 (Huangyuan County Museum, Qinghai Province), Qinghai sheng wenwu kaogu dui 青海省文物考古队 (The Cultural Relics and Archaeology Team of Quinghai Province), Qinghai sheng shehui kexueyuan lishi yanjiushi 青海省社会科学院历史研究室 (The Academy of Social Sciences and History Research Department, Qinghai Province). (1985). "Qinghai Huangyuan xian Dahuazhongzhuang Kayue wenhua mudi fajue jianbao 青海湟源县大华中庄卡约文化墓地发掘简报 (Preliminary Report on the Excavation of the Kayue Culture Cemetery of Dahuazhongzhuang, Huangyuan County, Qinghai)." *Kaogu yu wenwu* 考古与文物 (Archaeology and Cultural Relics) (5):11–34.

Quindlen, Anna. (2007). "Not Semi-Soldiers." *Newsweek*, November 12, 2007, p. 90.

Razhev, Dmitrii I. (2001). *Naseleniye lesosotepi Zapadnoi Sibiri rannego zheleznogo veka: rekonstruktsiya antropologicheskikh osobennostei* (Iron Age Population of Western Siberian Forest-Steppe: anthropological reconstruction). PhD Diss.: Ekaterinburg.

Reinhard, K. J., L. Tieszen, K. Sandness, L. Beiningen, E. Miller, A. Ghazi, C. Miewald, and S. Barnum. (1994). "Trade, Contact, and Female Health in Northeast Nebraska." In. C. Larsen and G. Milner (eds.), *The Wake of Contact: Biological Responses to Conquest*, pp. 63–74. New York: Wiley-Liss.

Renfrew, C. (1998). "All the King's Horses." In S. Mithen (ed.), *Creativity in Human Evolution and Prehistory*, pp. 260–284. London: Routledge.

———. (2002). "Pastoralism and Interaction: Some Introductory Questions." In K. Boyle, C. Renfrew, and M. Levine (eds.), *Ancient Interactions: East and West in Eurasia*, pp. 1–10. Cambridge: McDonald Institute.

Rhodes, J. A. and C. J. Knusel. (2005). "Activity-Related Skeletal Change in Medieval Humeri: Cross-Sectional and Architectural Alterations." *American Journal of Physical Anthropology* 128:536–546.

Rice, Tamara Talbot. (1957). *The Scythians*. New York: Praeger.

Rikushina, G. and V. Zaibert. (1984). "Predvaritelnoe Soobshchenie o Skeletnikh Ostatkakh Lyudeys Eneoliticheskovo Poseleniya Botay." In *Bronzoviy Vek Uralo-Irtishskovo Mezhdurechya*, pp. 121–135. Chelyabinsk, USSR: Bashkirskiy Gosudarstvenniy Universitet.

Robb, John. (2002). "Time and Biography: Osteobiography of the Italian Neolithic Lifespan." In Y. Hamilakis, M. Pluciennik, and S. Tarlow (eds.), *Thinking through the Body: Archaeologies of Corporeality*, pp. 153–177. London: Kluwer Academic.

Roes, Anna. (1963). *Bone and Antler Objects from the Frisian Terp-Mounds*. Haarlem, The Netherlands: H. D. Tjeenk Willink and Zoon N.V.

Rolle, Renate. (1989). *The World of the Scythians*. Berkeley: University of California Press.

Ross, Anne. (1967). *Pagan Celtic Britain: Studies in Iconography and Tradition*. London: Routledge and Kegan Paul.

Rostovtzeff, Michael I. (1929). *The Animal Style in South Russia and China*. Princeton: Princeton University Press.

Rubinson, Karen S. (2002). "Through the Looking Glass: Reflections on Mirrors, Gender, and Use among Nomads." In S. Nelson and M. Rosen-Ayalon (eds.), *In Pursuit of Gender: Worldwide Archaeological Approaches*, pp. 67–72. New York: AltaMira Press.

Rubinson, Karen S. and Michele Marcus. (2005). "Hasanlu IVB and Caucasia: Explorations and Implications of Contexts." In A. Çilingiroğlu and G. Darbyshire (eds.), *Anatolian Iron Age 5*, pp. 313–318. London: British Institute at Ankara.

Rudenko, S. I. (1960). *Kultura naselenia tsentralnogo Altaya v skifskie vremena* (The Culture of the Central Altai Population during the Scythian Period). Moscow-Leningrad: Nauka.

———. (1962). *Kul'tura Khunnov i Noinulinskie Kurgany* (Hun Culture and Noin Ula Kurgans). Moscow-Leningrad: Izd-vo Akademii Nauk SSSR.

———. (1970). *Frozen Tombs of Siberia: The Pazyryk Burials of Iron-Age Horsemen.* Berkeley: University of California Press.

———. (1979). *The Frozen Tombs of Siberia.* London: Dent.

Sansom, G. B. (1930). "An Outline of Recent Japanese Archaeological Research in Korea." *Transactions of the Asiatic Society of Japan* 7:5–19.

Sarianidi, Victor. (1985). *The Golden Hoard of Bactria: From the Tillya-tepe Excavations in Northern Afghanistan.* New York: Abrams.

———. (1989). *Khram I nekropol? Tillyatepe.* Moscow: Nauka.

Sasse, Werner. (2001). "Trying to Figure Out How Kings Became Kings in Silla." In *Mélanges Offerts à Li Ogg et Daniel Bouchez.* Cahiers d'Etudes Coréenes (7):229–244. Paris: Centre d'Etudes Coréenes.

Saul, F. and J. Saul. (1989). "Osteobiography: A Mayan Example." In M. İşcan and K. Kennedy (eds.), *Reconstruction of Life from the Skeleton*, pp. 287–301. New York: Liss.

Savunen, Liisa (1995). "Women in elections in Pompeii." In Richard Hawley and Barbara Levick (eds.), *Women in Antiquity: New Assessments*, pp. 194–206. London and New York: Routledge.

Saxe, Arthur Alan. (1970). Social Dimensions of Mortuary Practices. PhD thesis, University of Michigan.

Saxo Grammaticus. (ed. Ellis Davidson) (trans. Peter Fisher). (1979–1980) (reprint 1998). *Saxo Grammaticus: The History of the Danes Books I–IX.* H.R. Cambridge: Brewer.

Schiltz, Véronique. (2006). "Tillia tepe, la 'Colline de l'or,' une nécropole nomade." In Pierre Cambon, Jean-François Jarrige, Paul Bernard, and Véronique Schiltz (eds.), *Afghanistan: Les trésors retrouvés. Collections du musée national de Kaboul*, pp. 69–79. Paris: Musée national des Arts asiatiques-Guimet.

Schutkowski, H. (1993). "Sex Determination of Infant and Juvenile Skeletons 1: Morphognostic Features." *American Journal of Physical Anthropology* 90:199–205.

Seyock, Barbara (2004). *Auf den Spuren der Ostbarbaren.* Tübingen, Germany: Bunka, Band 8.

Scott, Eleanor. (1997). "Introduction: On the Incompleteness of Archaeological Narratives." In Jenny Moore and Eleanor Scott (eds.), *Invisible People and Processes: Writing Gender and Childhood into European Archaeology*, pp. 1–12. London: Leicester University Press.

Sebas'tjanova, E. A. (1977). "Raboty u stantsii Askiz (Works in the Askiz Station)." *Arkheologicheskie Otkrytie 1976 Goda* :241–242.

Shaanxi Sheng Kaogu Yangjiusuo 陕西省考古研究所 (Institute of Archaeology, Shaanxi Province). (1986). "Shaanxi Tongchuan Zaomiao Qin mu fajue jianbao 陕西铜川枣庙秦墓发掘简报 (Preliminary Report of the Excavation of Qin Tombs in Zaomiao, Tongchuan, Shaanxi)." *Kaogu yu Wenwu* 考古与文物 (Archaeology and Cultural Relics) 2:7–17.

Shelach, Gideon. (1999). *Leadership Strategies, Economic Activity, and Interregional Interaction: Social Complexity in Northeast China.* New York: Plenum Press.

————. (2000). "The Earliest Neolithic Cultures of Northeast China: Recent Discoveries and New Perspectives on the Beginning of Agriculture." *Journal of World Prehistory* 14 (4):363–413.

————. (2001). "Apples and Oranges? Cross-cultural Comparison of Burial Data from Northeast China." *Journal of East Asian Archeology* 3 (3–4):53–90.

————. (2005). "Early Pastoral Societies of Northeast China: Local Change and Interregional Interaction during c. 1100 to 600 BC." In R. Amitai and M. Biran (eds.), *Mongols, Turks and Others: Eurasian Nomads and the Outside World*, pp. 15–58. Leiden: Brill.

————. (forthcoming). "Violence on the Frontiers? Sources of Power and Sociopolitical Change at the Easternmost Parts of the Eurasian Steppes during the Late Second and Early First Millennium BCE." In Bryan K. Hanks and Katheryn M. Linduff (eds.), *Monuments, Metals and Mobility: Trajectories of Complexity in the Late Prehistoric Eruasian Steppe*.

Shennan, S. (1986). "Central Europe in the Third Millennium BC: An Evolutionary Trajectory for the Beginning of the European Bronze Age." *Journal of Anthropological Archaeology* 5:115–146.

————. (1989). *Archaeological Approaches to Cultural Identity*. London: Unwin and Hyman.

————. (1998). "Producing Copper in the Eastern Alps during the Second Millennium BC." In A. B. Knapp, V. C. Pigott, and E. W. Herbert (eds.), *Social Approaches to an Industrial Past: The Archaeology and Anthropology of Mining*, pp. 191–204. London: Routledge.

Shepherd, D. J. (1999). "The Elusive Warrior Maiden Tradition: Bearing Weapons in Anglo-Saxon Society." In J. Carman and A. Harding (eds.), *Ancient Warfare*, pp. 219–243. Stroud, UK: Sutton.

Shui Tao 水涛. (2001). "Gansu diqu qingtong shidai wenhua jiegou he jingji xingtai yanjiu 甘肃地区青铜时代的文化结构和经济形态研究 (The Cultures and Economic Adaptation in Gansu during the Bronze Age)." In Shui Tao (ed.), *Zhongguo xibei diqu qingtong shidai kaogu lunji* 中国西北地区青铜时代考古论集 (Collection of Papers on the Bronze Age of Northwest China), pp. 193–327. Beijing: Kexue Chubanshe.

Shultz, Edward J. (2004). "An Introduction to the *Samguk Sagi*." *Korean Studies* 28:1–13.

Sima Qian 司馬遷 (1959). *Shiji* 史記 (The Records of the Grand Historian). Beijing: Zhong hua shu ju 中華書局 (China Publishing House).

Simonenko, Aleksander V. (1991). "Der linkshändige Sarmatenfürst von Porgoi und die voernhme Dame aus dem Bogajčik-Kurgan." In R. Rolle, M. Müller-Wille, and K. Schietzel (eds.), *Gold der Steppe: Archäologie der Ukraine*, pp. 215–220. Schleswig: Archäologiches Landesmuseum.

————. (2001). "Chinese and East Asian Elements in Sarmatian Culture of the North Pontic Region." *Silk Road Art and Archaeology* 7:53–72.

Simpson, S., D. Hutchinson, and C. Larsen. (1990). "Coping with Stress: Tooth Size, Dental Defects and Age at Death." In C. Larsen (ed.), *The Archaeology of the Mission Santa Catalina de Guale: 2. Biocultural Interpretations of a Population in*

Transition, pp. 66–77. Anthropological Papers of the American Museum of Natural History No. 68. New York: American Museum of Natural History.

Sinitsyn, I. V. (1964). "K materialam po sarmatskoii kul'ture na territorii nizhnego Povolzh'ya (On the Materials of the Sarmatian Culture in the Lower Reaches of Volga River)." *Sovietskaya Arkheologiya* (Soviet Archaeology) (8):figs. 6, 7, 9, 13, 20.

Smirnov, Konstantin F. (1989). "Savromatskaya i rannesarmatskaya kultury (Sauromatian and Early Sarmatian cultures)." In Anna I. Melyukova (ed.), *Stepi evropeiskoi chasti SSSR v skifo-sarmatskoe vremya. Arkheologiya SSSR*, pp. 165–177. Moscow: Nauka.

Sofaer, J. (2006). *The Body as Material Culture: A Theoretical Osteoarchaeology.* Cambridge: Cambridge University Press.

Sohn, P., C. Kim and Y. Hong (1970). *The History of Korea.* Seoul: Korean National Commission for Unesco.

Sokefeld, Martin. (1999). "Debating Self, Identity, and Culture in Anthropology." *Current Anthropology* 40 (4):417–447.

Sosnovskii, G. P. (1934). *Nizhne-Ivolginskoe Gorodishche* (Lower Ivolga Fortresses), *PIDO* (Issues on Pre-Capitalist History), Nos. 7 and 8.

———. (1946). *Raskopki Il'Movoii padi* (The Excavation of Il'Movoii Valley). *Sovietskaya Arkheologiya* (8).

———. (1947). *O Poselenii Gunnskoii Epokhi v Doline r. Chikoya* (Residential Sites of the Hun Period in Chikoy Basin). *KSIIMK* (14).

Spector, Janet. (1993). *What This Awl Means: Feminist Archaeology at a Wahpeton Dakota Village.* St. Paul: Minnesota Historical Society.

Stambul'nik, E. U. (1983). *Novye pamyatniki gunno-sarmatskogo vremeni v Tuve* (New Remains of Hun-Sarmatia in Tuva). *Drevnie kul'tury Evraziiskikh stepeii* (Ancient Cultures on the Eurasian Steppe). Leningrad.

Stenton, Frank. (1968). *Anglo-Saxon England.* 3rd ed. Oxford: Clarendon Press.

Stevens, Susan T. (1991). "Charon's Obol and Other Coins in Ancient Funerary Practice." *Phoenix* 45 (3):215–229.

Stirland, A. J. (1993). "Asymmetry and Activity-Related Change in the Male Humerus." *International Journal of Osteoarchaeology* 3:105–113.

Stoodley, N. (2000). "From the Cradle to the Grave: Age Organization and the Early Anglo-Saxon Burial Rite." *World Archaeology* 31 (3):456–472.

Strabo. (trans. Horace Leonard Jones). (1917) (reprint 1969). *The Geography of Strabo.* Vol. I. Loeb Classical Library. Cambridge, MA: Harvard University Press.

———. (1938) (reprint 1969, 1988). *The Geography of Strabo.* Vol. V. Loeb Classical Library. Cambridge, MA: Harvard University Press.

Sullivan, Michael. (1984). *The Arts of China*, 3rd ed. Berkeley: University of California Press.

Sun, Ji 孙机. (1991). "Buyao, buyaoguan yu yaoye shipian 步摇, 步摇冠与摇叶饰片 (Buyao (Dangling Ornament Which Sways When the Wearer Walks) with Buyao and Its Accessories)." *Wenwu* 文物 (Cultural Relics) 11:55–64.

Sun, Shoudao 孙守道. (1960). "Xiongnu 'Xichagou wenhua' gumuqun de fajue 匈奴 '西岔沟文化' 古墓群的发掘 (The Excavation of the Ancient Tombs of the 'Xichagou Culture' of the Xiongnu)." *Wenwu* 文物 (Cultural Relics) (8–9):25–32.

Sun Yan. (2006). "Colonizing China's Northern Frontier: Yan and Her Neighbors during the Early Western Zhou Period." *International Journal of Historic Archaeology* 10 (2):159–177.

Sweely, T. (ed.) (1999). *Manifesting Power: Gender and the Interpretation of Power in Archaeology*. New York: Routledge.

Tacitus. (trans. Horace Leonard Jones). (1914) (reprint 1980). *Agricola, Germania, Dialogus*. Loeb Classical Library. Cambridge, MA: Harvard University Press.

———. (Clifford H. Moore and John Jackson, trans.) (1931) (reprint 2005). *The Histories: Books IV–V* (Clifford H. Moore, trans.). *The Annals: Books I–III* (John Jackson, trans.). Vol. III. Loeb Classical Library. Cambridge: Harvard University Press.

———. (trans. John Jackson). (1937) (reprint 1969). *The Annals: Books XIII–XVI*. Loeb Classical Library. Cambridge, MA: Harvard University Press.

Tairov, A. and A. Bushmakin. (2001). "Mineral'nye Poroshki iz Kurganov Uzhnogo Urala i Severnogo Kazakhstana i ikh Vozmozhnoe Ispol'zovanie." *Rossiiskaya Arkheologiya* 1:66–75.

———. (2002). "The Composition, Function and Significance of the Mineral Paints from the Kurgan Burial Mounds of the South Urals and North Kazakhstan." In A. Jones and G. MacGregor (eds.), *Colouring the Past: The Significance of Colour in Archaeological Research*, pp. 175–793. Oxford: Berg.

Tal'ko-Gryntsevich, Yu. D. (1898). "Sudzhinskoe Kladbishche v Il'movoii padi (The Sudzhin Prehistoric Cemetery in Il'movoi Valley)." *Trudy TKORGO* 1 (2).

Tan Ying-jui, Sun Xiu-ren, Zhao Hong-guang, and Gan Zhi-gang. (1995). "The Bronze Age of the Song-Nen Plain." In S. M. Nelson (ed.), *The Archaeology of Northeast China*, pp. 225–250. London: Routledge.

Taylor, Alison. (2001). *Burial Practice in Early England*. Stroud, UK: Tempus.

Taylor, Timothy. (1994). "Thracians, Scythians, and Dacians, 800 BC–AD 300." In Barry Cunliffe (ed.), *The Oxford Illustrated Prehistory of Europe*, pp. 373–410. Oxford: Oxford University Press.

———. (1996). *The Prehistory of Sex: Four Million Years of Human Sexual Culture*. New York: Bantam Books.

———. (2001). "Believing the Ancients: Quantitative and Qualitative Dimensions of Slavery and the Slave Trade in Later Prehistoric Eurasia." *World Archaeology* 33 (1):27–43.

Tedlock, Barbara. (2005). *The Woman in the Shaman's Body: Reclaiming the Feminine in Religion and Medicine*. New York: Random House.

Teploukhov, S. A. (1927) "Drevnie pogrebenija v Minusinskom krae (Ancient tombs of the Minusinsk region)." *Materialy po etnografii* 3(2):98–112.

———. (1929). "Opyt klassifikatsii metallicheskikh kul'tur Minusinskogo kraja (Tentative Classification of the Metal Cultures of the Minusinsk Region)." *Materialy Po Etnografii* 3 (2):98–112.

Thomas, J. (1991). "Reading the Body: Beaker Funerary Practice in Britain." In P. Garwood, D. Jenings, R. Skeates, and J. Toms (eds.), *Sacred and Profane: Proceedings of a Conference on Archaeology, Ritual and Religion, Oxford 1989*, pp. 33–42. Oxford: Oxford University Committee for Archaeology Monographs No. 32.

———. (1996). *Time, Culture, and Identity: An Interpretative Archaeology.* London: Routledge.

Tian Guangjin 田广金. (1976). "Taohongbala de Xiongnu mu 桃红巴拉的匈奴墓 (The Hsiung Nu Tombs at T'ao-hung-pa-la)." *Kaogu Xuebao* 考古学报 (Acta Archaeologica Sinica) 1:131–143.

———. (1982). "Xiongnu Muzang de leixing he niandai 匈奴墓葬的类型和年代 (The Patterns and Time of Huns Tombs)." *Nei Menggu Wenwu Kaogu* 内蒙古文物 考古 (Cultural Relics and Archaeology of Inner Mongolia) 2:8–17.

———. (1983). "Jinnian lai Neimenggu diqu de Xiongnu kaogu 近年来内蒙古地区 的匈奴考古 (Archaeological Studies on the Xiongnu People in Inner Mongolia in Recent Years)." *Kaogu Xuebao* 考古学报 (Acta Archaeologica Sinica) 1:7–24.

Tian Guangjin 田广金 and Guo Suxin 郭素新. (1980). "Nei Menggu Aluchaideng faxian de Xiongnu yiwu 内蒙古阿鲁柴登发现的匈奴遗物 (Objects of the Xiong-nu People Found at Aluchaideng in Inner Mongolia)." *Kaogu* 考古 (Archaeology) 4:333–338.

———. (1986). *E'erduosi Qingtongqi* 鄂尔多斯青铜器. Beijing: Wenwu chubanshe 文物出版社 (Cultural Relics Press).

———. (1988). "E'erduosi shi qingtongqi de yuanyuan 鄂尔多斯式青铜器的渊 源 (The Origins of the Ordos Style Bronzes)." *Kaogu Xuebao* 考古学报 (Acta Archaeologica Sinica) 3:257–274.

Tian Guangjin 田广金 and Han Jianye 韩建业. (2003). "Zhukaigou wenhua yanjiu 朱开沟文化研究 (Research of the Zhukaigou Culture)." In Beijing daxue kaogu wenbo xueyuan 北京大学考古文博学院 (Archaeological Museum of Historical and Cultural Relics, Beijing University) (ed.), *Kaoguxue yanjiu* 考古学研究 (Ar-chaeological Research). Vol 5. pp. 226–259. Beijing: Kexue chubanshe 科学出版 社 (Science Press).

Tian Yun 田耘 (1984). "Xichagou gumuqun zushu wenti qianxi 西岔沟古墓群族属 问题浅析 (A Simple Analysis to the Ethnic Attribute of the Ancient Cemetery in Xichagou)." *Heilongjiang Wenwu Congkan* 黑龙江文物丛刊 (Collected Works on Heilongjiang Cultural Relics) 1:29–34.

Treherne, P. (1995). "The Warrior's Beauty: The Masculine Body and Self-Identity in Bronze Age Europe." *Journal of European Archaeology* 3 (1):105–144.

Treister, Mikhail. (1997). "Sarmatian Treasures of South Russia." *Archaeology* 50 (1):49–51.

———. (1997/1978). "Further Thoughts about the Necklaces with Butterfly-Shaped Pendants from the North Pontic Area." *Journal of the Walters Art Gallery* 55/56:49–62.

Trever, K. V. (1931). *Nakhodki iz Raskopok v Mongolii 1924–1925* (Excavations of Mongolia in 1924–1925). *Soobshch, GAIMK*, Nos. 9 and 10.

Tseng Yung 曾庸. (1961). "Liaoning Xifeng Xichagou gumuqun wei Wuhuan wen-hua shiji lun 辽宁西丰西岔沟古墓群为乌桓文化史迹论 (Preliminary Identifica-tion of the Ancient Cemetery at Hsi Ch'a Kou, Hsi Feng County, Liaoning, as the Remains of the Wu Huan Tribe)." *Kaogu* 考古 (Archaeology) 6:334–336.

Tsevendorzh, D. (1985). *Novye dannye po Arkheologii khunnu* (New Data of Hun Archae-ology). In *Drevnie Kultury Mongolii* (Ancient Mongolian Cultures), Novosibirsk.

Tylor, E. B. (1989). *Primitivnaya kultura (Primitive Culture)*. Moscow: Politizdat.

Tyrell, Wm. Blake. (1984). *Amazons: A Study in Athenian Mythmaking*. Baltimore, MD: Johns Hopkins University Press.

Ucko, Peter J. (1969). "Ethnography and the Archaeological Interpretation of Funerary Remains." *World Archaeology* 1:262–290.

Umehara Sueji 梅原末治. (1960). "Môkô Noin Ura Hakken no Ibutsu 蒙古ノイン・ウラ発現の遺物 (Relics Discovered in Noin Ula, Mongolia)." *Tôyô Bunko Ronsô* 東洋文庫論叢 27.

Vadetskaja, E. B. (1986). *Arkheologicheskie Pamjatniki v Stepjakh Srednego Eniseja* (Archaeological Sites in the Steppes of the Middle-Enisej Region). Saint Petersburg: Nauka.

Virgil. (trans. H. Rushton Fairclough). (1916) (reprint 1978). *Virgil with an English Translation*. 2 vols. 1935 rev. ed. Loeb Classical Library. Cambridge, MA: Harvard University Press.

Vishnevskaya, O. A. (1973). *Kul'tura sakskikh plemen nizov'ya Syrdari v VII: V vv. do n.e. (po materialiam Uigaraka)*. Trudy Tuvinskoi kompleksnoi arkheologicheskoi ekspeditsii. Moscow: Nauka.

Wang Lixin 王立新. (2004). "Liaoxi qu Xia zhi Zhanguo shiqi wenhua geju yu jingji xingtai de yanjin 辽西区夏至战国时期文化格局与经济形态的演进 (The Evolution of Cultural Pattern and Economic Formation in the Western Liaoning Area from the Xia to the Warring States Period)." *Kaogu Xuebao* 考古学报 (Acta Archaeologica Sinica) 3:243–269.

Watts, James, An Jiayao, Angela F. Howard, Boris I Marshak, Su Bai, and Zhao Feng. (2004). *China: Dawn of a Golden Age, 200–750 AD*. New York: Metropolitian Museum and New Haven: Yale University Press.

Weedman, Kathryn and Lisa Frink. (2006). *Gender and Hide Production*. Walnut Creek, CA: AltaMira Press.

Weglian, E. (2001). "Grave Goods Do Not a Gender Make: A Case Study from Singen am Hohentwiel, Germany." In B. Arnold and N. L. Wicker (eds.), *Gender and the Archaeology of Death*, pp. 137–155. Walnut Creek, CA: AltaMira Press.

Wells, P. (1998). "Identity and Material Cutlure in the Later Prehistory of Central Europe." *Journal of Archaeological Research* 6 (3):239–298.

———. (2001). *Beyond Celts, Germans and Scythians*. London: Duckworth.

West, S. (1999). "Introducing the Scythians: Herodotus on Koumiss (4.2)." *Museum Helveticum* 56:76–86.

———. (2000). "Herodotus in the North? Reflections on a Colossal Cauldron (4.18)." *Scripta Classica Israelica* 19:15–86.

Whittle, A. (1996). *Europe in the Neolithic: The Creation of New Worlds*. Cambridge: Cambridge University Press.

Williams, H. (2003). *Archaeologies of Remembrance: Death and Memory in Past Societies*. New York: Kluwer Academic.

Wright, Rita P. (1989). "New Tracks on Ancient Frontiers." In C. C. Lamberg-Karlovsky, *Archaeology in the Americas and Beyond*, pp. 268–279. Cambridge: Cambridge University Press.

———. (1991). "Women's Labor and Pottery Production in Prehistory." In Joan Gero and Margaret Conkey, *Engendering Archaeology*, pp. 194–223. Oxford: Basil Blackwell.

———. (1996). "Technology, Gender and Class: Worlds of Difference in Ur III Mesopotamia." In Rita P. Wright (ed.), *Gender and Archaeology*, pp. 79–110. Philadelphia: University of Pennsylvania Press.

———. (2002). "Revisiting Interaction Spheres—Social Boundaries and Technologies on Inner and Outermost Frontiers." *Iranica Antiqua* 37:403–417.

———.(forthcoming). "Gendered Relations in Ur III: Kinship, Property and Labor." In Diane Bolger (ed.), *Gender through Time*. Lanham, MD: AltaMira Press.

Wu En 乌恩. (1985). "Yin zhi Zhouchu de beifang qingtongqi 殷至周初的北方青铜器 (Northern Bronzes from Yin to Early Zhou)." *Kaogu Xuebao* 考古学报 (Acta Archaeologica Sinica) 2:135–156.

———. (1989). "Shilun Han dai Xiongnu yu Xianbei yiji de qubie 试论汉代匈奴与鲜卑遗迹的区别 (Trial Analysis on the Differences between Xiongnu and Xianbei Remains)." In *Zhongguo Kaogu Xuehui Di Liu Ci Nianhui Lunwenji* 中国考古学会第六次年会论文集 (Proceedings of the Sixth Annual Conference of Archaeology Society of China), pp. 136–150. Beijing: Wenwu chubanshe 文物出版社 (Cultural Relics Press).

———. (1990). "Lun Xiongnu kaogu yanjiu zhongde jige wenti 论匈奴考古中的几个问题 (Questions of the Analysis on the Archaeology of the Xiongnu)." *Kaogu Xuebao* 考古学报 (*Acta Archaeologica Sinica*) 4:409–437.

Wu Jui-man. (2004). "The Late Neolithic Cemetery at Dadianzi, Inner Mongolia Autonomous Region." In Katheryn M. Linduff and Sun Yan (eds.), *Gender and Chinese Archaeology*, pp. 47–91. Walnut Creek, CA: AltaMira Press.

Wu Xiaolong. (2004). "Female and Male Status Displayed at the Maoqinggou Cemetery." In Katheryn M. Linduff and Sun Yan (eds.), *Gender and Chinese Archaeology*, pp. 203–236. Walnut Creek, CA: AltaMira Press.

Xiong Cunrui 熊存瑞. (1983). "Xianqin Xiongnu jiqi youguan de jige wenti 先秦匈奴及其有关的几个问题 (Xiongnu Living during the Period before the Qin Dynasty and Other Relevant Problems)." *Shehuikexue Zhanxian* 社会科学战线 (Social Science Front) 1:110–113.

Yablonsky, Leonid T. (1993). *Kurgany Levobereznhogo Ileka*. Vypusk 1. Moscow: Nauka.

———. (1994). *Kurgany Levobereznhogo Ileka*. Vypusk 2. Moscow: Nauka.

———. (1995a). *Kurgany Levobereznhogo Ileka*. Vypusk 3. Moscow: Nauka.

———. (1995b). "The Material Culture of the Saka and Historical Reconstruction." In Jeannine Davis-Kimball (ed.), *Nomads of the Eurasian Steppes in the Early Iron Age*, pp. 201–240. Berkeley: Zinat Press.

———. (1996). *Kurgany Levobereznhogo Ileka*. Vypusk 4. Moscow: Nauka.

———. (2000). "Scythian Triad" and "Scythian World," In J. Davis-Kimball, E. M. Murphy, L. N. Koryakova, and L. T. Yablonsky (eds.), *Kurgans, Ritual Sites and Settlements: Eurasian Bronze and Iron Age*, pp. 3–8. BAR International Series 890. Oxford: Archaeopress.

————. (2002). "Archaeological Mythology and Some Real Problems of the Current Archaeology," In K. Jones-Bley and G. B. Zdanovich (eds.), *Complex Societies of Central Eurasia from the Third to the First Millennia BC: Regional Specifics in the Light of Global Models*. Chelyabinsk State University, Chelyabinsk, Russian Federation/Journal of Indo-European Studies Monograph Series.Washington, DC: Institute for the Study of Man.

Yatsenko, Sergie A. (1987). "K Rekonstrukstii zhenskoi plechevoi odezhdy sarmatii (A Reconstruction of Sarmatian Womens Wear)." *Sovetskaya Arkheologiya* 3:166–176.

————. (2001). "The Costume of the Yuech-Chihs/Kushans and Its Analogies to the East and to the West" *Silk Road Art and Archaeology* 7:73–120.

YKZMWWGZZ [Yikezhao Meng Wenwu Gongzuozhan Nei Menggu Wenwu Gongzuodui] 伊克昭盟文物站 内蒙古文物工作队 (Archaeological Team of Yeke Joo League and the Archaeological Team of the Inner Mongolian Autonomous Region). (1981). "Xigoupan Han dai Xiongnu mudi diaocha ji 西沟畔汉代匈奴墓地调查记 (A Survey of the Graveyard of the Xiongnu during the Han Dynasty at Xi-Gou-Pan)." *Nei Menggu Wenwu Kaogu* 内蒙古文物考古创刊号 (Cultural Relics and Archaeology of Inner Mongolia, First issue.) 1:15–26.

YKZMWWGZZ [Yikezhao Meng Wenwu Gongzuozhan] 伊克昭盟文物工作站 (Archaeological Team of Yike League). (1981). "Yikezhao Meng Budonggou Xiongnu Mu Qingli Jianbao 伊克昭盟补洞沟匈奴墓清理简报 (Excavation of Xiongnu Tombs in Budonggou, Yike League)." *Nei Menggu Wenwu Kaogu Chuang kan hao* 内蒙古文物考古创刊号 (Cultural Relics and Archaeology of Inner Mongolia, First Issue) (1).

Yi Kedong (1998). "The Prehistory and Social Life of the Capital." In Korean National Commission for UNESCO (ed.), *Kyongju, City of Millenial History*. Elizabeth, NJ: Hollym.

Yoffee, Norman. (1993). "Too Many Chiefs? (or, Safe Texts for the '90s)." In N. Yoffee and A. Sherratt (eds.), *Archaeological Theory: Who Sets the Agenda*, pp. 60–78. Cambridge: Cambridge University Press.

————. (1995). "Political Economy in Early Mesopotamian States." *Annual Review of Anthropology* 24:281–311.

Zaibert, V. (1993). *Eneolit Uralo-Irtyshskogo Mezhdurechya*. Petropavlovsk, Kazakhstan: Academiya Nauk Kazakhstana.

Zdanovich, G. B. (ed.) (1995). *Arkaim*. Chelyabinsk, Russia: Kamennyi Poyas.

Zeymal, Evgeny V. (1999). "Tillya-Tepe within the Context of the Kushan Chronology." In M. Alram and D. Klimburg-Salter (eds.), *Coins, Art and Chronology: Essays on the Pre-Islamic History of the Indo-Iranian Borderlands*, pp. 239–244. Vienna: Verlag der Österreichischen Akademie Der Wissenschaften.

Zhangjiakou Shi Wenwu Shiye Guanlisuo 张家口市文物事业管理所. (1987). "Hebei Xuanhuaxian Xiaobaiyang mudi fajue baogao 河北宣化县小白杨墓地发掘报告 (Report on the Excavations at the Xiaobaiyang Graveyard, Xuanhua County, Hebei)." *Wenwu* 文物 (Cultural Relics) 5:41–51.

Zheng Long 郑隆 and Li Yiyou 李逸友. (1964). "Cha You Hou Qi Erlanhugou mudi 察右后旗二兰虎沟墓地 (The Erlanhugou Cemetery in Qahar Right Rear

Banner)." *Nei Menggu Wenwu Ziliao Xuanji* 内蒙古文物资料选辑 (Selected Works of Materials of Cultural Relics from Inner Mongolia), pp. 99–101. Hohhot: Neimenggu Renmin chubanshe 内蒙古人民出版社 (Inner Mongolia People's Press).

Zhong Kan 钟侃. (1986). "Ningxia Kaogu Faxian he Yanjiu 宁夏考古发现和研究 (Ningxia's Archaeological Discoveries and Research)." *Ningxia Wenwu* 宁夏文物 (Ningxia Cultural Relics) 1:16–25, 38.

Zhongguo Kexueyuan Kaogu Yangjiusuo 中国科学院考古研究所 (Institute of Archaeology, Academia Sinica). (1962). *Feng-hsi fa-chüeh pao-kao* 沣西发掘报告 (Excavations at Feng Hsi (1955–1957)). Beijing: Wenwu chubanshe 文物出版社 (Cultural Relics Press).

———. (1996). *Dadianzi: Xiajiadian xiaceng wenhua yizhi yu mudi fajue baogao* 大甸子:夏家店下层文化遗址与墓地发掘报告 (Dadianzi: Excavations of the Domestic Site and Cemetery of the Lower Xiajiadian Period). Beijing: Kexue chubanshe 科学出版社 (Science Press).

ZGKXYKGYJSZ [Zhongguo Kexueyuan Kaogu Yanjiusuo Nei Menggu Wenwu Gongzuodui] 中国科学院考古研究所内蒙古工作队 (The Inner Mongolia Archaeological Team, Institute of Archaeology, Academia Sinica). (1964). "Nei Menggu Balin Zuo Qi Nan Yangjiayingzi de yizhi he muzang 内蒙古巴林左旗南杨家营子的遗址和墓葬 (Excavations of a Dwelling Site and Burials at Southern Yang Chia Ying Tzu, Barin Left Banner, Inner Mongolia)." *Kaogu* 考古 (Archaeology) 1:36–43, 53.

———. (1974). "Chifeng Yaowangmiao, Xiajiadian yizhi shijue baogao 赤峰药王庙夏家店遗址试掘报告 (Report on the Test Excavations at Yaowangmiao and Xiajiadian Sites, in the Chifeng Area)." *Kaogu Xuebao* 考古学报 (Acta Archaeologica Sinca) 1:111–144.

———. (1975). "Ningcheng Nanshangen yizhi fajue baogao 宁城南山根遗址发掘报告 (Report of the Excavations at the Nanshan'gen Site in the Ningcheng Area)." *Kaogu Xuebao* 考古学报 (Acta Archaeologica Sinca) 1:117–140.

———. (1979). "Chifeng Zhizhushan yizhi de fajue 赤峰蜘蛛山遗址的发掘 (Excavations at the Zhizhushan Site in the Chifeng Area)." *Kaogu Xuebao* 考古学报 (Acta Archaeologica Sinca) 2:215–244.

Zhongguo shehui kexueyuan kaogu yanjiusuo 中国社会科学院考古研究所 (Chinese Academy of Social Sciences and Archaeology Research Institute) and Qinghaisheng wenwu kaogu yanjiusuo 青海省文物考古研究所 (Cultural Relics and Archaeology Research Institute, Qinghai province) (2004). "Qinghai Huzhu Fengtai Kayue wenhua yizhi fuxuan jiegou fenxi baogao 青海互助丰台卡约文化遗址浮选结果分析报告 (Report on the Analysis of Flotation Results from the Kayue Culture Site of Fengtai, Huzhu, Qinghai)." *Kaogu yu wenwu* 考古與文物 (Archaeology and Cultural Relics) 2:85–91.

Zhu Yonggang 朱永刚. (1987). "Xiajiadian shangceng wenhua de chubu yanjiu 夏家店上层文化的初步研究 (Research of the Upper Xiajiadian Culture)." In Su Bingqi 苏秉琦 (ed.), *Kaoguxue wenhua lunji* 考古学文化论集 (Discourses on Cultural Archaeology), pp. 99–128. Beijing: Wenwu chubanshe 文物出版社 (Cultural Relics Press).

————. (2004). "Xiajiadian shangceng wenhua xiang nan de fenbu taishi yu diyu wenhua bianqian 夏家店上层文化向南的分布态势与地域文化变迁 (The Spread of the Upper Xiajiadian Culture Southward and Local Cultural Changes)." In Jilin daxue bianjiang kaogu yanjiu zhongxin 吉林大学边疆考古研究中心 (Center for Archaeological Research of the Border Areas, Jilin University) (ed.), *Qingzhu Zhang Zhongpei xiansheng qishi sui lunwen ji* 庆祝张忠培先生七十岁论文集 (Essays Celebrating Zhang Zhongpei at 70 years), pp. 422–436. Beijing: Kexue chubanshe.

Zjablin, L. P. (1977). *Karasukskij mogil'nik Malye Kopjony 3* (The Karasuk Cemetery of Malye Kopjony 3). Moscow: Nauka.

Zohary, Daniel and Maria Hopf. (2000). *Domestication of Plants in the Old World*: *The Origin and Spread of Cultivated Plants in West Asia, Europe and the Nile Valley*. New York: Oxford University Press.

Index

255

About the Contributors

Natalia Berseneva is a research fellow of the Department of Archaeology and Ethography at the Institute of History and Archaeology (Ural Division, Russian Academy of Sciences, Ekaterinburg). She earned her PhD from the same institute in 2005, and since 1996, she has participated in fieldwork and research projects in Ural and Western Siberia including "Settlements and Burials of the Iron Age on Eurasian Crossroad" and "The Iron Age Society and Environment." Presently she is involved in a new project that aims to study social dynamics in the Bronze and Iron ages. Most of her academic papers address the archaeology of the Trans-Urals and Western Siberia during the Bronze and Iron ages.

Bryan Hanks is an assistant professor in the Department of Anthropology at the University of Pittsburgh. He graduated with a PhD in archaeology from the University of Cambridge in 2003. His theoretical interests include trajectories of development connected with early complex societies and anthropological perspectives on death and burial traditions and prehistoric warfare and violence. He has been actively engaged in collaborative archaeological fieldwork with the Russian Academy of Sciences in north-central Eurasia since 1998 and has published a number of articles focusing on the Bronze and Iron ages of the Eurasian steppe region. He is currently writing a book on the Eurasian steppe Iron Age and is editing a monograph on trajectories of societal complexity based on papers delivered at a recent international conference he organized at the University of Pittsburgh.

Deborah G. Harding is the collection manager for anthropology at the Carnegie Museum of Natural History in Pittsburgh, Pennsylvania. She earned her master's degree in anthropology at the University of Pittsburgh in 1994. She learned to weave in the late 1960s, and has been teaching textile and basketry-related technologies since the mid-1970s. Harding has, until recently, concentrated on North and South American weaving traditions. She is currently working with the Museum of the Cherokee Indian to revive 18th-century textile techniques and feather cape making among the eastern band of the Cherokee.

Karlene Jones-Bley is a research associate in the Indo-European Studies program at the University of California, Los Angeles, where she earned her PhD in 1989 and has taught a number of courses in European archaeology. She is also archaeology book review editor for the *Journal of Indo-European Studies*. Her book, *Early and Middle Bronze Age Pottery from the Volga-Don Steppe* (1999), provides not only the first corpus of Steppe pottery published in English but also an introduction to Steppe archaeology. She has excavated in Russia, England, Northern Ireland, Germany, and the United States. Her papers have been published in Russian and English and include works on ceramics and Indo-European burial, ritual, and culture. She is currently working on a comparative study of women in ancient Indo-European societies.

Sophie Legrand is a doctoral candidate in the Archaeology Department at the University of Paris. She is preparing her PhD on the Final Bronze Age culture in the Minusinsk Basin (South Siberia). She took part in an archaeological fieldwork project in Anchil Chon (Minusinsk Basin) from 1998 until 2000. Her latest publications are "Karasuk Metallurgy: Technological Development and Regional Influence" in *Metallurgy in Ancient Eastern Eurasia from the Urals to the Yellow River* (2004), and "The Emergence of the Karasuk Culture" in the journal *Antiquity* (2006).

Katheryn M. Linduff is University Center for International Studies professor of art history and archaeology, specializing in the study of early China and Inner Asia, at the University of Pittsburgh. She is interested in the rise of complex society and especially in the interplay of ethnic, cultural, and gender identity with social, economic, and political life in ancient China and eastern Eurasia. Her publications include *Gender and Chinese Archaeology* (2004; in Chinese in 2006), *Metallurgy in Ancient Eastern Eurasia from the Urals to the Yellow River* (2004), *Ancient Bronzes of the Eastern Eurasian Steppes: The Arthur M. Sackler Collection* (1997), and many papers on the intersection of peoples at the ancient borders of dynastic China. She has engaged in a large settlement pattern study of the Neolithic, Bronze, and Iron Age peoples of northeast China for the past ten years.

Sarah Milledge Nelson is a John Evans Professor in the Department of Anthropology at the University of Denver, and earned her PhD from the University of Michigan. Nelson has conducted fieldwork in eastern Eurasia and related areas in northeast China and Korea. Her most relevant books are *The Archaeology of Korea* (1993), *The Archaeology of Northeast China* (1995), and *Gender in Archaeology: Analyzing Power and Prestige* (1997, 2004). Her most recent book is *Handbook of Gender in Archaeology* (2006). Here she provides the first look at the region of ancient Korea and its Eurasian roots and how that informs and genders symbolism of the early Korean state.

Sandra Olsen, a curator in the Section of Anthropology, Carnegie Museum of Natural History, Pittsburgh, is a Eurasian steppe archaeologist, specializing in zoo-archaeology and the origins of horse domestication. She earned her PhD in archaeology in 1984 from the Institute of Archaeology, University of London and has conducted fieldwork in many locations, including Europe and Africa, but most recently in northern Kazakhstan. She has published over fifty articles, mostly on faunal analysis, bone artifacts, and Kazakh archaeology, as well as three edited volumes, one on SEM in archaeology and two on horses in prehistory and history. Her recent work has shed light on early horse pastoralists of the Botai culture, in north-central Kazakhstan, including evidence for the control and corralling of horses and a variety of ritual patterns.

Karen S. Rubinson is a research scholar in the Department of Anthropology at Barnard College. She earned her MA in East Asian art and archaeology and her PhD in ancient Near Eastern art and archaeology from the Department of Art History and Archaeology at Columbia University. Rubinson is coeditor of *Ceramics in Transition: Chalcolithic through Iron Age in the Highlands* (2007), a book based on an international symposium held at Barnard College in 2003, and *Archaeology in the Borderlands: Investigations in Caucasia and Beyond* (2003). She is also an associate editor of the multivolume *Civilizations of the Ancient Near East* (1995). Long interested in the interconnections in Eurasia, she has published widely on the subject, particularly on the Bronze Age in the Caucasus and Ancient Near East and on the Iron Age in the Eurasian Steppe. She has conducted excavations in Turkey, Iran, and Armenia, as well as in the northeastern United States. Currently president of the American Research Institute in the South Caucasus, she has also served as vice president of the Archaeological Institute of America.

Gideon Shelach is a professor and chair of the Department of East Asian Studies at the Hebrew University of Jerusalem and director of the Louis Frieberg Center of East Asian Studies. He earned his PhD from the Department of Anthropology at the University of Pittsburgh in 1996 and has been engaged, since 1994, in archaeological fieldwork projects in the Chifeng area of northeast China. His latest book, *Prehistoric Societies on the Northern Frontiers* *of China: Archaeological Perspectives on Identity Formation and Economic Change during the First Millennium BCE*, will be published in 2008. His academic papers address the archaeology of northeast China from the Neolithic to the end of the Bronze Age as well as other aspects, such as the formation of the Qin state in Northwest China.

Rita P. Wright, a professor in the Department of Anthropology at New York University, earned her PhD from Harvard University. She is one of the leading scholars on gender in archaeology. She also has a strong interest in cultural heritage and stewardship issues and has written articles about Afghanistan, as well as other areas. She edited *Gender and Archaeology* (1996) and coedited *Craft and Social Identity* (1998). Her most recent book, *The Ancient Indus: Urbanism, Economy and Society* (forthcoming), is an overview of the Indus civilization, part of the Case Studies in Early Society by Cambridge University Press, of which she is series editor. A recipient of a John D. and Catherine T. MacArthur Fellowship, she has excavated in the ancient Near East and South Asia, most recently directing a long-term survey in Pakistan.